access to history

The USA in Asia 1945–75

Vivienne Sanders

Study Guide authors: Sally Waller (AQA), Angela Leonard (Edexcel) and Sheila Randall (OCR)

The Publishers would like to thank the following for permission to reproduce copyright material:
Photo credits: p43 Time & Life Pictures/Getty Images; **p50** Hulton-Deutsch Collection/CORBIS; **p63** Getty Images; **p105** *t* Bettmann/CORBIS, *b* Getty Images; **p116** Corbis; **p127** AP/EMPICS; **p149** Bettmann/CORBIS; **p161** AP/EMPICS; **p163** Time & Life Pictures/Getty Images; **p164** AP/EMPICS; **p165** Bettmann/ CORBIS; **p169** AFP/Getty Images; **p184** AP/EMPICS; **p189** Bettmann/CORBIS; **p213** Bettmann/CORBIS.
Acknowledgements: p75 Fourth International Publishing Association for an extract from *Fourth International*, Vol. XII, No. 3 (Whole No. 110), May–June 1951, published bimonthly by the Fourth International Publishing Association; **p196** Edexcel Limited; **p226** *St. Louis Post Despatch* for an extract from an editorial; **p226** Excerpted from an editorial originally appearing in the *Toronto Star* January 24, 1973.
Every effort has been made to trace all copyright holders, but if any have been inadvertently overlooked the Publishers will be pleased to make the necessary arrangements at the first opportunity.

Hachette UK's policy is to use papers that are natural, renewable and recyclable products and made from wood grown in sustainable forests. The logging and manufacturing processes are expected to conform to the environmental regulations of the country of origin.

Orders: please contact Bookpoint Ltd, 130 Milton Park, Abingdon, Oxon OX14 4SB. Telephone: (44) 01235 827720. Fax: (44) 01235 400454. Lines are open 9.00–5.00, Monday to Saturday, with a 24-hour message answering service. Visit our website at www.hoddereducation.co.uk

© Vivienne Sanders
First published in 2010 by
Hodder Education,
An Hachette UK Company
338 Euston Road
London NW1 3BH

Impression number   5 4 3 2
Year   2014 2013 2012

Cover image: The Vietnam Memorial in Washington, © Jon Arnold Images Ltd/ Alamy
Typeset in Baskerville 10/12pt and produced by Gray Publishing, Tunbridge Wells
Printed and bound by CPI Group (UK) Ltd, Croydon, CR0 4YY

A catalogue record for this title is available from the British Library.

ISBN: 978 1444 110098

Contents

Dedication

Keith Randell (1943–2002)

The *Access to History* series was conceived and developed by Keith, who created a series to 'cater for students as they are, not as we might wish them to be'. He leaves a living legacy of a series that for over 20 years has provided a trusted, stimulating and well-loved accompaniment to post-16 study. Our aim with these new editions is to continue to offer students the best possible support for their studies.

Ashfield School Library

Ashfield School

Sutton Road

Kirkby In Ashfield

Notts

NG17 8HP

The last date entered is the date by which the
book must be returned

Introduction: The Cold War Context

POINTS TO CONSIDER

From 1950 to 1953 the United States fought Communist forces in Korea, and from 1950 to 1973 it poured monetary and then military aid into fighting Communists in Vietnam. This military intervention in Asia was part of the Cold War. This chapter looks at the origins of the Cold War in Europe and the arrival of the Cold War in Asia.

Key dates

1917	Russian Revolution, which led to the establishment of the Communist USSR
1941–5	USA fought in Second World War against Japan and Germany; USA and USSR allies
1944–8	Soviet takeover of Eastern Europe
1949	China became Communist
1950–3	Korean War
1950–73	US involvement in Vietnam War
1975	Communists took over the whole of Vietnam

1 | Overview: Two US Wars in Asia

Key question
When and why was the United States involved in Asia?

Key dates

Korean War: 1950–3

US involvement in Vietnam War: 1950–73

Key term

Communist
A believer in economic equality brought about by the revolutionary redistribution of wealth.

By the end of 1945, the United States was the most powerful nation in the world. It had defeated its Second World War foes, Germany and Japan, and was the sole possessor of the atomic bomb. Nevertheless, security fears soon led the United States into two bloody wars in Asia, the Korean War (1950–3) and the Vietnam War (1950–73). The United States fought in Korea and Vietnam because of the Cold War (c. 1947–c. 1989) between the United States and its Western allies on the one side, and **Communist** Russia and China on the other.

The Cold War (c. 1947–c. 1989)

In the half-century of the Cold War era, a state of extreme tension existed between the Western world and the Communist world. The West was led by the United States, which had allies such as Britain, France, Italy and West Germany. The Communist world was led by the USSR, and, to a lesser extent, China. Although armed to the hilt, the United States and USSR never met directly in combat – hence the 'cold' war.

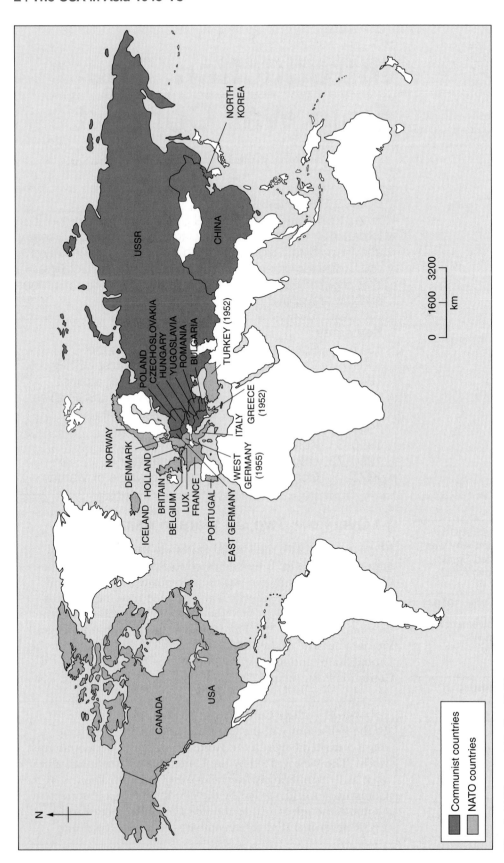

The Cold War world in the 1950s.

Key question
When and why did the United States fall out with the USSR?

Key dates

Russian Revolution, which led to the establishment of the Communist USSR: 1917

USA fought in Second World War against Japan and Germany; USA and USSR allies: 1941–5

Soviet takeover of Eastern Europe: 1944–8

Key terms

USSR
Union of Soviet Socialist Republics.

Ideologies
Sets of political beliefs, for example, Communism.

Capitalist
One who believes in a free market economy with no state intervention – the opposite of the Communist economic philosophy.

Multi-party state
Nation in which voters have a free choice between several political parties.

Expansionist
In the Cold War, each side considered the other to be aggressive and anxious to expand its power and influence.

2 | The Cold War to 1949

a) Ideological opponents

Prior to the Russian Revolution that began in 1917, relations between the United States and Russia had often been quite friendly. However, after the Revolution that established the Communist government in Russia (which then called itself the **USSR**), relations between the two nations deteriorated rapidly.

The United States and the USSR had very different **ideologies**. Americans favoured a **capitalist** economy, in which there was minimal government control, and market forces were left as the main regulator of jobs, companies and trade. The American definition of democracy was dominated by the concept of one man, one vote, and the United States was a **multi-party state**. In contrast, the USSR favoured a government-controlled economy, in which wealth was equally distributed (at least in theory). The Soviet definition of democracy emphasised economic equality, without which it was felt the vote was virtually worthless. The Soviets believed that the Communist Party was the party of the people and that consequently there was no need for several political parties.

The ideological differences made the United States and USSR suspicious of and hostile towards each other. Both countries believed their ideology was superior and should be exported, and both perceived the other as an **expansionist** security threat.

In 1918–19, the United States was one of several countries that made a half-hearted and small-scale intervention in Russia. The reasons for this intervention included anger at Russia's withdrawal from the First World War, the desire to recover war supplies and anti-Communism. The intervention achieved little, apart from antagonising the Soviets, who never forgot what they described as this US attempt to 'strangle Communism in its cradle'. When the US then refused to give diplomatic recognition to the new Communist nation, relations remained tense throughout the 1920s.

In 1933, the new US president, Franklin D. Roosevelt, was one of many Americans who felt it was time for a change of policy. Relations with the USSR improved until the outbreak of the Second World War, when Stalin and Hitler's attack on Poland alienated the United States. However, in 1941, Hitler turned on and invaded the USSR, and Japan attacked the United States. The USA and USSR then became wartime allies.

b) Wartime allies

At times, the Soviet–American wartime alliance (1941–5) appeared to be working well, although there were underlying ideological tensions and disagreements over strategy. Almost as soon as the Second World War ended, Soviet–American relations deteriorated, and the two countries embarked on the Cold War because:

- There were great ideological differences between the USA and USSR.
- The United States disliked the Soviet takeover and Communisation of Eastern Europe (1944–8).
- The Soviets resented the fact that the United States had kept its atomic bomb programme secret while the two countries were supposedly allies in the Second World War. Stalin was fearful of American power once the effects of the bomb were demonstrated in 1945.
- There was a war of words from 1946 onwards, as spokesmen from both sides were critical of the other.
- There were clashes of interest over several geographical areas, including Iran, Germany, Greece and Turkey.

Prior to 1949, Cold War tensions were concentrated on Europe, but in 1949 the focus switched to Asia.

Summary diagram: The Cold War to 1949

USA		USSR
Capitalism, political democracy	1917+	Communism, economic democracy
No diplomatic relations with USSR	1920s	No diplomatic relations with USA
Diplomatic relations with USSR	1933+	Diplomatic relations with USA
Anti-Hitler	1939	Pro-Hitler
Allied with USSR against Hitler and (1945) Japan	1941–5	Allied with USA against Hitler and (1945) Japan
Sole possessor of atomic bomb	1945	Intimidated by US nuclear power
Angry about Eastern Europe	1944–8	Took over Eastern Europe

3 | The Cold War Comes to Asia (1949)

a) The United States and China to 1945

From the late nineteenth century, some influential Americans developed a sentimental attachment to China, based on dreams about converting millions of Chinese to Christianity and selling them American products. In 1911, the Chinese Imperial dynasty was replaced by a republic. This increased American affection for China because Americans believed that the Chinese were trying to emulate the American development from monarchical government to a more democratic system.

By the 1920s, the leader of the Chinese republic was Chiang Kai-shek (Jiang Jieshi), head of the Chinese Nationalist Party or *Kuomintang* (*Guomindang*). His was a rather ineffective regime, and one of its many opponents was the slowly growing Chinese Communist Party under Mao Zedong.

Key question
What was the relationship between the USA and China from the nineteenth century to 1945?

In 1931, Japan invaded China. The Japanese conquest of much of eastern China was fuelled by Japanese imports of iron and steel from the United States. So, the United States put economic sanctions on Japan in order to help Chiang and China. Japanese resentment at those American sanctions was a major reason behind the Japanese attack on Pearl Harbor that brought the United States into the Second World War. In that war, the US considered Chiang's China to be an ally, if a rather ineffective one.

So, for much of the first half of the twentieth century, the US attitude toward China was friendly, although rather patronising and sometimes impatient.

Key question
Did Truman 'lose' China?

Key date

China became Communist: 1949

b) The United States and China 1945–9

After the defeat of Japan in the Second World War, China was ravaged by its civil war, in which Chiang Kai-shek's Nationalists fought Mao's Communists. Initially, the US continued to give financial and military aid to Chiang. For example, 50,000 American marines helped Chiang between 1945 and March 1947. However, in December 1948, the United States cancelled all aid to Chiang, convinced that the United States would have to take over China in order to ensure Chiang's victory. In 1949, Mao's Communist forces were triumphant and Mao declared the establishment of the People's Republic of China (PRC), the world's second great Communist state. Chiang and the remnants of his Nationalist forces fled to the island of Formosa, now more commonly called Taiwan.

The 'fall' of China to Communism had a dramatic impact on American politics. President Truman, a Democrat, faced a great deal of Republican criticism for having 'lost' China. Truman was in some ways a victim of his own 'Truman Doctrine', enunciated in 1947. That doctrine depicted a frightening world in which the United States faced the evil Communist ideology. Convinced by the Truman Doctrine, many Americans wondered why, if the Communists were such a threat, their President had allowed China to fall to Communism. In reality, any attempt to save Chiang Kai-shek would have required a large-scale American intervention. In the unlikely event that the American public would have accepted this, Chiang was probably beyond salvation. Most well-informed American observers in China were convinced of the inevitability of Mao's victory. Nevertheless, exasperated by more than a decade of Democrats in the White House, the Republicans made a great deal of political capital out of Truman's 'loss' of China, which put Truman on the defensive and contributed to his involvement in the Korean War.

So, China's becoming Communist brought the Cold War to Asia. Fearful of a further expansion of Communism in that region, the United States became involved in the Korean War (1953) and in Vietnam (c. 1950–73).

Summary diagram: The Cold War comes to Asia (1949)

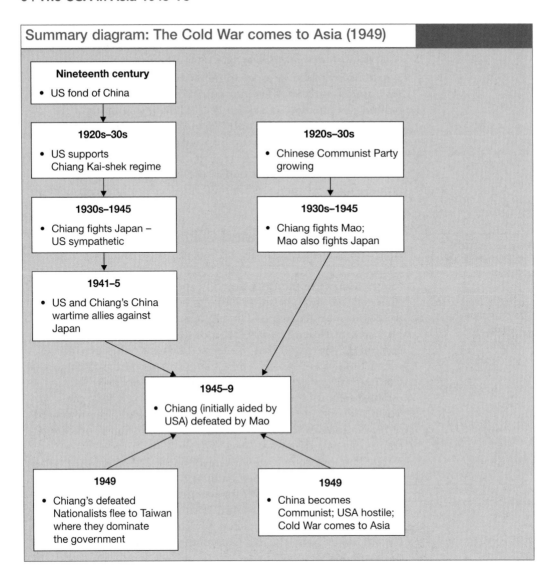

Nineteenth century
• US fond of China

1920s–30s
• US supports Chiang Kai-shek regime

1920s–30s
• Chinese Communist Party growing

1930s–1945
• Chiang fights Japan – US sympathetic

1930s–1945
• Chiang fights Mao; Mao also fights Japan

1941–5
• US and Chiang's China wartime allies against Japan

1945–9
• Chiang (initially aided by USA) defeated by Mao

1949
• Chiang's defeated Nationalists flee to Taiwan where they dominate the government

1949
• China becomes Communist; USA hostile; Cold War comes to Asia

4 | Overview of the Korean War (1950–3)

After the Second World War, two Korean states developed:

• Communist North Korea, led by Kim Il Sung, was supported by the USSR and the People's Republic of China.
• Anti-Communist South Korea, led by Syngman Rhee, was supported by the United States.

In summer 1950, Communist North Korea attacked South Korea. The United States, under the aegis of the **United Nations (UN)**, entered the war to protect South Korea, then invaded North Korea in the autumn of 1950. That brought China into the war to protect its Communist neighbour.

Key question
Who fought whom and when in Korea?

United Nations (UN)
The UN was set up in 1945. The 50 nations that signed its founding charter pledged to assist any other member that was a victim of aggression.

Key term

The bitter fighting between the US/UN/South Korea on the one side, and North Korea and China on the other, resulted in stalemate. As a result, an **armistice** was signed and the *status quo* restored in 1953.

The Korean War helped to convince the United States that Communism was in an expansionist phase in Asia and had to be resisted, which led to the American involvement in Vietnam.

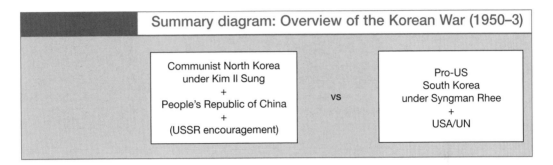

Summary diagram: Overview of the Korean War (1950–3)

Communist North Korea under Kim Il Sung

+

People's Republic of China

+

(USSR encouragement)

vs

Pro-US South Korea under Syngman Rhee

+

USA/UN

Key term

Armistice
The laying down of arms in a war, usually as a prelude to a peace treaty.

Key question
Who fought whom and when in Vietnam?

Key date

Communists took over the whole of Vietnam: 1975

Key term

Guerrillas
Soldiers who try to avoid conventional warfare (that is, one army directly confronting another), preferring methods such as sabotage to counter the enemy's superior forces.

5 | Overview of the Vietnam War (1946–75)

From 1946 to 1954 the Vietnamese people struggled for independence against their French colonial masters. When the French left Vietnam in 1954 the country was temporarily divided into two. Almost immediately the Americans moved in, helping to create and support an anti-Communist Vietnamese regime in the south against the Communist Vietnamese regime in the north.

From 1954, the United States made increasingly strenuous efforts to support the government of South Vietnam in its struggle against Communist **guerrillas** who were supported by North Vietnam, China and the USSR. However, by 1973 the United States had given up the struggle against the Vietnamese Communists. The latter proceeded to take over the whole of Vietnam in 1975.

Summary diagram: Overview of the Vietnam War (1946–75)

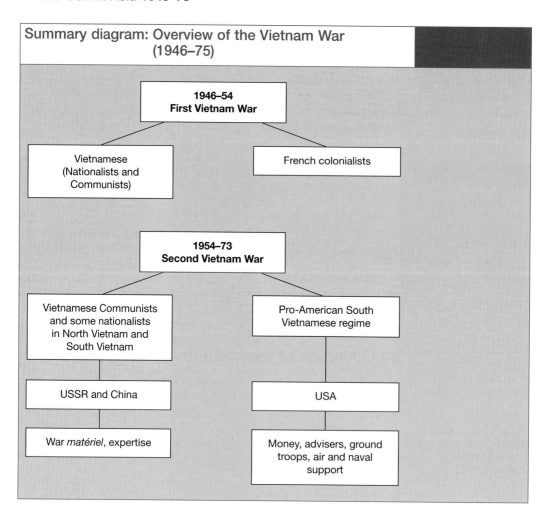

1

Causes of the Korean War

POINTS TO CONSIDER
This chapter covers the creation of the two Korean nations and the motivation of the participants in the Korean War through the following sections:

- Korea before 1945
- Korea 1945–9
- The US position on Korea in early 1950
- The Korean civil war
- The Soviets, the Chinese and the outbreak of the Korean War
- The US entry into the Korean War

Key dates

1941–5		USA and USSR allies in the Second World War
1945	August 12	Soviet troops entered northern Korea
	September 8	American troops entered southern Korea
	November	USA and USSR began talks on reunifying Korea
1948	May	Republic of Korea (South Korea) established
	September	Democratic People's Republic of Korea (North Korea) established
1948–9		Border clashes between North Korea and South Korea
		Soviet then American troops left Korea
1950	January 12	Acheson's 'defence perimeter' speech
	February	Senator McCarthy's speech generated hysterical anti-Communism
	April	National Security Council planning paper set out US position in Cold War
	June 25	North Korea attacked South Korea

1 | Korea Before 1945

Korea, a small East Asian country, had a long history of being dominated by foreign powers. Prior to 1895, Korea's giant northern neighbour China was the greatest threat. Then, from 1910 to 1945, Korea was controlled by Japan.

During the Second World War, from 1941 to 1945, the United States and USSR were allies. Although Korea was very low on their list of priorities, they discussed its future. It was suggested that after Korea was liberated from the Japanese occupation, **trustees** might guide it towards independence. The proposed trustees were the United States, China and the USSR. There were more concrete proposals for the taking of the Japanese surrender, which the Soviets were to take in the north of Korea, the Americans in the south.

After Japan was defeated, Soviet troops, as agreed, entered the northern half of Korea (12 August 1945) and American troops entered the southern half of Korea (8 September 1945).

By the time the Russian and American troops finally left (1948–9), two Koreas had been created, one pro-Soviet, the other pro-American. It could be said that the origins of the Korean War lay in these pragmatic military decisions taken in 1945, which became highly significant because of the development of the Cold War.

Key question
How did the Second World War contribute to the outbreak of the Korean War?

Key dates

USA and USSR allies in the Second World War: 1941–5

Soviet troops entered northern Korea: 12 August 1945

American troops entered southern Korea: 8 September 1945

USA and USSR began talks on reunifying Korea: November 1945

Republic of Korea (South Korea) established: May 1948

2 | Korea 1945–9

In late 1945, the USA and USSR began 18 months of what proved to be unsuccessful negotiations on the issue of Korean reunification. Meanwhile, Korea was effectively divided into two by their occupying forces. Initially, the USA was keen to get its troops out of southern Korea: in September 1947, the **JCS** said it was pointless keeping them there, as Korea had no strategic significance. However, as Cold War tensions increased (see pages 3–5), President Truman, fearing domestic criticism and damage to US credibility, rejected JCS arguments for early withdrawal.

As both great powers had troops stationed in Korea, it is not surprising that the USA tried to create a state in its own image in the southern part of the country, and that the Soviets did likewise in the northern part. The USA wanted to gain international approval for its policies and ambitions for Korea. So, in November 1947, the USA successfully pressured the UN into issuing a resolution favouring reunification following nationwide elections in Korea. Under further US pressure, the UN then supervised elections, but only in the American-controlled south. As a result of these elections, the pro-American anti-Communist Syngman Rhee was elected leader of the newly established Republic of Korea (**ROK**) in May 1948. The ROK was more commonly known as South Korea.

Key question
How and why did the creation of two Koreas contribute to the Korean War?

Key terms

Trustees
In an international context, countries who take responsibility for another country.

JCS
The Joint Chiefs of Staff were the heads of the US armed forces.

ROK
The Republic of Korea, also known as the ROK or South Korea.

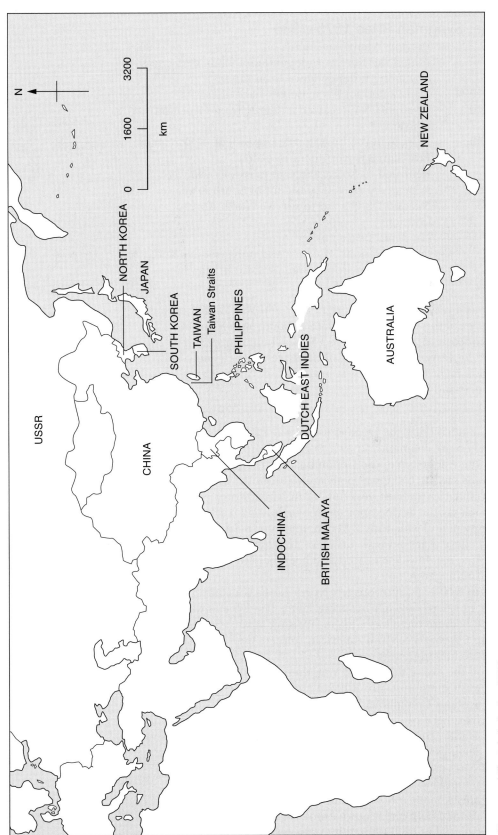

Korea and East Asia in the 1950s.

Profile: Syngman Rhee 1875–1965

1875	– Born in Whanghae, Korea
1896	– Joined the Korean Independence Club, dedicated to gaining independence from Japan
1898–1904	– Imprisoned for his nationalist activities
1904–10	– Lived in USA; received a degree from Princeton University
1912–45	– In exile in the USA; elected president of Korean Provisional Government in exile
1945	– Returned to Korea; built up mass following
1948–60	– Repeatedly elected president of South Korea
1950–3	– Needed US/UN aid to survive North Korean invasion
1953	– Hindered peace talks
1960	– Demonstrations, violence and universal demands for his resignation; resigned; exile in Hawaii
1965	– Died

Rhee was a very important figure in the Cold War, in that he was the leader of the US-sponsored state of South Korea, for the independence of which the United States fought in 1950–3. Despite his fervent anti-Communism, Rhee was a frequent embarrassment to the United States, as his government was usually unpopular and dictatorial.

In September 1948, the Democratic People's Republic of Korea (**DPRK**), more commonly known as North Korea, was established under the leadership of the Communist Kim Il Sung. Some historians say the USSR was determined from the first to establish and dominate a Stalinist government in North Korea. Other historians say the Soviets sponsored North Korean self-government and wide-ranging economic and social reforms. Many believe that Kim had considerable popular support, and that if free nationwide elections had been held in Korea, he would have won (narrowly).

In late 1948, Soviet troops left North Korea. In contrast, the American troops only left in spring 1949. The US exit was delayed because there was a major uprising against Syngman Rhee in October 1948 and American soldiers were needed to help keep him in power.

So, on the eve of the Korean War, there were two Koreas: North Korea was Communist, pro-Russian and pro-Chinese; South Korea was anti-Communist and pro-American. North Korea was militarily superior to South Korea, having been armed to the hilt by the USSR. The USA, fearful that Rhee might prove aggressive in his dealings with North Korea, gave him far less military aid than the Soviets gave to Kim. The creation of these two Korean nations, moulded in the image of the two great Cold War protagonists, made a Korean War very likely, especially as Rhee and Kim were both ambitious nationalists. Both wanted reunification, but each wanted it on his terms.

Key term

DPRK
The Democratic People's Republic of Korea, also known as the DPRK or North Korea.

Key dates

Democratic People's Republic of Korea (North Korea) established: September 1948

Soviet then American troops left Korea: 1948–9

Profile: Kim Il Sung 1912–94

1912	– Born near Pyongyang, Korea
1930s	– Joined Korean guerrilla resistance movement against Japanese colonialism; Soviets gave him military and political training
1941–5	– Led a Korean contingent in the Soviet Army
1945	– Returned to Korea; established a Communist government backed by the USSR in what became known as North Korea
1948	– First Prime Minister of North Korea
1950–3	– Invaded South Korea, which triggered the Korean War; US/UN help saved South Korea
1953	– After Korean War, became oppressive dictator of an isolated and impoverished country
1994	– Died; his son succeeded him as ruler

Kim was a very important figure in the Cold War in that his nationalism and Communism triggered off the only Cold War conflict in which the armies of two major powers (the USA and the People's Republic of China) faced each other on the battlefield. Theoretically, the USA fought as part of the UN force in Korea, but in practice, that force was dominated by the Americans. After the Korean War, having failed in his attempt to reunify the peninsula, his Communist North Korean state was a propaganda disaster for Communism.

Summary diagram: Korea before 1949

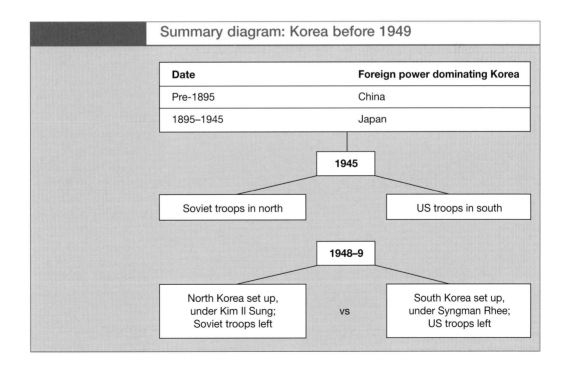

3 | The US Position on Korea in Early 1950

The British historian Peter Lowe contends that an 'unquestionably foolish' combination of US statements and acts contributed greatly to the outbreak of the Korean War. These were:

- On 12 January 1950, US **Secretary of State** Dean Acheson defined the American 'defence perimeter' in the Pacific. This 'defence perimeter' was an imaginary line drawn from north to south, through the Pacific Ocean. Acheson said that any attack on any country to the east of that line would be interpreted by the United States as an attack on America itself. Acheson's 'defence perimeter' speech required careful listening. On the one hand, he excluded Korea from the US defence perimeter, but on the other hand, he envisaged US/UN action to help South Korea against Communist aggression.
- The **Democrat** chairman of the influential Senate Foreign Relations Committee, Senator Connally, made a speech in which he seemed willing to accept a Communist takeover of the whole peninsula. Rhee criticised the speech as foolish.
- In January 1950, the Republican-dominated **Congress** rejected a **bill** that gave aid to Korea. Here, the **Republicans** were trying to make the point that they opposed the Democrat Truman's China policy (they accused Truman of having 'lost' China to Communism). Congress then passed the bill in February, but the damage had probably been done: the initial rejection of the bill must have suggested to some Communists that Korea did not greatly matter to the United States and that an attack on South Korea would not be opposed.

Key question
To what extent did the USA contribute to the outbreak of the Korean War?

Acheson's 'defence perimeter' speech: 12 January 1950

Secretary of State
The US equivalent of Britain's Foreign Secretary, he had responsibility for foreign policy and was in charge of the State Department.

Democrat
Member of a US political party characterised by greater sympathy for the poor.

Congress
The US equivalent of the British Parliament; Congress makes laws and grants money to fund the President's policies.

Bill
In order to make a measure law, the suggested measure has to be presented to Congress. Once this bill is passed by both houses of Congress, and assented to by the President, the bill becomes an act or law.

Republicans
US political party characterised by conservatism on domestic issues.

Summary diagram: The US position on Korea in early 1950

Acheson says outside defence perimeter, but …

Does Korea matter?

Chairman of the Senate Foreign Relations Committee seems relaxed about a Communist Korea

Congress rejects Korea aid bill, but …

4 | The Korean Civil War

Key question
Was a Korean civil war underway before the North Korean attack?

Most historians now agree that the two Koreas were already waging civil war before North Korea's attack triggered the full-scale **internationalised Korean War**. The Korean civil war was caused by the nationalism and ambition of Kim Il Sung and Syngman Rhee, both of whom wanted their country reunified. There had been frequent border clashes, mostly initiated by South Korea, beginning in the summer of 1948, and peaking in the summer of 1949. It seems that Kim Il Sung thought that his June 1950 invasion of South Korea would inspire a popular rebellion against the autocratic Syngman Rhee.

Key dates
Border clashes between North Korea and South Korea: 1948–9

North Korea attacked South Korea: 25 June 1950

At the time, the West was certain that North Korea was the aggressor, but even some Western historians remain unconvinced that it was all the Communists' fault. Whatever the reality, the United States was convinced that the USSR and China were behind an aggressive North Korean attack on South Korea.

Key term
Internationalised Korean War
The war between North Korea and South Korea led to intervention by the US/UN and China.

5 | The Soviets, the Chinese and the Outbreak of the Korean War

a) Stalin's role

Key question
Was it Stalin's war?

It was essential that Kim had Stalin's approval for the invasion of South Korea: the North Korean leader could not have made an effective attack without Soviet fighter planes. Throughout 1949, Stalin repeatedly stopped Kim from attacking South Korea, probably because the Soviet leader feared such an attack might lead to US intervention.

However, in the end, Stalin gave Kim the go-ahead. Suggested reasons for Stalin's approval include:

- After China became Communist in late 1949, Communist parties throughout the world were keen to see Korea become totally Communist.

Profile: Joseph Stalin 1879–1953

1879	–	Born in Georgia
1929	–	Became the dominant figure in Soviet politics
1939	–	Stalin and Hitler collaborated in the Second World War – initially
1941	–	USSR attacked by Nazi Germany
1941–5	–	USSR and USA allies in the Second World War
1944–8	–	Took control of Eastern Europe, which antagonised the USA and triggered the Cold War
1950 January	–	Recognised Ho Chi Minh's Democratic Republic of Vietnam
June	–	Gave Kim Il Sung the go-ahead to attack South Korea
October	–	Encouraged Communist China to enter the Korean War
1953	–	Died

Stalin had a massive influence on US policy in Asia after 1950. Firstly, he played an important role in the Korean War. He gave his approval to Kim Il Sung's attack on South Korea, which was the trigger event for the war. Then he was important in the internationalisation of the war. His domination of Eastern Europe (achieved between 1944 and 1948) and his policies towards Germany had alienated the USA and helped to ensure that the United States would enter the Korean War. Also, Stalin encouraged Mao Zedong to enter the war after US forces crossed the 38th parallel. Secondly, although Stalin was far less active in his support of Ho Chi Minh and Communism in Vietnam, the US thought otherwise. The American belief that Ho was Stalin's puppet, coupled with Stalin's actions in Europe and Korea, helped to stimulate the US involvement in Vietnam. So, Stalin had a vital role in motivating US intervention in two wars in Asia.

- The Yugoslav representative at the UN said Stalin (who feared Mao Zedong as a potential rival for the leadership of world Communism) encouraged Kim in order to get the US embroiled with Communist China. With China and the United States thus occupied and weakened, the USSR would naturally become more powerful.
- Stalin was anxious about a resurgent Japan, which seemed to be speedily changing from US foe to US friend. Japan was only about 100 miles from Korea, and the Soviet Union and Communism would be safer if the whole Korean peninsula were Communist.
- It is possible that what Lowe called the 'unquestionably foolish' combination of US words and deeds in early 1950 (see above) encouraged Stalin to think that he and Kim could get away with the attack.
- A Korean War would distract the United States from Europe, enabling Stalin to feel more secure in that region.

Key question
Was it Mao's war?

b) Mao's role

The United States believed that Moscow and Beijing colluded in the North Korean attack on South Korea. Mao certainly feared a resurgent Japan, and his concern for his frontiers was demonstrated by his invasion of Tibet a few days before Chinese troops poured into Korea.

Profile: Mao Zedong 1893–1976

1893		– Born in Hunan province, China
1921		– Became a Communist
1930s–1945		– Fought against Chiang Kai-shek's Nationalist regime and against Japanese aggression in China
1949		– Finally defeated Chiang Kai-shek and established the Communist People's Republic of China
1950	January	– Recognised Ho Chi Minh's Democratic Republic of Vietnam
	June	– Assented to Kim Il Sung's attack on South Korea
	October	– Entered the Korean War after American forces crossed the 38th parallel into North Korea
1953		– Korean War ended
1960s		– **Sino-Soviet** relations deteriorated due to ideological differences, traditional great power rivalry, and a personality clash between Mao and the Soviet leader Khrushchev; Mao increasingly aided Ho Chi Minh's struggle against the US in Vietnam
1972		– Relations with US improved
1976		– Died

Key term

Sino-Soviet
Chinese–Soviet.

Mao, like Stalin, was a very important factor in US involvement in Asia. When Mao's Communist forces were victorious in the Chinese civil war in 1949, the United States was horrified and began to turn its attention to Asia (as opposed to Europe) as the storm centre of the Cold War. Mao, like Stalin, gave his assent to Kim Il Sung's invasion of South Korea, which triggered off the Korean War. The American belief that Mao and Stalin were behind this invasion was an important motivation for the US intervention in Korea. When American troops neared the Chinese border, this brought China into the Korean War and into three years of bitter fighting against the Americans. The American conviction that Mao was behind Ho Chi Minh helped bring about US intervention in Vietnam. Although Ho Chi Minh had needed no encouragement from Mao to fight for Vietnamese independence, Ho relied heavily on Mao's material aid in his wars against the French and the Americans. So, Mao had been vitally important in the US intervention in two Asian wars.

On the other hand, a surely more persuasive argument is that it was not 'Mao's war'. China had only recently emerged from civil war, the new Communist regime was still not fully established, and were Mao to undertake any foreign adventures, Taiwan was surely a greater priority. Furthermore, Kim Il Sung preferred Stalin to Mao, partly because he feared China more: China was closer and had historically worked to dominate its smaller neighbour. Finally, although Mao followed Stalin in giving Kim his approval for the attack, Stalin clearly took the lead. This was surely not 'Mao's war'.

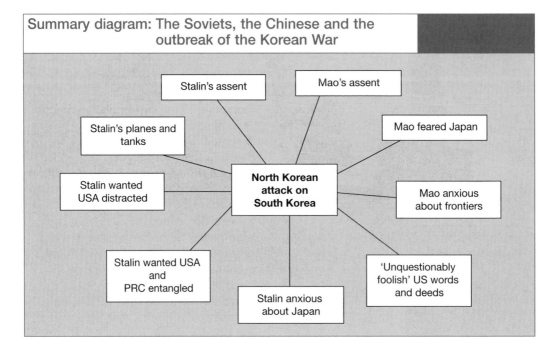

Summary diagram: The Soviets, the Chinese and the outbreak of the Korean War

6 | The US Entry into the Korean War

There were many reasons why President Truman led the United States into the Korean War.

Key question
Why did the US enter the Korean War?

a) Reason 1: American anti-Communism

Underlying all the other reasons was American anti-Communism. The United States feared an ideology that rejected capitalism and political democracy. Americans believed that their security would be greatly threatened in a world where more and more countries went Communist. It was anticipated that those countries would refuse to trade with the United States and thereby damage the US economy. More importantly, it was believed that those countries would try to export their ideology (either by persuasion or by force) to all other countries, including the United States.

Profile: Harry Truman 1884–1972

1884		– Born on a Missouri farm
1935		– Elected senator for Missouri (Democrat)
1941–5		– United States in the Second World War: Truman excelled on Senate Committee investigating National Defence
1945	April	– President Roosevelt died; Vice-president Truman became president
1947		– Effectively declared Cold War in 'Truman Doctrine' speech: said United States would help any country that resisted Communism
1949		– Set up NATO (North Atlantic Treaty Organisation), the Western anti-Communist military alliance. When China became Communist, Republicans accused Truman and the Democrats of 'losing China'
1950	February	– Senator Joseph McCarthy (Republican) said Truman's State Department contained Communists; beginning of paranoid Cold War period
	May	– Truman offered financial aid to the French in their struggle against Communism in Vietnam
	June	– When Communist North Korea invaded non-Communist South Korea, Truman sent United States forces to restore the *status quo*
1950–3		– Korean War, often known as 'Truman's War'; both Truman and the war became increasingly unpopular
1953		– Retired to Missouri
1972		– Died

Truman's decision to oppose Communism resulted in US involvement in the Cold War and in the wars in Korea and Vietnam. His decision to send American troops to Korea after North Korea attacked South Korea resulted in a three-year war involving many countries that might have led to a Third World War. Although initially he aimed only to restore the *status quo* in South Korea, he changed US war aims in September 1950 and attempted the reunification of the peninsula. When he allowed General MacArthur to cross the 38th parallel into North Korea, he brought China fully into the war. The conflict between the Chinese and the Americans in Korea confirmed that the Cold War had dramatically arrived in Asia, and ensured that **Sino-American** relations were exceptionally hostile until the early 1970s. When Truman aided the French in their struggle to defeat the Communist Ho Chi Minh's fight for Vietnamese independence, he started the American involvement in Vietnam, although it could be argued that the commitment was still reversible at his death.

Key term

Sino-American
Chinese–
American.

b) Reason 2: The world balance of power

From the time that Russia became Communist, the United States feared a Communist-dominated world, and by 1950 that eventuality seemed likely.

Prior to the Second World War, the USSR remained the world's only Communist country. However, towards the end of the Second World War, as Soviet troops marched across Eastern Europe towards Berlin to deliver the final blow to Hitler, they began to create pro-Soviet regimes in Poland, Romania, Bulgaria, Hungary and Czechoslovakia.

By 1950, all of Eastern Europe and the Soviet half of Germany (see below) were Communist. Eastern Europe had effectively disappeared behind Stalin's '**Iron Curtain**'.

US resentment and fear at the loss of Eastern Europe was exacerbated by several events between 1948 in 1949 that suggested that the world balance of power had tilted in favour of Communism:

Iron Curtain
After the Second World War, the USSR established Communism in, and took control of, Eastern Europe. Churchill said that it was as if an 'iron curtain' had come down across the European continent.

Key term

- Early in 1948, opposition to Communism in Czechoslovakia was snuffed out. The West perceived this as further proof of Soviet expansionism.
- In spring 1948, Stalin blocked Western road, rail and canal access to West Berlin. The West perceived his actions to be a highly aggressive attack on the *status quo*. The British historian Peter Lowe emphasises that these two great European crises, in Czechoslovakia and Germany, played a big part in persuading Truman that Communist aggression had to be contained in Korea. According to Lowe, Europe's battles were fought on the battlefields of Korea.
- In August 1949, the US monopoly of the atomic bomb came to an end. The Soviet testing of their first bomb was a great and frightening blow to US confidence and security.
- In October 1949, China became Communist. Truman, having depicted Communism as a terrifying evil in his 'Truman Doctrine' speech of March 1947, was now vulnerable to Republican accusations that by ceasing aid to Chang Kai-shek, he had 'lost China' for the United States (see page 5). These accusations left Truman on the defensive, needing to prove his anti-Communist credentials somehow.
- After the fall of China, Communism seemed to be entering a dynamic expansionist phase. Not only had North Korea attacked South Korea, but there were also Communist insurgencies in Vietnam (see page 85), British Malaya and the Philippines.
- Some historians emphasise US Cold War credibility as a major cause of US entry into the war. The US ambassador to the USSR, Alan Kirk, cabled Washington on 25 June 1950, that the attack represented:

a clear-cut Soviet challenge which [the] US should answer firmly and swiftly as it constitutes [a] direct threat [to] our leadership of [the] free world against Soviet Communism.

Key dates

Senator McCarthy's speech generated hysterical anti-Communism: February 1950

National Security Council planning paper set out US position in Cold War: April 1950

Key terms

Congressional mid-term elections
The US president and some members of Congress are elected every fourth year, but the US Constitution (aiming to prevent a single party dominating US politics) requires that the other members of Congress are to be elected in the middle of that four-year cycle.

National Security Council
Established in 1947 to co-ordinate US government work on internal and external security; members included the president, vice-president, secretary of state, secretary of defence, and the chiefs of the CIA and JCS.

The Philippines and the Cold War

After the Spanish–American war of 1898, the USA took possession of the Philippine Islands. In 1934, the US promised the Philippines independence after 1945. During the 1930s, there was a small Filipino Communist party (PKP). In the Second World War, a PKP leader headed the anti-Japanese resistance on the most densely populated island, Luzon. The resistance movement was known as *Hukhalahap* (Huk).

The Philippines became independent in 1946, and the Huks led the rebellion against the new government. By late 1948 there were at least 5000 guerrillas in Central Luzon. Most of the Huks were Communist, so by 1948, the USA had given $72.6 million to help the Filipino government oppose the rebels.

By 1950 there were at least 12,000 Huk insurgents in central Luzon. The Americans suggested that Ramon Magsaysay be appointed Secretary of Defence, and he proved popular and successful. He persuaded the government to introduce agrarian reforms that helped the peasants and thereby decreased Huk support. American financial aid ($500 million between 1951 and 1956) was vital in the defeat of the Huks. Few Huks remained by 1960.

c) Reason 3: McCarthyism and domestic political concerns

In February 1950, Republican Senator Joseph McCarthy declared that there were Communists in the State Department. He generated large-scale anti-Communist hysteria. In this atmosphere, Truman had to be seen to be tough in handling the Communist threat, otherwise the Republicans might win a great victory over the Democrats in the **Congressional mid-term elections** of November 1950. Initially, wars tend to make the American people rally around their president, so Truman's political motivation in entering the Korean War has long been emphasised by historians, although others deny that he went to war to increase his own popularity.

d) Reason 4: NSC-68

Early in 1950, a beleaguered Truman, haunted by the Soviet bomb, the establishment of the People's Republic of China, and McCarthy, commissioned the **National Security Council** (NSC) to produce a planning paper. He wanted this paper to summarise where the United States stood, and in which direction it should move, in relation to Communism.

NSC-68 was a classic Cold War document in that it described a polarised world, in which the enslaved (in Communist countries) faced the free (in countries such as the USA). This 68th planning paper of the NSC (hence 'NSC-68') claimed that the USSR had a 'fanatic faith' and that its leaders wanted total domination of Europe and Asia. The paper recommended:

- the development of a hydrogen bomb, even more powerful than the atomic bombs dropped on Japan, so that the United States could resist Communist attempts at domination
- the build-up of US conventional forces (soldiers, tanks, ships, etc.), in order to defend American shores and to enable the USA to fight limited wars abroad
- higher taxes to finance the struggle
- alliances that would gain help for the United States
- the mobilisation of the American public, in order to create a Cold War consensus, as the country needed to be united in the waging of this war.

The recommendations of NSC-68 make it easy to see why the United States was ready to intervene in Korea.

e) Reason 5: Fears for Japan

After the Second World War, the American occupation under General MacArthur had revitalised Japan, which was beginning to develop from American foe into American friend (see the box opposite on page 23). Japan was only 100 miles from South Korea and was within Acheson's defence perimeter. The safety of Japan would be jeopardised if it were to be faced by a totally Communist Korean peninsula with Communism apparently on the march. Historians such as Peter Lowe emphasise that US anxiety about Japan was a major cause of the Korean War. The Defence Department told Truman that Japan was vital for the defence of the West against Communism. In June 1950, several of Truman's leading advisers emphasised that Communist control of South Korean airbases would greatly threaten Japanese security, although, according to Patterson (1996), most of them 'were not much concerned about Japan'.

The United States, Japan and the Cold War

The US occupation of Japan
After the US victory in the Second World War, President Harry Truman (see page 19) put General Douglas MacArthur (see page 34) in charge of the 'Allied' (in reality, American) occupation. MacArthur was Supreme Commander for the Allied Powers, and he and his administration became known as SCAP. In 1948, 3200 American personnel in SCAP governed 86 million Japanese.

The United States occupied Japan for nearly seven years. From 1945 to 1947, the emphasis was on demilitarisation, democratisation and retribution (for war crimes). After 1947, the new US Secretary of State, George Marshall, took a much greater interest in Japan. As a result of this change in personnel and of the developing Cold War, the nature of American rule changed.

Key question
How successfully did the US contain Communism in Japan?

The impact of the Cold War on the US occupation of Japan

The Cold War had a dramatic impact on US policy towards Japan. It led many in Washington to view Japan as vital to American security. When China went Communist in 1949, Truman's National Security Council promoted the policy of economic recovery in Japan to ensure that a prosperous Japan would see the advantages of capitalism and be a bulwark against Chinese Communism. Under the pressure of the Cold War, the United States decided that Japan should develop from foe to friend, which led to rapid American moves to end the occupation. The Korean War further speeded up the process, so a Japanese–American peace treaty was signed in September 1951 in San Francisco. The treaty restored Japanese independence. In allowing the USSR to retain its post-war gains (as promised by President Roosevelt) of the Kurile Islands, it also guaranteed Soviet–Japanese tension, which suited the United States. Along with the peace treaty, a security treaty was signed. This allowed the United States to retain military bases in Japan. Stimulated by the outbreak of the Korean War, SCAP had created a 75,000-strong police reserve which was, in all but name, a military force, in defiance of the American-written Japanese constitution. So, because of the Cold War, the United States was building up Japanese power militarily and economically.

Japanese Prime Minister Yoshida described the Korean War as 'the gift of the gods'. Japan became a vital source of supplies for the Americans fighting in Korea. This triggered the post-war Japanese 'economic miracle', especially through US purchase of Japanese vehicles.

Would Japan have gone Communist?

Established in 1922, the Japanese Communist Party (JCP) was Japan's oldest political party. Prior to the Second World War, it was repressed, but it revived in the early years of the American occupation, when it concentrated on becoming 'lovable' by aiming to achieve political power through the ballot box rather than through revolution. In the 1949 election, the JCP received 10 per cent of the popular vote, but then Moscow urged it to become more militant. The Korean War accelerated that militancy, and the Japanese government and SCAP used the militancy as an excuse to crush the party. Some Japanese Communist leaders went underground, others fled to China. Some ordinary members engaged in terrorism and sabotage. Without leaders, and perceived as too militant, the JCP lost electoral importance until 1969 and 1972, when being 'lovable' again won it 6.8 per cent then 10.4 per cent of the popular vote.

Although the JCP was reasonably popular, it was never that important or influential. Japan and China were traditional enemies, and for many Japanese, Communism was too closely associated with a hostile neighbour after 1949. Also, US policies helped to ensure that Japan did not become Communist. There was little overt antagonism or resistance to the American occupation. This was due to a combination of factors, including:

- Japanese war weariness.
- The unexpected benevolence of the American regime.
- American generosity in feeding the urban population which faced starvation after the war.
- **SCAP** control of the Japanese media.
- MacArthur's insistence on retaining Japan's beloved emperor, who was used to promote American policies.
- Japan's traditionally conformist and controlled society.

Then, in order to develop Japan as a Cold War ally, the US speedily ended the occupation. Furthermore, the association with the United States quickly brought prosperity. The Korean War gave a massive fillip to the Japanese economy. Thus, for all these reasons, Japan was 'saved' for the West.

The end of the story
Japan prospered greatly because of internal factors (such as the hard work ethos) and because of the United States, which bore the financial burden of Japan's defence. By 1965, Japan was the world's second largest economy (the United States was first). By the 1970s, Japanese nationalist antipathy towards the United States was often quite strong, while the perceived economic threat from Japan aroused American antagonism. However, it was not until the 1980s that Japanese–American relations deteriorated dramatically. Significantly, that deterioration paralleled the winding down of the Cold War.

Key terms

SCAP
General MacArthur was Supreme Commander for the Allied Forces (SCAP) in Japan. The acronym was used to describe the whole US occupation regime.

Collective security
An international system whereby all countries agree to collectively protect any one of their number that is a victim of aggression.

f) Reason 6: The United Nations and lessons from history

Collective security had been tried in the years between the two world wars, in the form of the League of Nations. The failure of that body was thought to have played a role in the outbreak of the Second World War. Truman, a keen student of history, felt that the 1930s had taught that collective security needed to be supported and appeasement (as when Britain and France gave in to Hitler) needed to be avoided. When North Korea attacked South Korea, Truman believed that the League of Nations' successor, the UN, was being tested, and that if he failed to support it, and if he appeased aggressors, the results might be another world war. He felt certain of support from Western allies such as Britain and France, as they were anxious about Communist unrest in their colonial possessions (British Malaya and French Indochina).

Malaya, Korea and the Cold War

Britain provided a small number of troops to fight alongside the United States in Korea, but the main British struggle against Communism took place in Malaya.

In the late eighteenth century, Britain had become interested in Malaya, which became a British colony in 1867. In the Second World War, the Japanese took Malaya from the British (1942–5). The Japanese conquerors were particularly harsh on the Chinese, who constituted 44.7 per cent of the population of Malaya. In 1945, in the four-week gap between the time that the defeated Japanese left and the British returned, the Chinese Communist Party of Malaya (MCP) murdered Malays who had collaborated with the Japanese. The British thus returned to a nation divided by racial animosity. In 1948, inspired by Mao's successes in China, the MCP began to rebel against British rule. The British were (probably wrongly) convinced that the Communist uprising was sponsored by the USSR. The arrival of some Chinese army officers confirmed the British and American belief that the Communist insurgency in Malaya was orchestrated by Beijing and Moscow.

The British, supported by the indigenous Malays (who constituted 43.5 per cent of the population), fought a successful counter-insurgency war against the Chinese Communist guerrillas. The counter-insurgency was partially financed by the prosperity generated by increased Malayan exports of rubber and tin, which were much in demand during the Korean War. Britain granted Malaya independence in 1957.

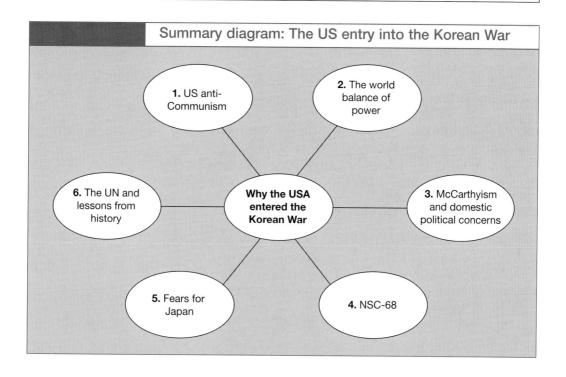

Summary diagram: The US entry into the Korean War

1. US anti-Communism

2. The world balance of power

6. The UN and lessons from history

Why the USA entered the Korean War

3. McCarthyism and domestic political concerns

5. Fears for Japan

4. NSC-68

7 | Key Debates on the Korean War

For around two decades after the end of the Korean War, American historians demonstrated relatively little interest in the war, hence Clay Blair's phrase, 'the forgotten war' (1987). Others referred to the Korean War as 'the war before Vietnam' or 'the unknown war'. Nevertheless, the war has generated considerable debate among historians – although nowhere near as much as the Vietnam War.

Debate 1: A war of Communist aggression?

For many years, the traditional **orthodox viewpoint on the Korean War** among Western historians was that this was a war of Communist aggression. However, in 1981, the US historian Bruce Cumings, with a **revisionist viewpoint on the Korean War**, emphasised that this was, initially, a Korean civil war. The consensus that has emerged since then is that the North Korean attack was motivated more by Korean nationalism and by the desire for the reunification of the peninsula, than by Communist aggression. Cumings and Lowe also emphasised that US policies in Korea after 1945 bore a great deal of responsibility for the Korean civil war, and therefore for the internationalised Korean War. This was because the United States stopped a left-wing revolution in Korea in 1945 and imposed the unpopular Syngman Rhee's reactionary regime on the south. Kim Il Sung, well aware of Rhee's unpopularity, therefore decided that his invasion of South Korea had an excellent chance of success.

Debate 2: Chinese and Soviet motivation

There has been much disagreement about the roles played by Stalin and Mao in Kim's invasion. Some historians still agree with the Truman administration and believe that the USSR ordered North Korea to attack, despite the general consensus that the US intervened in a civil war. New evidence that has emerged since the opening up of the Chinese and Soviet archives in the 1980s has illuminated Chinese and Soviet motivation. Soviet documents released in the 1990s confirm that before 1950, Stalin repeatedly refused to approve the invasion, but that after Mao's victory in China, pressure grew on the Soviet leader to facilitate a similar victory in Korea by unleashing Kim. Whatever Stalin's motivation, few doubt that without his go-ahead, Kim would have – or even could have – invaded South Korea.

Western historians were once willing to believe the contemporary Chinese contention that Chinese aims were purely defensive, but Chinese historians working with these new sources, such as Chen Jian (1994), have emphasised other factors, such as China's desire to restore its world status, Stalin's pressure on China to enter the war, and the Chinese desire to repay Korean military aid during the Chinese civil war.

Key terms

Orthodox viewpoint on the Korean War
US historians who see the Korean War as a war of Communist aggression have the orthodox viewpoint.

Revisionist viewpoint on the Korean War
Historians who see the origins of the Korean War in a Korean civil war, rather than blaming the North Korean attack on Communist aggression, have a revisionist viewpoint.

Debate 3: US motivation in East Asia

The traditional interpretation of US intervention in East Asia remains popular (for example, Dockrill and Hopkins, 2006). According to this interpretation, the US was motivated by anti-Communism, containment and the Cold War. However, **revisionist historians** (such as Robert Wood, 2005) accuse the United States of a neocolonialist policy, aimed at achieving US economic hegemony in East Asia. This **neocolonialism** can be said to explain the strong Washington support for the British efforts to reassert British colonial rule over Malaya after 1946. Of course, the US support for the European colonial powers in East Asia, whether the British in Malaya, the Dutch in the Dutch East Indies (until 1949) or the French in Indochina, can all be attributed to anti-Communism, as the British, Dutch and French all faced Communist opponents. (The Communists were frequently the most numerous and determined opponents of the colonial regimes, as with the Malay Communist Party.) US policy in post-war Japan is similarly debated. Some historians see the USA as a benevolent occupying power, some see the USA as restructuring Japan to serve US economic needs, and some see the Cold War dictating US policy in Japan. **Post-revisionists** such as John Lewis Gaddis (2005) see US policy as combining the several elements, especially the desire to promote democracy and capitalism during the Cold War.

US intervention in Korea is variously interpreted. Again, there are those who emphasise containment, and those who emphasise US economic ambitions. Some emphasise very specific factors. Leffler (2001) concentrates on the importance of Japan in the US intervention in Korea. The USA believed that Japan's economic revival required access to markets and raw materials in other countries such as Korea and Malaya. The US also had to intervene in Korea to demonstrate to Japan that the US was a credible power and ally. Gaddis (2005) stressed that the US intervention was a response to a Communist 'challenge to the entire structure of post-war collective security', and quotes Truman 'repeatedly' telling his advisers, 'We can't let the UN down'.

Key terms

Revisionist historians
American historians who criticise US motives in the Cold War as aggressive and acquisitive.

Neocolonialism
Whereas old-style colonialism was usually openly exploitative, neocolonialism had a kinder face.

Post-revisionists
Historians who do not 'blame' one side of the Cold War.

Some key books in the debates

Bruce Cumings, *The Origins of the Korean War* (Princeton, 1981–90).
John Lewis Gaddis, *The Cold War* (Penguin, 2005).
Melvyn Leffler, in Odd Arne Westad (editor), *Reviewing the Cold War* (London, 2001).
Peter Lowe, *The Korean War* (Macmillan, 2000).
James Patterson, *Grand Expectations: The United States, 1945–1974* (Oxford, 1996).
Zhang Shuguang and Chen Jian (editors), *Chinese Communist Foreign Policy and the Cold War in Asia: New Documentary Evidence, 1944–1950* (Chicago, 1996).
Robert Wood, in Melvyn Leffler and David Painter (editors), *The Origins of the Cold War* (New York, 2005).
Vladislav Zubok and Constantine Pleshakov, *Inside the Kremlin's Cold War* (Harvard, 1996).

2 The Course of Events in the Korean War in 1950

POINTS TO CONSIDER
With the advantage of surprise, the North Korean invasion force pushed the ROK (South Korean) and US troops down to the southeastern corner of the Korean peninsula. General MacArthur then turned the war around in brilliant fashion: US/UN and ROK forces crossed into North Korea itself, prompting China to enter the war. Chinese troops forced US/ROK/UN forces back into South Korea. The front lines then stabilised near the 38th parallel. This chapter covers the rapidly changing military situation in 1950 with sections on:

- The internationalisation of the war
- The military situation, June–September 1950
- Inchon and new American war aims
- Chinese intervention in the Korean War
- The fighting in Korea, October–December 1950
- The debates about General MacArthur

Key dates

1950	June 25	North Korea attacked South Korea
	June 27	Security Council resolution declared UN should oppose North Korea
	June 30	South Korean troops in headlong retreat; Truman sent US troops to Korea
	July 3	US 7th Fleet arrived in Taiwan Straits
	August	US/ROK/UN forces driven behind Pusan Perimeter
	September 15	Successful US assault on Inchon
	October	Chinese forces poured into Korea
	November	US/UN/ROK forces retreated back into South Korea

1 | The Internationalisation of the War

a) The course of events in summer 1950

On 25 June 1950, North Korea attacked South Korea, which prompted the UN Secretary-General, Trygve Lie, to assert, 'This is war against the United Nations'. The attack was debated in the UN **Security Council**. In the absence of the USSR (which had been boycotting the UN because Communist China had no UN seat) and encouraged by the USA, the Security Council passed a resolution that asked the aggressor, North Korea, to withdraw. On 27 June, another Security Council resolution declared that the UN should oppose North Korea.

At this time, the USA had 500 advisers in South Korea as part of its Korea Military Advisory Group (KMAG). These advisers joined South Korean forces and civilians in such a rapid retreat that they nicknamed KMAG: 'Kiss My Ass Goodbye'.

On hearing of the North Korean attack, President Truman had said to his Secretary of State, Dean Acheson, 'We've got to stop the sons of bitches, no matter what.' Truman responded to the 27 June UN resolution with an **executive order** authorising US air and naval forces to attack North Korea, telling the nation:

> The attack upon Korea makes it plain beyond all doubt that Communism has passed beyond the use of subversion to conquer independent nations and will now use armed invasion and war.

Years later he elaborated on that in his memoirs, saying that if the 'free world' had not opposed the Communists in South Korea, 'no other small nation[s] would have the courage to resist threats and aggression by stronger Communist neighbours'.

Truman did not ask Congress to declare war, prompting Republican Senator Robert Taft to point out that he was supposed to do so under the US constitution. However, Congress was very supportive, extending the **draft** by one year. Another Republican Senator, William F. Knowland, criticised Truman for not allowing the United States air force to operate in North Korea itself, saying that no one would stop a policeman chasing a thug away from a crime scene: 'The action this government is taking is a police action against the violator of the law of nations and the charter of the United Nations.' Truman used the 'police action' phrase in a press conference on 27 June:

> *Reporter*: Mr President, everybody is asking in this country, are we or are we not at war?
>
> *Truman*: We are not at war … The members of the United Nations are going to the relief of the Korean Republic to suppress a bandit raid on the Republic of Korea.
>
> *Reporter*: Mr President, would it be correct under your explanation to call this a police action under the United Nations?
>
> *Truman*: Yes, that is exactly what it amounts to.

Key question
How and why did the Korean civil war become internationalised?

Key dates

North Korea attacked South Korea: 25 June 1950

Security Council resolution declared UN should oppose North Korea: 27 June 1950

South Korean troops in headlong retreat; Truman sent US troops to Korea: 30 June 1950

Key terms

Security Council
The UN chamber that contained the great powers; the other members were only represented in the General Assembly.

Executive order
In certain areas, such as military matters, the US constitution gives the president the power to act alone, through issuing executive orders.

Draft
The US term for what the British call conscription (the enforced call-up of civilians to be soldiers).

As the South Korean capital, Seoul, fell to the Communists, Truman sent US troops to Korea on 30 June. General Douglas MacArthur had warned him that without them, the Communists would take over the whole of Korea. Truman also ordered the US 7th Fleet to the **Taiwan Straits**, where it arrived on 3 July. When on 7 July, a UN Security Council resolution called for the creation of a United Nations Command (**UNC**), the UN asked Truman to appoint a UNC commander, and Truman appointed MacArthur. The UN asked that the UNC commander have direct access to the UN, but Truman insisted that MacArthur communicate only with Washington.

From the first, there were major tensions between MacArthur and Truman. Truman was wedded to his Cold War doctrine of containment of Communism: he wanted a limited, defensive war in South Korea in order to forestall Soviet or Chinese intervention. MacArthur on the other hand wanted to go all out against North Korea and, later, against Communist China.

b) Analysis of events in summer 1950

> **An old Korean proverb …**
> 'When whales collide, the shrimp suffer.' In the Cold War between the USA and the USSR, some Koreans recognised that they were the shrimp.

The internationalisation of the Korean civil war in the summer of 1950 raises several questions, including why the United States entered the war (see pages 18–25 and 27), the significance of the US entry into the war, whether MacArthur was a wise choice as UNC commander, and whether the war was a US war or a UN war.

i) The significance of the US entry into the Korean War
The USA was taking a significant risk in entering into the Korean War. General Omar Bradley, chairman of the JCS, was convinced that the USSR and China would not get involved in the war, but was aware that if they did, the war would effectively become a Third World War.

When Truman ordered American forces to Korea he was 'significantly expanding and militarising' US foreign policy in Asia, according to American historian James Patterson (1996). Similarly, when Truman sent the 7th Fleet to the Taiwan Straits, he was reinjecting the United States into a Chinese civil war from which the United States had extricated itself in 1947, according to Chinese–American historian Gordon Chang. While the dispatch of the 7th Fleet was motivated by the US fear that a Chinese Communist takeover of Taiwan or a similar move by Chiang against the mainland would threaten US security, Communist China naturally interpreted it as an aggressive move. Chinese fears were confirmed when General MacArthur, to the dismay of the State Department, made a high-profile visit to Taiwan to see Chiang Kai-shek on 30 July and publicly praised him. Britain, a

Key date

US 7th Fleet arrived in Taiwan Straits: 3 July 1950

Key terms

Taiwan Straits
The stretch of water between mainland (Communist) China and Chang Kai-shek's island of Taiwan.

UNC
The United Nations Command, under MacArthur, co-ordinated the US/UN/ROK forces in the Korean War.

Key question
What was the significance of the US entry into the Korean War?

Profile: Douglas MacArthur 1880–1964

1880		– Born in Little Rock, Arkansas
1917–19		– Brave and able leader in the First World War
1930–5		– Appointed army chief of staff
1935–41		– Built up the Filipino army
1937		– Retired from the US Army
1941		– Recalled to active service in the Second World War
1942–5		– Commanded US troops in the successful island-hopping strategy that took them close to Japan by 1945
1945–51		– Allied Commander of the Japanese occupation: effectively demilitarised Japan, restored its economy, and introduced liberal democracy. Also head of Far East command
1950	June	– Appointed Commander of UN forces in Korea
	September	– His brilliant landing at Inchon drove the North Korean invaders out of South Korea; led US/UN/South Korean troops into North Korea
	October	– Chinese entered Korean War and drove MacArthur's forces back into South Korea
1951	April	– President Truman controversially sacked MacArthur
1952–64		– Relative seclusion until his death

Key terms

Containment
Truman's policy of seeking to prevent the spread of Communism, for example, in Korea.

Europe-firster
An American who, during the Cold War, thought that Europe was the most important arena of conflict.

Asia-firster
An American who, during the Cold War, thought that Asia was the most important arena of conflict.

MacArthur was of great importance in the Korean War, not so much because he was the leader of the US and UN forces, but because that leadership, coupled with his great reputation, gave him the opportunity to influence American Cold War policy. President Truman believed in the policy of **containment** of Communism, and this led him to favour limited war in Korea. MacArthur, however, was keen to take on Communist China and to use all available American resources, including atomic weapons. While Truman was a **Europe-firster**, MacArthur was an **Asia-firster**. What added to MacArthur's importance was that he made his opinions public. Public disagreements over US policy greatly damaged Truman, but it was the president's policies that eventually prevailed. There was no all-out war against Communist China.

close US ally, criticised this extension of the Korean conflict to China. Furthermore, the dispatch of the 7th Fleet created confusion as to US war aims. On 10 July 1950, Secretary of State Dean Acheson declared that the US war aim in Korea was simply the restoration of the *status quo* – that is, to get North Korea out of South Korea. However, as Britain recognised, the combination

Profile: Chiang Kai-shek 1887–1975

1887	– Born into a moderately prosperous trading and farming family
1906–11	– Trained for a military career
1909–11	– Served in the Japanese army, but returned to China to support the revolution against the imperial dynasty
1918	– Joined the Nationalist Party or *Kuomintang*
1925–7	– As commander in chief of the Revolutionary Army, made great progress towards the reunification of China
1930	– Converted to Christianity
1930–1	– Decided not to resist the Japanese invasion of China until he had crushed the Chinese Communists
1937	– Gave up fighting the Communists to concentrate on war against the Japanese invaders
1941–5	– Allied with the Americans against Japan
1946	– Chinese civil war fully under way
1949	– Mao's Communists finally defeated Chiang, who, with the remainder of his Nationalist forces, moved to, and ruled, Taiwan
1950	– US became more friendly to Chiang as a result of the Korean War
1950–5	– US–Taiwanese defence treaty
1975	– Died

Chiang was important to US policies in East Asia for over half a century. When it seemed that he was likely to reunite China (which had been torn apart by warlords and foreign invaders), the Americans admired him, and gave him aid to combat the Japanese. During the Second World War, the Americans accepted him as one of the 'Big Four' (USA, USSR, Britain and China). However, the Americans became exasperated with Chiang when he failed to defeat Mao and the Communists after the end of the Second World War. The Americans had ceased to give him aid for many months before Mao's final victory in 1949. After the fall of China to Communism, President Truman said that the United States had little interest in Taiwan. However, when the Korean War broke out, American policy changed. The United States then considered Chiang a vital and important ally in the struggle against Communism.

of the fleet deployment and MacArthur's public support for Chiang Kai-shek suggested that another US war aim was at the very least to defend Chiang and perhaps even to promote his aggression against the People's Republic of China.

Within the context of American domestic politics, Truman was taking a great risk. Initially the war seemed to have a great deal of support. Polls showed three-quarters of Americans approved of Truman's assistance to South Korea. Second World War hero Dwight D. Eisenhower said, 'We'll have a dozen Koreas soon if we don't take a firm stand.' When Truman's decision to send in troops was announced, members of Congress stood up and cheered. When he asked them for $10 billion in July 1950, they did the same again. A *Christian Science Monitor* reporter said, 'Never before have I felt such a sense of relief and unity pass through the city [of Washington, DC].'

Truman had concerns as to whether he needed a congressional declaration of war. He asked Senator Tom Connally, head of the influential Senate Foreign Relations Committee, for his opinion. Senator Connally assured him that he did not need such a declaration, even though Truman thought it was stipulated by the US constitution. Connally said:

> If a burglar breaks into your house, you can shoot at him without going down to the police station and getting permission. You might run into a long debate by Congress, which would tie your hands completely. You have the right to do so as Commander in Chief and under the UN Charter.

Subsequently, however, when the war went badly, Truman's failure to get a congressional declaration of war caused him great political difficulties, and gave his opponents the opportunity to call the Korean War 'Truman's war'.

ii) The choice of MacArthur as UNC commander

General Douglas MacArthur was a career soldier with a great reputation. Americans considered him to be one of the heroes of the Second World War, when he had led the US Army in the Pacific. He had taken the Japanese surrender in 1945 and from 1945 to 1950 had been in charge of the US occupation of Japan (see pages 23–4). He had handled the remaking of Japan as a peace-loving democracy with great skill. Already commander of US forces in the Pacific, with a reputation as a great soldier and an expert on East Asia, he seemed to be the logical choice as UNC commander.

However, MacArthur had his faults. The leading Republican spokesman on foreign affairs, John Foster Dulles, warned Truman that tact would be needed by the UN commander, and that tact was not MacArthur's strong point. JCS Chairman Omar Bradley considered MacArthur to be domineering, vain and arrogant. For example, MacArthur was convinced that he understood what he called the 'mind of the Oriental' better than anyone else. Also, MacArthur surrounded himself with sycophants and friendly members of the press, always ensuring that they took flattering pictures of him. Truman himself had great reservations about MacArthur. In his diary in 1945, Truman had referred to MacArthur as 'Mr Prima Donna, Brass Hat', a 'play actor and **bunco man**'. When asked if he knew MacArthur, the modest Eisenhower said, 'Not only have I met him, I studied dramatics under him for five years in Washington and four in the Philippines.'

Key question
Was MacArthur a wise choice as UNC commander?

Key term

Bunco man
A con-man.

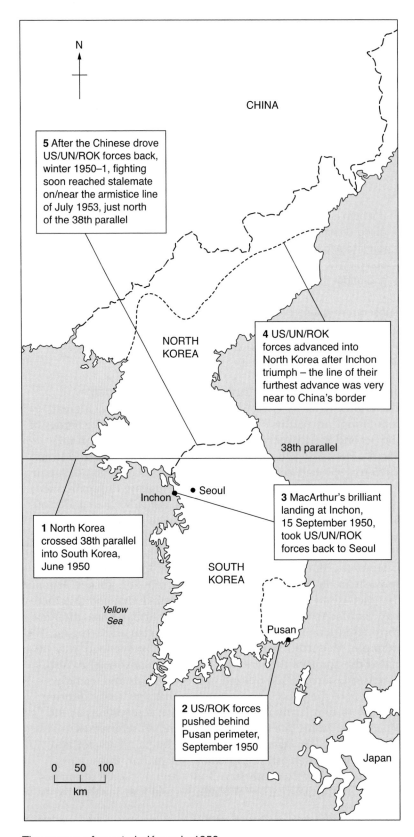

N

CHINA

5 After the Chinese drove US/UN/ROK forces back, winter 1950–1, fighting soon reached stalemate on/near the armistice line of July 1953, just north of the 38th parallel

NORTH KOREA

4 US/UN/ROK forces advanced into North Korea after Inchon triumph – the line of their furthest advance was very near to China's border

38th parallel

Inchon • Seoul

3 MacArthur's brilliant landing at Inchon, 15 September 1950, took US/UN/ROK forces back to Seoul

1 North Korea crossed 38th parallel into South Korea, June 1950

SOUTH KOREA

Yellow Sea

Pusan

2 US/ROK forces pushed behind Pusan perimeter, September 1950

Japan

0   50   100

km

The course of events in Korea in 1950.

Key question
Was this a UN war or
a US war?

iii) Key debate: A US war or a UN war

President Truman frequently maintained that the Korean War was a UN war, a UN 'police action'. US troops painted 'Harry's police' on the sides of their tanks and jeeps. Fifteen other nations fought alongside the United States and South Korea. These were Britain, Australia, New Zealand, South Africa, Canada, France, Holland, Belgium, Colombia, Greece, Turkey, Ethiopia, the Philippines, Thailand and Luxembourg. Other nations helped in other ways. For example, India, Italy, Norway, Denmark and Sweden sent medics, while Chile, Cuba, Ecuador, Iceland, Lebanon, Nicaragua, Pakistan and Venezuela sent food and economic aid. Panama provided transportation.

On the other hand, the United States and South Korea provided 90 per cent of the fighting men, and although MacArthur headed UNC, he never communicated directly with the UN. Furthermore, there was disagreement among America's allies over issues such as the dispatch of the US 7th Fleet to the Taiwan Straits. There is no doubt that throughout the war the US always did what it wanted to do, usually without reference to the UN and its allies. Prior to the Korean War, Truman had shown little interest in the UN, only using it to legitimise elections in South Korea (see page 10).

In some ways, MacArthur's refusal to deal with the UN is understandable, as there were difficulties enough in co-ordinating the war effort. Around 40,000 troops from other UN countries joined American troops in Korea. Roughly half of the 40,000 were from Britain, Australia, New Zealand and Canada. Communications between forces of different nationalities proved difficult. Some of the problems were amusing, if irritating (see the box below), but others were more serious. For example, a British brigade took a hill, then called for an American air strike against North Korean positions. The British identified themselves with white panels on the ground, but the North Koreans did that too, so the Americans bombed the British. American '**friendly fire**' caused 60 British casualties. In the rapid retreat of late November 1950, the British needed a translation of the American phrase 'Haul ass' ('retreat fast')! There were further communication problems when the British Commonwealth Brigade tried to free some ambushed Americans: the Americans did not know the British radio frequency. The Turks could not understand what the US commanders were telling them, and they sometimes captured South Koreans instead of Chinese.

Key term

Friendly fire
When a force's own side or an ally fires on the force by mistake.

UN problems
American quartermasters had interesting dietary problems with which to deal in the Korean War. Different countries had different requirements:

- Greeks – extra olive oil, 15 live and virgin lambs for Easter, no corn.
- Turks – no pork, no corn, no spices, no sauces, extra bread, lots of American canned spinach.

- Thais – three times more spices and sauces than Americans, no beets/cake mix/dry cereals/citrus fruit/sweet pickles.
- French – no American bread (they insisted on baking their own).

General Matt Ridgway recalled:

a thousand petty headaches. The Dutch wanted milk where the French wanted wine. The Muslims wanted no pork and the Hindus no beef. The Orientals wanted more rice and the Europeans more bread. Shoes had to be extra wide to fit the Turks. They had to be extra narrow and short to fit the men from Thailand and the Philippines. Only the Canadians and Scandinavians adjusted easily to United States rations and clothes.

Summary diagram: The internationalisation of the war

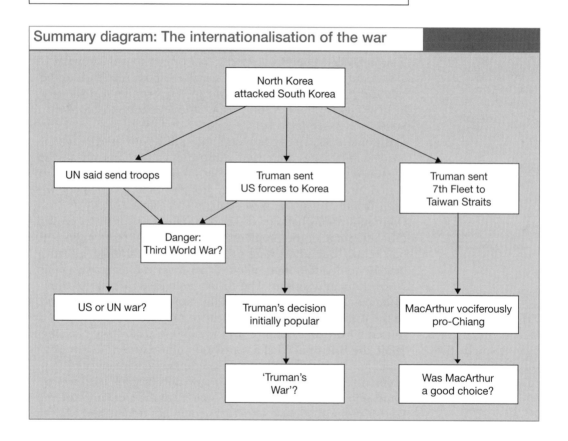

2 | The Military Situation, June–September 1950

a) American troop preparation and motivation

Not surprisingly, the American, South Korean and UN forces struggled throughout the summer of 1950. They were on the defensive, having been unprepared for the attack. The US Army had been rapidly run down after the Second World War. Although under the experienced and aggressive Major General Walton 'Bulldog' Walker, the US 8th Army had gone soft on occupation

Key question
How and why did the US/UN/ROK forces struggle early in the Korean War?

duty in Japan. For five years, they had been like policemen in a crime-free society. 'We were, in short, in a state of shameful unreadiness', said Lieutenant General Matt Ridgway, the army's deputy chief of staff. Roy Appleman, the official army historian, said the occupation divisions 'were not trained, equipped or ready for battle', and that 'the great majority of the enlisted men were young and not really interested in being soldiers'. Lieutenant Colonel John 'Iron Mike' Michaelis told the *Saturday Evening Post* about some of his troops' initial problems:

> When they started out, they couldn't shoot. They didn't know their weapons. They have not had enough training in plain-old-fashioned musketry. They'd spent a lot of time listening to lectures on the difference between Communism and Americanism and not enough time crawling on their bellies on manoeuvres with live ammunition singing over them … The US Army is so damn roadbound that the soldiers have almost lost the use of their legs. Send out a patrol on a scouting mission and they load up in a three-quarter ton truck and start riding down the highway.

Nevertheless, morale was high at first: 'We thought they would back off as soon as they saw American uniforms', said one soldier. General George Barth said the US troops had 'overconfidence that bordered on arrogance'.

However, as the war dragged on, there was the little to provide inspirational motivation for the American soldiers who fought in Korea. Fighting a limited war for ideology made it difficult to maintain morale. There had been no motivating attack on American soil, as at Pearl Harbor. There were no strong ancestral links to Korea as there had been for many American soldiers fighting in Europe in the Second World War.

Furthermore, Korea seemed to be a particularly unpleasant place in which to fight. In August, the temperature was over 38°C, and that accentuated the smells that characterised the country, such as the *kimchi* (fermenting cabbage) buried along the roadsides. Even worse were the 'honey wagons', ox-drawn carts of human excrement used to fertilise Korean rice paddies. Thirsty American soldiers, ignorant of Korean agricultural methods, drank water from those rice fields, and caught chronic dysentery. Americans could not tell who was North Korean or South Korean or, later, Chinese. The GIs began to call all Asians 'gooks', from the Korean word for 'Korean people', *han'guk saram*. The word 'gooks' began to take on an increasingly derogatory tone. In short, the only things that inspired many American soldiers was the desire to stay alive and the determination not to let their fellow American soldiers down.

Early in the war, co-ordination between the US air force and American troops on the ground was very poor. On 3 July, US planes bombed an ROK train and two train depots, killing 200 ROK soldiers. An American soldier wounded by an attack by his own air force, asked, 'What kind of screwy war is this?'

b) Early retreat, July 1950

American confidence was soon dissipated as the US forces failed to halt the North Korean tanks. As yet, the Americans and South Koreans had no tanks. US military planners had previously decided that the mountains and rice paddies of Korea made the Korean landscape unsuitable for tanks, so none had been given to Syngman Rhee (see page 12). The performance of the North Korean Soviet-built T-34 tanks proved those US military planners wrong. The retreat became chaotic, and inexperienced American troops frequently fled, a phenomenon that became known as 'bugout fever'.

The North Koreans were a tough enemy, and from the first there was great American bitterness about North Korean tactics and atrocities. For example, the North Koreans hid soldiers among streams of South Korean civilians fleeing southward from the North Korean advance. That tactic enabled the North Koreans to get behind the US defences and fire at unsuspecting Americans often using South Korean refugees as human screens, from behind which they could throw hand grenades.

The fighting was brutal, and the number of casualties very high. For example, in late July, Walton Walker had to make a stand at Taejon, because it had an airstrip and was the hub of five roads, all of which the Americans desperately needed as men and equipment were pouring in from Japan. Of the 4000 Americans who fought at Taejon, one in three ended up dead, wounded or missing.

c) The Pusan Perimeter, August 1950

During August, the retreating US and ROK troops were pinned behind the **Pusan Perimeter**, an area 100 miles by 50 miles in the southeastern corner of the Korean peninsula. Within the area were the only port and airfield left where the US could land more troops and supplies. Walker told his troops, 'There will be no more retreating.' An ROK 'bugout' looked imminent, but the ROK commander rallied his troops, and he and Walker managed to hold the line of the Pusan Perimeter, enabling the bitter fighting to continue. One area, known as 'Battle Mountain', changed hands 19 times, sometimes two or three times in a single day.

By late August, the North Koreans also had problems. They were outnumbered (they had lost 58,000 men in their charge to the south) and down to around 40 tanks. The Americans still controlled the skies and seas, and the North Korean supply lines were overstretched. Within the Pusan Perimeter, the North Koreans could not use their favourite tactic of flanking the enemy, as the Americans and South Koreans were bordered by the sea to the south and the east. The Americans and South Koreans now had less territory to defend, and more troops with which to defend it. Furthermore, the arrival of six US tank battalions was soon to make a great difference to the war.

d) September 1950

By September, there had been 8000 US casualties, and although 50 countries had pledged some kind of support, only the British had arrived. The military situation naturally aroused a considerable degree of doubt in the United States as to the wisdom of the involvement, but supporters of the war were still in the majority in Washington in the summer of 1950. There were some American fears that the Korean War could escalate into a Third World War, but the Truman **administration**, assured by MacArthur, remained convinced that the USSR and China would not enter the war. In a speech on 1 September 1950, Truman tried to reassure Moscow and Beijing that the United States did not want a Third World War. At that point, the US military effort looked unimpressive, and there was little for the USSR or China to fear. However, on 15 September 1950, the military situation was suddenly and miraculously revolutionised by a stroke of MacArthur genius. Against the advice of other military experts, MacArthur undertook what proved to be a highly successful assault on Inchon.

Key terms

Administration
Rather than refer to a president's 'government', Americans refer to a president's 'administration'.

Amphibious assaults
Attacks using land and sea forces.

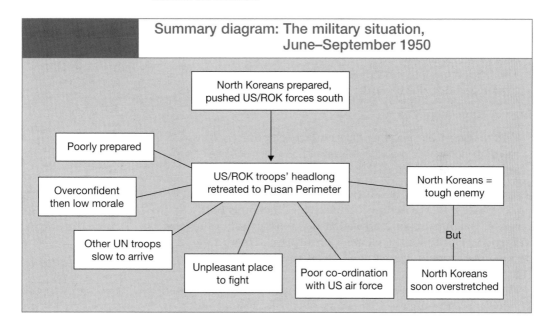

Summary diagram: The military situation, June–September 1950

North Koreans prepared, pushed US/ROK forces south

Poorly prepared

Overconfident then low morale

US/ROK troops' headlong retreated to Pusan Perimeter

North Koreans = tough enemy

Other UN troops slow to arrive

Unpleasant place to fight

Poor co-ordination with US air force

But

North Koreans soon overstretched

3 | Inchon and New American War Aims

a) Inchon

In the Second World War, MacArthur's strategy had been to bypass enemy strongholds with **amphibious assaults** that left enemy forces cut off and surrounded. In September 1950, he suggested using that idea in Korea. He advocated a landing 200 miles behind the North Korean lines at Inchon, but generals, admirals, staff officers and the JCS all told him not to do it. There were many objections:

Key question
What was the significance of Inchon?

Key date
Successful US assault on Inchon: 15 September 1950

- In 1949, JCS Chairman Omar Bradley had dismissed assaults from the sea as obsolete.
- The reluctant US Navy said if there had to be a landing, 50 miles south of Inchon would be a preferable location, but MacArthur insisted on Inchon because it was 20 miles from Seoul and had airfields, roads and railroads.
- The navy said the massive tidal variation (32 feet between high tide and low tide) would mean that the first US landing craft and men would be stuck ashore for 12 hours on exposed mudflats, before the tides would allow the rest of the force to join them.
- It was rumoured that the Soviets had mined the harbour.
- There were only four days in September on which the water levels would be suitable for the operation (after September, the weather would be turning bad).
- The approach to Inchon was a narrow, dangerous seaway called the Flying Fish Channel. If that seaway were to be blocked, say, by a sunken ship, the assault would stall.
- There was an island in the seaway that would have to be seized before the main landing, which would then be delayed until the evening, with only two hours of daylight remaining.
- Inchon had no beach, just a 15-foot sea wall that would need to be scaled or blown up.
- The US force would land in the middle of a city of 250,000 civilians, who would be at the mercy of North Korean forces.

Bradley subsequently wrote:

> I had to agree that it was the riskiest military proposal I had ever heard of. Inchon was probably the worst possible place ever selected for an amphibious landing.

Ridgway said it was a '5000-to-1 gamble', while Rear Admiral James Doyle told MacArthur in Tokyo that 'Inchon is not possible.' MacArthur contended that the 'impracticalities involved will tend to ensure for the element of surprise'. He won the backing of President Truman and Defence Secretary Louis Johnson, so the assault went ahead.

MacArthur watched the assault from his boat, wearing his gold-braided cap and sunglasses, smoking his corncob pipe, and accompanied by his trademark press following. The amphibious force had a bad start, when Typhoon Kezia's 125 mph winds scattered some ships and caused severe seasickness among the ground troops, but after that, luck was with MacArthur. Despite every South Korean and American seeming to know and talk freely about the landing, the North Koreans were still taken by surprise. Although the first wave of men was isolated for several hours on stinking mud, waiting for the tide to enable reinforcements to join them, the North Koreans did not attack. In the afternoon, more marines landed and scaled or blew up the sea wall. One nervy Marine reported the smell of poisonous gas, but it turned out to be Korean garlic. Despite all the doubt and problems, MacArthur's plan succeeded: Inchon was soon taken.

As the Americans who had landed at Inchon advanced towards Seoul, other Americans and South Koreans worked their way out of the Pusan Perimeter by late September. By now, they had been joined by some British troops.

As the **US/UN**/ROK forces advanced from behind the Pusan Perimeter, they came across more North Korean atrocities, including two American **POWs** who had been in a group of around 100 South Korean POWs. The POWs had been put into shallow trenches, and shot and buried there. The two Americans pretended to be dead, and were buried alive, but they punched air holes in the soil above them and waited until they were rescued.

Meanwhile, the South Korean capital, Seoul, was retaken. On 27 September, MacArthur ceremoniously handed the capital building over to a grateful Syngman Rhee, who thanked him profusely on behalf of the South Korean people for saving their nation, saying, 'We love you.' Inchon had proved MacArthur right. 'In hindsight', said Bradley, 'the JCS sounded like a bunch of Nervous Nellies to have doubted.' MacArthur had triumphed. This would have dramatic political and military implications in the months to come.

b) Confused and confusing war aims, September 1950

The Communist position had so deteriorated that Stalin was considering whether to dump North Korea or to encourage Chinese intervention. He chose the latter option, and the Chinese proved willing to intervene because the triumphant Americans had dramatically changed their war aims. The USA had entered the war to restore the *status quo*, that is, to evict the North Koreans from South Korea. The declared UN war aim had been, 'To repel armed invasion and restore peace and stability in the area', but that wording was sufficiently vague to give respectability to the US/UN/ROK forces crossing the 38th parallel into North Korea following Inchon. US/UN/ROK war aims were now to destroy the North Korean forces and to reunify the Korean peninsula. Indeed, South Korean forces did not wait for UN approval before crossing. 'We will not allow ourselves to stop', said Syngman Rhee.

At this stage, MacArthur's orders were not very clear. On 27 September, the JCS passed to him a modified version of a UN Security Council resolution, which said his military objective was 'the destruction of the North Korean Armed Forces'. The resolution authorised him to conduct military operations in North Korea. On 29 September, the new Secretary of Defence George Marshall told MacArthur, 'We want you to feel unhampered tactically and strategically to proceed north of the 38th parallel.' A UN resolution of 7 October, passed by a margin of 45 to seven, said, 'all appropriate steps [should] be taken to ensure conditions of stability throughout Korea'. There was no clarification of 'appropriate steps'.

Marguerite Higgins: a Korean War heroine?

Marguerite Higgins was an experienced war correspondent who had covered the fall of Nazi Germany for the *New York Herald Tribune*. In 1950, the paper sent her to Tokyo, which she considered a dead-end posting, until the Korean War broke out. She flew to Seoul and joined the US forces in their headlong retreat. The main bridge leading out of Seoul was destroyed, so Higgins boarded a raft. When it sank, she swam the rest of the way. She described the US retreat as 'the most appalling example of panic I've ever seen … It was routine to hear comments like, "Just give me a jeep and I'll know which direction to go in. This mama's boy ain't cut out to be a hero".'

Higgins wrote dramatic accounts of her experiences with the American forces, often sleeping on the ground with whatever unit she was following. 'Maggie's the only gal you can brag about sleeping with and not be a cad', said one soldier. With her tennis shoes, baggy fatigues, aviator sunglasses and big cap, she survived with few luxuries – a typewriter, toothbrush, towel, lipstick and flea powder. Frequently covered in mud and lice, she relied on what she called 'friendly bushes' when in need of a toilet. She quickly developed a range of ailments (ranging from athlete's foot to bronchitis, acute sinusitis, malaria, dysentery and jaundice) that put her in hospital when she finally got back to the United States.

General Walton Walker thought the Korean War was not the sort of place for a woman, so he sent her back to Japan. Communist cartoons mocked Walker, showing Higgins being driven out, with a headline, 'MacARTHUR's FIRST VICTORY'. Higgins appealed to MacArthur ('I walked out of Seoul. I want to walk back in'), who allowed her to return. She managed to land at Inchon and waded ashore with the marines. She was not allowed back on the ships, because she was a woman, so she slept on the beachhead. When the Chinese entered the war, she joined the US retreat, then went home to the USA.

Higgins was the sole female battlefield reporter in the Korean War and the first woman to win the Pulitzer Prize for international reporting. She swore never to marry, 'Until I find a man who is as exciting as war', then married US Air Force General William Hall. 'Bill is the most exciting thing', she affirmed – 'next to war'.

c) New US war aims

In September 1950, the United States changed its war aims from the restoration of the *status quo* in Korea to the destruction of North Korea. There were several reasons for the change. After the great victory at Inchon and the military surge towards Seoul, military momentum and a surge of optimism made the idea of stopping at the 38th parallel seem ridiculous to most Americans

Key question
Why had the US changed its war aims?

Marguerite Higgins and General MacArthur talking in South Korea in 1950.

and South Koreans. A halt at the 38th parallel would certainly have damaged American and South Korean morale. The war had evoked a bitterness that engendered more conflict. There was a great American desire for revenge against the North Korean aggressor, because so many Americans had died or been wounded, and because of the North Korean atrocities. Important individuals such as the South Korean leader Syngman Rhee and General MacArthur were desperately keen to reunify the Korean peninsula. Subsequently, when the invasion of North Korea went wrong, the Truman administration 'tried to deflect blame' (historian James Matray) by emphasising MacArthur's role in changing the war aims. MacArthur's advice was certainly taken very seriously, especially given his great triumph at Inchon.

There was considerable political calculation and motivation in Truman's decision. Republican attacks on him for his 'loss' of China (see page 5), coupled with the McCarthy scare (see page 21), made him anxious to maintain his anti-Communist credentials. Another factor pushing him towards the more aggressive war aims was the forthcoming congressional mid-term elections. If he was seen to be failing to push home the advantage against the Communists, it might have an adverse impact on Democratic candidates in those elections, as the American public was keen to 'finish the job'. Finally, American credibility was at stake in Korea. The war in Korea had come to represent US determination to stand up to Communism. It was felt that US credibility and prestige would be best served by the defeat of North Korea.

However, the change in war aims presented several problems. Although the UN approved the decision to invade North Korea in October, some of America's allies were not keen on the change. Britain, for example, felt that the UN would lose the moral high ground if it were to change war aims in the middle of the war. Britain felt that while the initial aim (the restoration of the *status quo*) was clearly defensive, this new aim (the destruction of North Korea) could be perceived as aggressive. A minority in Washington were also unhappy. For example, the State Department Soviet specialist George Kennan recommended that the US get out of Korea as soon as possible, as he believed that Korea was not that important, and that the US could get into trouble there. He was proved right: Communist China now intervened, completing the internationalisation of the war.

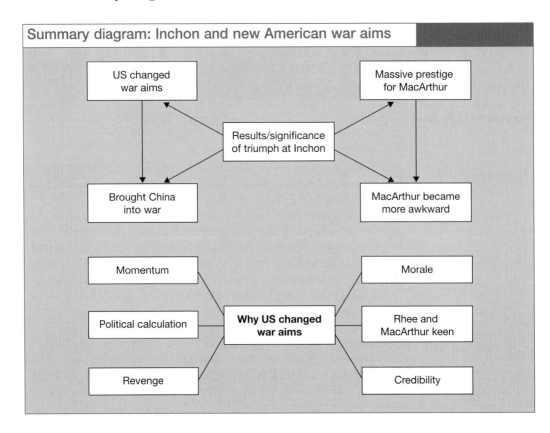

Summary diagram: Inchon and new American war aims

Key question
Why did China
intervene?

4 | Key Debate: Why China Intervened in the Korean War

On several occasions the Chinese warned the United States that if American troops crossed the 38th parallel, China would intervene in the war, but Truman ignored these warnings.

Western historians lack access to Chinese sources, so there has been a great deal of guesswork involved in their suggestions as to why China intervened. They have found it easy to believe the contemporary Chinese diplomats, who said that Chinese intervention was motivated by security reasons:

- the US had sent the 7th Fleet to Taiwan
- MacArthur had defied orders that said he should not send US troops too close to the Yalu River (the border between China and North Korea) and
- MacArthur had made his support for Chiang and his opposition to Communist China very clear in many public words and deeds.

Recently, Chinese historians such as Chen Jian (2001), Zhang Shu Guang (1995) and Shen Zhihua (2000), with unprecedented access to their national archives, have emphasised factors other than security. Firstly, like many other countries, China traditionally believed that it was a superior power, to which others (including Korea) were supposed to defer. China called itself the 'middle kingdom' or 'central kingdom', which was another way of saying that China was the centre of the world and the most important country within it. During the nineteenth and early twentieth centuries, China had been exploited, dominated and humiliated by other countries. The Korean War offered an opportunity for China to re-establish its prestige and status on the world stage.

Secondly, when Mao and his Communists had fought Chiang Kai-shek and his Nationalists in the Chinese civil war, North Korea had sent thousands of soldiers to help, so Mao felt an obligation to help North Korea.

Thirdly, this new Chinese research has proved, as Western historians have always suspected, that Stalin pressed and encouraged Mao to enter the war. This was probably because he knew that if China and the United States fought each other, it would strengthen his position in relation to both of them. China would rely on Soviet financial and material aid, and both China and United States would be weakened by the conflict. Entering the Korean War was not a decision that was taken lightly. Mao had a very difficult job in obtaining **politburo** unanimity, as there was still a great deal of work to be done in establishing the Communist regime.

It would soon become clear that China's entry into the war would greatly change its course and consequences.

Key term

Politburo
The Chinese
Communist
government's
equivalent of the
British or US
cabinet.

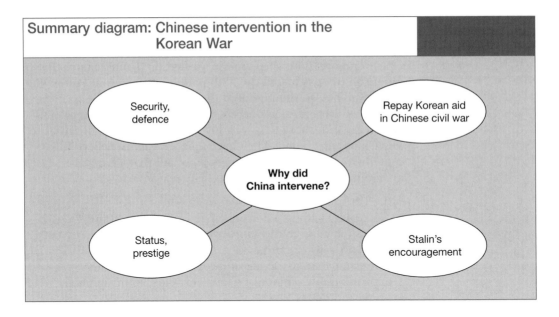

Summary diagram: Chinese intervention in the Korean War

- Security, defence
- Repay Korean aid in Chinese civil war
- **Why did China intervene?**
- Status, prestige
- Stalin's encouragement

5 | The Fighting in Korea, October–December 1950

a) Changing fortunes in October 1950

In October, while the Chinese prepared to enter the war, US/ROK/UN forces moved northwards. MacArthur ignored General Walker's advice, and split his ground forces. He removed the inspired forces who had taken Seoul from the battlefield just when they could have chased the enemy further north and sent some of them off by sea for an amphibious assault on Wonsan. The plan was to surround the North Koreans once more, but splitting forces in this way was against all conventional military operational procedure. MacArthur also moved the troops for the Wonsan landing southward, so that they could sail out through Inchon. Those troops clogged roads and stopped remaining US/UN/ROK troops from moving swiftly north. When the diverted troops finally got to Wonsan Harbour, it contained 3000 Soviet mines, so by the time the Americans were finally able to land there, ROK ground troops and US entertainer Bob Hope were there before them. It had taken two weeks to clear the mines, and meanwhile the American troopships had sailed up and down the coast so often that they joked about 'Operation yo-yo'. A severe outbreak of dysentery on board the ships had made it possible to smell them many miles downwind.

On 15 October, with both men still thinking victory was imminent, Truman and MacArthur flew to Wake Island, a US base in the middle of the Pacific Ocean. MacArthur was confident, saying, 'Formal resistance will end in North and South Korea by Thanksgiving [23 November].' When Truman asked him if the Chinese or Soviets were likely to intervene, MacArthur said that there was 'very little' chance of this, but that the Chinese would not fight very well anyway. Truman responded with an equally

Key question
What was the impact of China's entry into the war?

Chinese forces poured into Korea: October 1950

Key date

optimistic public statement about the 'complete unity in the aims and conduct of our foreign policy'.

The optimism seemed justified, for on 19 October American and South Korean forces 'liberated' the North Korean capital, Pyongyang. MacArthur's reputation soared further: a Communist capital had been liberated by the West (a feat never to be repeated in the Cold War). MacArthur declared, 'The war will soon be over.'

In mid-October, MacArthur had given orders that only ROK forces should operate near the Chinese border, but on 24 October he reversed the order and US forces headed for the Yalu River, the border between North Korea and China. MacArthur said this was a military necessity, but it represented a great change in US policy. The JCS said it was 'a matter of concern', but did not stop him. 'It was really too late', said Bradley.

American and South Korean troops reached the Yalu River with a great sense of triumph. It became a tradition to urinate in the water on arrival. The ROK troops filled a bottle of the Yalu River water to take back to Syngman Rhee (hopefully before they relieved themselves). It was at this point that the Chinese stealthily moved 150,000 men into North Korea. The US was blind to all the signals: on 12 October, the **CIA** said that despite Chinese troop movements to the border, statements and charges of border violations, 'there are no convincing indications of an actual Chinese Communist intention to resort to full-scale intervention in Korea'.

American air surveillance struggled to detect Chinese troop movements, because they marched overnight and had no cumbersome artillery and very few trucks. They used mountain trails, not roads. Even when Walton Walker was faced with the first Chinese POWs, he thought they were Chinese who lived in Korea: 'After all, a lot of Mexicans live in Texas.' The battle-hardened Chinese troops (they had fought a bitter civil war for many years) proved to be formidable opponents.

At the same time that the Chinese had their dramatic impact on the war, the weather turned dramatically. The North Korean winter arrived before the US/UN/ROK forces received the proper winter clothing. The Americans were also taken by surprise at having suddenly to build defensive lines. By 1 November, they were surrounded by Chinese, some of whom marched into the middle of American positions wearing ROK clothing discarded in the rapid South Korean retreat.

MacArthur complained that the Chinese were 'lawless', in that they had not declared war. He wanted to bomb the Korean ends of the Yalu bridges in order to halt the Chinese troops at the Chinese border. He was furious when the JCS overruled him, but Truman sided with him and the bombing began. However, after one month of bombing, only four of the 12 bridges had been destroyed, and by then the Yalu River was frozen and the Chinese could cross it at many more points. Persuading himself that the Chinese were in retreat, MacArthur decided that a big offensive would end the Korean War.

Key term

CIA
The Central Intelligence Agency, established in 1947, was responsible for collecting and evaluating intelligence data for the federal government.

b) MacArthur's November offensive

MacArthur wanted the offensive to begin on 15 November, but 8th Army commander Walton Walker knew that he had insufficient supplies, so the attack was delayed until 25 November. Even then, Walker's army was still short of ammunition, winter equipment and rations. MacArthur talked of 'getting the boys back [home to America] by Christmas', but he made speedy victory unlikely when he broadcast the battle plan on Armed Forces Radio! That infuriated his commanders and made the Chinese task a lot easier. In the broadcast, MacArthur reiterated US war aims. He said his offensive:

> should for all practical purposes end the war, restore peace and unity to Korea, enable the prompt withdrawal of United Nations military forces and permit the complete assumption by the Korean people and nation of all sovereignty and international equality. It is that for which we fight.

Truman subsequently recalled:

> What we should have done was stop at the neck of Korea … But [MacArthur] was commander in the field. You pick your man, you've got to back him up. That's the only way a military organisation can work. I got the best advice I could and the man on the spot said this was the thing to do … So I agreed. That was my decision – no matter what hindsight shows.

Looking back on the failed offensive, Acheson explained why, even though all the president's advisers knew that MacArthur should have been restrained, they did nothing: 'It would have meant a fight with MacArthur, charges by him that they had denied his victory.'

c) The Chinese November offensive

Truman tried to reassure the Chinese that there was no threat to Chinese territory, but the Chinese thought otherwise, and took advantage of the November delay to prepare their offensive. The Chinese (300,000 men) and the North Koreans (100,000) outnumbered the 270,000 US/UN/ROK forces. The Chinese pretended to retreat, then awaited the US/UN/ROK forces with eager anticipation, believing that:

Key date

US/UN/ROK forces retreated back into South Korea: November 1950

> [the Americans'] infantry is weak. Their men are afraid to die … They depend on their planes, tanks and artillery … Their habit is to be active during the daylight hours. They are very weak at night … When transportation comes to a standstill, the infantry loses the will to fight.

The Chinese believed that the South Koreans were even worse, puppets 'deficient' in warfare, so they attacked the South Koreans and opened up the UN lines. MacArthur now admitted that he faced 'an entirely new war', an 'undeclared war by the Chinese', which necessitated more US forces. Colonel Paul Freeman said the Chinese were 'making us look a little silly in this God-awful country'.

The American troops in that 'God-awful country' were astounded by the cold, which sometimes hit −30°C, and frequently froze motor oil and weapons. Warming tents had to be used to defrost the men before they were sent out into the cold again. Hair oil and urine kept frozen rifles going some of the time. Plasma froze in the tubes of the medics, who had to dip their fingers into patients' blood in order to keep their hands warm. 'The only way you could tell the dead from the living was whether their eyes moved. They were all frozen stiff as boards', said one American surgeon. The Chinese suffered even more. Many froze to death in their foxholes. One Chinese officer was surprised to see thousands of snowmen on the horizon: on closer inspection, they turned out to be entire platoons of Chinese soldiers who had frozen to death on the spot.

American turkeys in Korea

UN troops from other countries were amazed at the American ability to give troops their traditional Thanksgiving turkey, accompanied by the usual cranberry sauce, sweet potatoes, buttered corn and gravy, all followed by pumpkin pie. However, the weather was so cold that the hot turkey was nearly frozen by the time any **GI** ate it.

Key terms

GIs
US soldiers were issued with certain equipment by their superiors. 'GI' stood for 'government issue' and was used to describe American soldiers.

Napalm
Flammable liquid used in warfare.

One of the hardest fought battles was that waged by the 25,000 Americans who were surrounded by 120,000 Chinese in the mountains of North Korea, near the Chosin Reservoir. Their chief of staff criticised the 'insane plan' that had sent them there. One captain felt as if they had run 'smack into what seemed like most of the Chinese from China. I always wonder why they sent us up into all that.' US air supremacy saved many American lives at 'frozen Chosin', but 12 GIs were burned by **napalm** dropped from their own planes. 'Men all around me were burned. They lay rolling in the snow. Men I knew, marched and fought with begged me to shoot 'em. I couldn't', said one private. In one division, 'Many were crying and hysterical. Some were sick and vomiting. Some had so many wounds you could hardly touch them.' Of the 25,000 American troops who fought in the Chosin Reservoir campaign, 6000 were killed, wounded or captured, while 6000 others suffered from severe frostbite. This 50 per cent casualty rate was far higher than that of the Second World War. Survivors of 'frozen Chosin' told the American press the Chinese burned wounded POWs alive and danced around the flames, then bayoneted others who tried to surrender. However, General Smith scolded the press when they used the word 'retreat': 'We are not retreating. We are merely attacking in another direction.'

This group of marines struggles through the snow at Chosin Reservoir carrying a wounded colleague to be flown from the battle zone for medical treatment.

The US/UN/ROK retreat was bad enough, but it would have been even worse without their superior mobility. The Chinese were on foot and could not keep up with the pace of the retreat, which the Americans christened 'the big bugout'. Colonel Freeman was despondent:

> Look around here. This is a sight that hasn't been seen for hundreds of years – the men of a whole United States Army fleeing from a battlefield, abandoning their wounded, running for their lives.

MacArthur desperately wanted to use atomic weapons and also repeatedly demanded more troops, but none was available in the US or in any other UN nation. MacArthur wanted to use Chiang Kai-shek's forces, but Washington did not want to crank up the war with China even further. In any case, Chiang's army had been bested by Mao's in the Chinese civil war. When MacArthur was also denied permission to bomb Chinese territory, he complained that he was having to fight with 'an enormous handicap' that was 'without precedent in military history'. Truman subsequently wrote that:

> I should have relieved General MacArthur then and there. The reason I did not was that I did not wish to have it appear as if he

were being relieved because the offensive failed. I have never believed in going back on people when luck is against them, and I did not intend to do it now. Now, no one is blaming General MacArthur, and I certainly never did, for the failure of the November offensive … [But] I do blame General MacArthur for the manner in which he tried to excuse his failure.

d) Trouble in Washington DC

The strain of war

Truman's mistakes, such as his declaration that MacArthur had the option to use atomic weapons, owed much to the tremendous pressure under which the war put him. On 5 December 1950, his best friend died, but Truman went off as previously arranged to hear his daughter Margaret's singing concert. The *Washington Post* critic declared her to be lacking in talent, and Truman sent that critic a letter, saying:

Some day I hope to meet you. When that happens you'll need a new nose, a lot of beefsteak for black eyes, and perhaps a supporter below.

The *Washington News* published the letter, and Truman received a great deal of hostile mail. One letter asked:

How can you put your trivial personal affairs before those of 160 million people. Our boys died while your infantile mind was on your daughter's review. Inadvertently you showed the whole world what you are. Nothing but a little selfish pipsqueak.

Another letter arrived with a Purple Heart [medal] enclosed, and said:

Mr Truman: As you have been directly responsible for the loss of our son's life, you might just as well keep this emblem on display in your trophy room, as a memory of one of your historic deeds. One major regret at this time is that your daughter was not there to receive the same treatment as our son received in Korea.

Back home, Truman was in considerable political trouble: his poll ratings were falling and his Democratic Party suffered losses in the November 1950 elections. He was also in trouble with America's allies: in a press conference he said he had 'always' considered using atomic weapons in Korea, and that 'the military commander in the field will have charge of the use of weapons, as he always has'. British Prime Minister Clement Attlee rushed to Washington, fearful that MacArthur had his finger on the nuclear button. Truman hastily reassured everyone that he was in ultimate control of the use of all weapons.

The atmosphere in Washington was one of panic. The JCS feared a Soviet attack in Europe, while on 15 December 1950, Truman declared a state of national emergency. He said, 'This danger has been created by the rulers of the Soviet Union', and promised that the United States would continue to defend the UN and the free world.

e) US military leadership, Christmas 1950

Instead of being 'home for Christmas', as MacArthur had promised, the forces of the United States and its allies were once more behind the 38th parallel by early December 1950. The US/UN/ROK forces had abandoned Pyongyang, and MacArthur seemed to be a beaten general. One of his officers wrote home that:

> When a gambler [MacArthur] pulls one off [Inchon] he is hailed as a genius, and when he fails, he is a bum. This time [MacArthur has] failed and he has to take the consequences of failure as I see it.

However, the split US forces were now reunited, and the US/UN/ROK forces would soon make a recovery, which owed a great deal to the arrival of the new field commander. General Walton Walker was killed when his jeep crashed on icy Korean roads at Christmas, 1950. Walker's replacement, General Matt Ridgway, was a brilliant leader who raised the morale and improved the performance of his troops. Ridgway's performance served to show up MacArthur's failings.

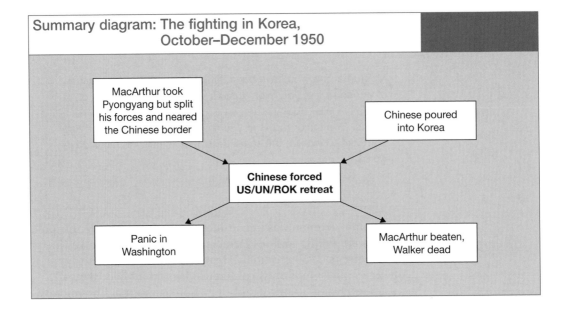

Summary diagram: The fighting in Korea, October–December 1950

MacArthur took Pyongyang but split his forces and neared the Chinese border

Chinese poured into Korea

Chinese forced US/UN/ROK retreat

Panic in Washington

MacArthur beaten, Walker dead

6 | Key Debate: How well did General MacArthur do in Korea?

MacArthur entered the Korean War with a great reputation, gained in the Philippines in the Second World War, and in the post-war Japanese occupation. His reputation was even greater after the triumph at Inchon. However, there have been many criticisms.

Some accuse MacArthur of waging 'war by remote control', in that he spent most of the war in Tokyo (Weintraub, 2000). In his defence, it could be argued that he visited Korea several times during the war, that Korea was a dangerous place and a dead commander was no use to anyone, and that he had other great responsibilities in the Pacific, especially Japan (see page 23).

Some have said that MacArthur failed to relieve ineffective officers, or pointed out that MacArthur was dangerously overconfident when he repeatedly assured the Truman administration that China would never enter the Korean War. This assurance proved incorrect, so it could be argued that MacArthur had misled the Truman administration into disaster. On the other hand, although MacArthur was considered to be an Asian specialist, it could be argued that Truman and his advisers should have investigated and considered the possibility more carefully. After the crossing of the 38th parallel proved to be a disaster, the Truman administration put the blame on MacArthur's advice and demands. It may be that they were simply trying to 'pass the buck', and, as was written on the plaque that stood on Truman's desk in the Oval Office, 'THE BUCK STOPS HERE'. The ultimate responsibility lay with the president.

It could also be argued that MacArthur received some confused and confusing instructions from Washington. During October 1950, he was ordered not to use US troops near the Chinese border, but he was also told by Secretary of Defence George Marshall that he could do as he liked. It could also be said that MacArthur was a poor choice on Truman's part, as John Foster Dulles had pointed out from the first (see page 36).

Peter Lowe (2000) contends that MacArthur was simply too powerful, because of his prestige, his command of US forces in the Pacific, his role in Japan and his command of UNC. All these positions made it difficult for any politician or military leader to oppose him, and help to explain the Truman administration's ambiguity in handling him. Lowe contends that as well as being too powerful, he was simply too old: aged over 70, he was probably past his best by the time of the Korean War.

Summary diagram: General MacArthur – an assessment	
✓	✗
• Second World War hero • Inchon success • Truman: 'The buck stops here' • Confused orders from Washington	• War by remote control • Did not relieve ineffective officers • Overconfident • Too old, too powerful

Some key books in the debates

Chen Jian, *Mao's China and the Cold War* (North Carolina, 2001).
Peter Lowe, *The Korean War* (Macmillan, 2000).
James Patterson, *Grand Expectations: The United States, 1945–1974* (Oxford, 1996).
Shen Zhihua, Sino-Soviet relations and the origins of the Cold War. *Journal of Cold War Studies* (2000).
Kathryn Weathersby, in Melvyn Leffler and David S. Painter (editors), *Origins of the Cold War: An International History* (New York, 2005).
Stanley Weintraub, *MacArthur's War* (New York, 2000).
Zhang Shu Guang, *Mao's Military Romanticism: China and the Korean War* (Kansas, 1995).

Study Guide: AS Questions

In the style of OCR

(a) **Study Sources B and C.**
Compare these sources as evidence for the behaviour of the USA during the outbreak of the Korean War in 1950.

(b) **Study all of the sources.**
Use your own knowledge to assess how far the sources support the interpretation that the UN in Korea was the puppet of the USA.

Source A

From: Report of the UN Commission on Korea, September 1950. The UN explains some of the background to the Korean War.

The Security Council has acted in response to unprovoked aggression, invoking the Charter to defend the independent and free state of South Korea. The origin of the conflict lies in the artificial division of Korea and the failure in 1945 of the USA and USSR to reach agreement on how to give independence to Korea. This failure was due to fundamental differences in outlook which have become such a feature of the international scene. This artificial division was made worse by the exclusion from North Korea of the UN commission to observe Korean elections. If supervised elections had been allowed across all of Korea and a unified independent Korea been created, the present conflict could never have arisen.

Source B

From a speech by the Soviet Deputy Foreign Minister, 4 July 1950. A Russian politician explains the behaviour of the UN and the USA during the outbreak of the Korean War.

Events in Korea started on 25 June as a result of a provocative attack by troops of South Korea on North Korea. This was the outcome of a deliberate plan. The US tries to justify intervention by alleging that it was undertaken by the UN Security Council. What really happened? It is known the US started its intervention before the Council was summoned to meet on 27 June. Thus, the US confronted the Council with an accomplished fact and it merely accepted the US-proposed resolution and approving the aggressive actions already undertaken. The illegal resolution of 27 June shows the UN is acting not as a body for maintaining peace, but as a tool of the USA.

Source C

From President Truman's radio and TV address to the nation, 19 July 1950. The American president explains the behaviour of the UN and the USA during the outbreak of the Korean War.

On 25 June, Communist forces attacked South Korea. This attack has made it clear that the International Communist movement is willing to use armed invasion to conquer independent nations. Communist leaders have demonstrated their contempt for the basic moral principles on which the UN is founded. As soon as word of the attack was received, I approved a request for a meeting of the UN Security Council. One of the main reasons the Council was set up was to act in such cases as this – to stop outbreaks of aggression in a hurry before they develop into general conflicts. In this case, the Council passed a resolution calling for North Korea to withdraw. North Korea ignored the request. The Council recommended that UN members help South Korea repel the attack and restore peace.

Source D

From an interview in 1961 with Dean Acheson, who had been US Secretary of State in 1950. A senior US official explains the attitude of the USA to the UN during the outbreak of the Korean War.

To call a meeting of the Security Council seemed the only sensible alternative at the time. This was true for several reasons. It was the proper procedure to take under the UN Charter. Here there was an aggression, the invasion of South Korea, by North Korea. An aggression was contrary to the Charter. The Charter had provisions for dealing with it, and for the US to ignore the Charter and act without the UN would have indicated that the US thought the Charter was worth nothing. Also, this was something which could be done immediately: other things would take time. One of the main considerations in my mind was the need for decisive, immediate action.

Source E

A modern North Korean author explains, in 2003, the outbreak of war in Korea.

In 1945 the US established a military government in South Korea. The US kept military bases in South Korea and a large advisor corps to command the South Korean army. This was part of a US plan for a northward expedition against North Korea. On 25 June 1950, the US and South Korea launched their armed attack. The US even organised a UN multinational force of satellite countries to bring them into this aggressive war. The purpose of this provocative act was to exterminate North Korea and turn the whole of Korea into an American colony. This was to be the springboard for US world domination.

Exam tips

(a) Here you need to compare not just the content of the two sources but also their authorship, date, typicality and reliability. You must do this because the question asks for comparison 'as evidence for …'. Let the introductory headings and the attributions at the start of each source lead you in the right direction. You are looking for similarities as well as contrasts.

For provenance, the two sources could not be more different, coming from very senior politicians on opposite sides. For date, both are contemporary with the first stage of the war but, by the time of Source C, North Korean forces were making serious gains. Put together, each is typical of the attitude of the side it comes from, reflecting the political position of the Cold War power backing each side. As evidence for attitudes and positions, the strong contrasts between Sources B and C help our understanding of how the Cold War influenced the start of the conflict.

Given their different origins and the context in which they were written, it is not surprising that the interpretation offered by each is so different. In Source B, North Korea is the victim of a deliberate plot by the USA, which is using the UN Security Council as a cover. Against that, North Korea is the aggressor in Source C and the USA has appealed to the UN Security Council to help South Korea. Source B argues that UN action is illegal while C sees the UN behaviour as acting properly in the way it was set up to do.

(b) Your task is to give a clear judgement on the question. No set conclusion is expected, but do not sit on the fence. If your essay is to score a high mark, it must use all five sources. Judge them against your own knowledge (pages 10, 14, 25, 27 and Chapter 2) and evaluate their strengths and weaknesses as a set, including any serious limitations they offer as evidence for or against the question (but do not go overboard on this as you can pick holes in any group put together as an exercise).

Like the question, your focus must always be on US policy and behaviour in 1950. The sources offer a variety of useful pointers, explicitly or implicitly. If your answer is to be strong, you need to sort the sources out, grouping them according to the view they give on the question.

- Sources A and C both reject the claim in the question, arguing that it was the UN that made the decision to get involved in Korea.
- Against that, Sources B and E agree with the proposition in the question. Both are highly critical of the UN, seeing it as the puppet of the USA during the Korean crisis of 1950.
- On the other hand, Source D takes a more subtle view, arguing that the USA had to act, but what Acheson says about how that action had to be taken might be read in several ways. Each can be seen as trying to justify its position.
- In the context of the debate on the independence of the UN, Source A criticises both the USA and USSR, blaming them clearly for the divide between North and South and, implicitly, holding both partially responsible for the outbreak of the war.

3 Ending the Korean War, 1951–3

POINTS TO CONSIDER

Thanks to the new ground commander, General Matt Ridgway, the anti-Communist forces managed to stabilise the military situation in early 1951. With the opposing troops facing each other near the 38th parallel, the pre-war *status quo* was effectively restored. Both sides suggested peace talks in spring 1951, but the armistice was not signed until 1953. This chapter considers the impact of the new commander, analyses MacArthur's dismissal, explains the long, drawn-out peace negotiations, and assesses the results and significance of the Korean War. It does this through sections on:

- The change of leadership in winter 1950–1
- MacArthur's dismissal
- Chinese aims in 1951
- The signing of the armistice in 1953
- The results and significance of the Korean War: the impact on American society, politics and foreign policy

Key dates

1950	December	Appointment of Ridgway as ground commander
1951	January	Chinese forces crossed into South Korea
	March	Chinese driven back to 38th parallel
	April 11	Truman dismissed MacArthur
	June	Armistice talks began
1953	July	Armistice signed

Key question
What was the significance of Ridgway's appointment?

Key dates

Appointment of Ridgway as ground commander: December 1950

Chinese forces crossed into South Korea: January 1951

Chinese driven back to 38th parallel: March 1951

Key term

Ground commander
While MacArthur was in charge of US forces in the Pacific, Walker then Ridgway commanded the American troops in Korea.

1 | Winter 1950–1: A Change of Leadership

a) The new US ground commander

The winter of 1950–1 was one of the turning points of the Korean War: US/UN/ROK fortunes revived, a revival partly due to a new US **ground commander**. Just before Christmas, Walton Walker presented a Silver Star to his soldier son. Soon afterwards, he was killed when his jeep collided with a truck. Truman declined Syngman Rhee's offer to put the South Korean truck driver to death. Walker had defended the Pusan Perimeter brilliantly, but his accidental death brought an even better leader to the forefront.

The 55-year-old Matt Ridgway had earned a great reputation in the Second World War, and was the army's deputy chief of staff in December 1950. When appointed ground commander in Korea, Ridgway set about evaluating the morale of the 365,000 US/UN/ROK troops. 'This was a bewildered army, not sure of itself or its leaders, not sure what they were doing there', he wrote later, 'There was obviously much to be done to restore this army to a fighting mood.' The troops liked him: he had a hand grenade taped on the right side of his chest, and a first-aid kit on the left, so they nicknamed him 'Iron Tits'. He had the knack of making them feel that he cared, as when he handed out the extra winter gloves or stationery for writing home that he carried in his jeep. His actions became legendary. One radio man, burdened by equipment and stuck in the mud, said 'Thanks, pal' to the man who bent down to tie up his bootlaces for him, and was surprised to see it was a three-star general – Ridgway. Ridgway did not seek easy popularity: he kept his officers on their toes, sacking one who gave him a plan for a second retreat to the Pusan Perimeter.

b) Ridgway's task

The JCS told Ridgway that his brief was basically to secure South Korea. They told him, 'Korea is not the place to fight a major war', and that fighting the Chinese in Korea constituted an 'increased threat of general war'. MacArthur disagreed with the JCS. He wanted to destroy North Korea, unleash Chiang Kai-shek's forces on China, and institute an American blockade of China. The JCS chairman Omar Bradley subsequently guessed at MacArthur's motivation:

> The only possible means left to MacArthur to regain his lost pride was now to inflict an overwhelming defeat on those Red Chinese generals who had made a fool of him.

By now the Chinese were caught up in the same kind of optimism and military momentum that had encouraged the Americans to cross the 38th parallel into North Korea in autumn 1950. In January 1951, the Chinese crossed the 38th parallel into South Korea – 'just walking there' would take it, said Peng, their top general. Nearly half a million Chinese drove for Seoul, in the vicinity of which were American, ROK, British, British

Commonwealth, Greek and Filipino forces. The Chinese aimed at the ROK forces, whose panicky retreat shocked Ridgway. Seoul was lost to the Communists yet again, and hundreds of thousands of South Korean refugees poured southward for the second time in six months.

By now, the war was highly unpopular in the USA: a January 1951 poll revealed that 49 per cent of Americans felt sending troops to Korea had been a mistake, and 66 per cent believed the United States should abandon South Korea. However, Truman had no intention of getting out. Truman and the JCS told MacArthur the bottom line:

> It is important to United States prestige worldwide, to the future of UN and NATO organisations, and to efforts to organise anti-Communist resistance in Asia that Korea not be evacuated unless actually forced by military considerations, and that maximum practicable punishment be inflicted on Communist aggressors.

Ridgway's task was not easy. Faced with the Chinese onslaught, US troop morale was low in January 1951. There was much talk that the 8th Army was about to evacuate Korea, and one captain wrote home that Korea 'holds no value now, military, political or idealistic'. Ridgway responded with a statement to be read to all the soldiers. It was headed, 'Why are we here? What are we fighting for?' In the statement he explained that the 'issue is whether Communism or individual freedom shall prevail', and warned the troops that unless the Communists were opposed, Americans might some day find themselves in the same position as the South Koreans, that is, victims of aggression in their own homeland.

The tide now turned in favour of the US/UN/ROK forces, for several reasons. The Chinese had overstretched themselves: their supply lines had reached their outer limits. The flatter lands of South Korea favoured the tanks and artillery that the Chinese lacked but that Ridgway had in abundance. Michaelis (see page 40) attributed the dramatic turnaround to Ridgway himself:

> Ridgway took that defeated army and turned it around. He was a breath of fresh air, a showman, what the army desperately needed.

General Walton Collins, sent by the JCS to check morale, agreed:

> 8th Army in good shape and improving under Ridgway's leadership. Morale very satisfactory considering conditions.

Ridgway was a thorough and imaginative commander. He improved reconnaissance and the supply system, and initiated a series of carefully thought out counter-attacks. By February 1951, 8th Army was moving forward again.

Not the least of Ridgway's tasks was to manage MacArthur, whose influence was now rather limited. Tensions were beginning to develop between MacArthur and Ridgway. For example,

Operation Killer
Ridgway's February
1951 plan to inflict
morale-damaging
losses on the
Chinese.

MacArthur tried to claim credit for initiating '**Operation Killer**', which was Ridgway's idea: 'an unwelcome reminder of the MacArthur that I'd known but had almost forgotten', said Ridgway later. By March, when Seoul was retaken and the 8th Army was back at the 38th parallel, the MacArthur problem was about to come to a head.

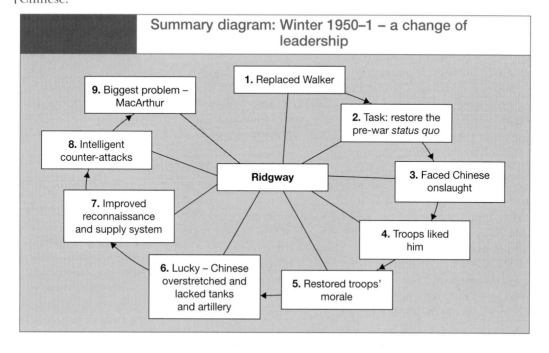

Summary diagram: Winter 1950–1 – a change of leadership

Key question
Why and with what
results did Truman
dismiss MacArthur?

Key date

Truman dismissed
MacArthur: 11 April
1951

2 | MacArthur's Dismissal

a) Disagreements and dismissal

Truman and MacArthur had long had major disagreements over:

- the relative strategic importance of Asia as opposed to Europe
- the use of nuclear weapons in the war
- whether or not the United States should further provoke Communist China.

In short, Truman was committed to waging limited war in Korea, while MacArthur was spoiling for an all-out fight against Communist China. They had clashed as early as August 1950, when MacArthur issued an unauthorised statement on the need for the United States to defend Taiwan – a highly sensitive foreign policy question (see page 33). Truman subsequently said he should have sacked MacArthur then and there. Then, in December 1950, MacArthur told journalists that Asia was the main Cold War battleground and that 'limited' war was wrong. When Ridgway asked the air force chief why the JCS did not tell MacArthur what to do, the chief replied, 'What good would that do? He would not obey the orders. What can we do?' Shocked, Ridgway replied, 'You can relieve any commander who won't obey orders, can't you?' At last, on 11 April 1951, Truman relieved MacArthur of his command in the Far East, saying:

With deep regret I have concluded that General MacArthur is unable to give his wholehearted support to the policies of the United States government and of the United Nations in matters pertaining to his official duties. In view of the specific responsibilities imposed upon me by the Constitution of the United States and the added responsibilities entrusted to me by the United Nations, I have decided that I must make a change of command in the Far East.

b) MacArthur's popularity

At the time, Truman's dismissal of MacArthur was a highly unpopular decision. Truman's **approval rating** sank as MacArthur and his admirers engaged in emotional farewells. When MacArthur left Tokyo for the last time, around two million Japanese people lined his route to the airport, to demonstrate their respect. A leading Japanese newspaper lamented, 'We feel as if we have lost a kind and loving father.' Then, when the old general returned to the United States, he was met by over half a million supporters in San Francisco and given a record-breaking **ticker-tape parade** in New York City. An unprecedented 3249 tons of ticker-tape, shredded paper and confetti rained down on him in his triumphal motorcade through the city. His 20 April 1951 speech to Congress is rightly famous. In that speech, he gained impressive and repeated congressional applause with his references to 'your sons' whom he had just left on the battlefields of Korea, to the 'feisty' South Koreans who had begged him 'don't scuttle the Pacific', and to his lifetime of service to his country. His final flourish was brilliantly dramatic:

> I am closing my 52 years of military service. The world has turned over many times since I took the oath on the Plains at West Point, but I still remember the refrain of one of the most popular barracks ballads of that day which proclaimed most proudly that, 'Old soldiers never die; they just fade away.' And like the old soldier of that ballad, I now close my military career and just fade away – an old soldier who tried to do his duty as God gave him the light to see that duty. Goodbye.

The applause was rapturous. Some congressmen wept openly. A conservative Republican said, 'We heard God speak here today, God in the flesh, the voice of God.' Ex-President Hoover described MacArthur as a 'reincarnation of St Paul'. A Gallup poll revealed 69 per cent of Americans believed Truman was wrong to sack him. Truman, who described the speech as '100 per cent bullshit', received 27,000 letters and telegrams, the vast majority of which criticised him. Over 100,000 letters reached Congress, many demanding Truman's **impeachment**. Senator McCarthy called Truman a 'son of a bitch' and blamed the firing on Truman's Missouri friends, all 'stoned on bourbon and Benedictine' (the president was famous for entertaining old friends from his home state in the White House).

Key terms

Approval rating American pollsters continually check the public's opinion (approval) of the president's performance.

Ticker-tape parade When national heroes returned to the United States, the citizens of New York City would shower them with bits of paper (ticker-tape) as they drove through the streets of the city in an open-top car.

Impeachment Process whereby Congress has the constitutional power to remove an errant president.

MacArthur, standing, being driven along Broadway, New York, on 23 April 1951. Many contemporaries thought the ticker-tape parade demonstrated MacArthur's popularity. Would you agree?

c) Support for the dismissal

Some contemporaries supported Truman. One Democratic senator said:

> I do not know how many thousand American GIs are sleeping in unmarked graves in North Korea. But most of them are silent but immutable evidence of the tragic mistake of 'The Magnificent MacArthur' who told them that the Chinese Communists just across the Yalu would not intervene.

Leading newspapers, some of which had been hostile to Truman, felt that the president had preserved the constitutional principle of civilian control over the military, MacArthur having committed two acts of insubordination. The first related to Truman's March 1951 peace initiative plan. Truman had made it clear that as the situation was highly delicate, no one was to release policy statements without State Department clearance. Some felt that when MacArthur then issued a **communiqué** that publicly insulted China as facing 'imminent military collapse', he had sabotaged Truman's plan. Truman later recalled that MacArthur had issued that controversial communiqué:

> in open defiance of my orders as President and commander-in-chief. By this act, MacArthur left me no choice. I could no longer tolerate his insubordination.

Key term

Communiqué
In diplomatic and military terms, a statement issued by a commander or leader.

Privately, Truman told a Democratic senator, 'I'll show that son of a bitch who's boss. Who does he think he is? God?'

MacArthur's second act of insubordination in spring 1951 came when he sent a letter to Republican congressman Joseph W. Martin and gave Martin permission to read it out in Congress. In the letter, MacArthur wrote that 'if we lose this war to Communism in Asia', the fall of Europe would inevitably follow. The letter made it very clear that he opposed Truman's doctrine of containment (which he likened to appeasement) and policy of limited war in Korea: 'There is no substitute for victory.' In allowing this letter to be read out in public, MacArthur violated the JCS directive of 6 December 1950, which said that all government officials had to obtain clearance before they published any comments on the war.

The JCS was fully supportive of Truman. They feared that MacArthur might deliberately provoke an incident in order to widen the war into an all-out conflict between the United States and Communist China, and their position was evident in the congressional hearings on the war in May 1951. JCS chairman Omar Bradley explained that he disagreed with MacArthur over the importance of China and Secretary of Defence George Marshall registered his disapproval of MacArthur's rejection of a limited war strategy. After the JCS testimonies, the MacArthur controversy died down.

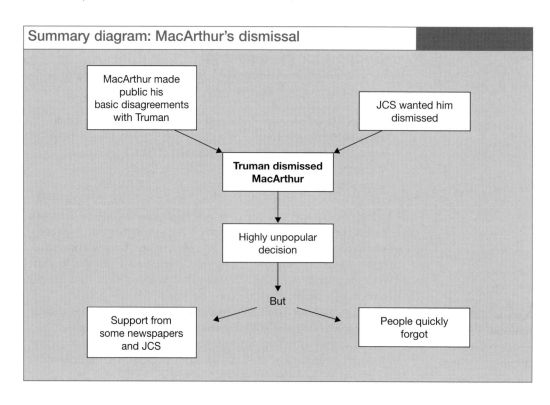

Summary diagram: MacArthur's dismissal

Key question
What were the
Chinese aims in
1951?

3 | Chinese Aims in 1951

In February 1951, the UN proposed peace talks, but the Chinese rejected the proposal. Under US pressure, and to the irritation of some US allies such as Britain, the UN then denounced China as an aggressor. This prompted the Chinese to articulate demands that help to explain Chinese motivation in the war. China wanted:

- the United States to get out of Korea
- the US 7th Fleet to leave the Taiwan Straits
- the UN seat for China, which was currently held by Chiang Kai-shek's Taiwan.

China launched another great offensive in Korea on 22 April 1951, but the cost in lives proved too high: 12,000 Chinese troops died on the first day of the offensive, and this helped prompt China to request an armistice in June 1951. China now modified its aims, concentrating on an armistice, which might get most of the American troops out of Korea.

Key question
Why was the
armistice finally
signed in 1953?

4 | The Signing of the Armistice in 1953

Key dates

Armistice talks began:
June 1951

Armistice signed: July
1953

Although China proposed an armistice in June 1951, it was not finally signed until July 1953. In those two years, the bitter fighting continued: it was calculated that two soldiers died for every minute the peace talks were on. The military situation had reached stalemate, and the front lines of the combatants had stabilised near the 38th parallel (Ridgway's replacement, General Matt Clark, wanted to attack Chinese Manchuria and use atomic weapons, but Washington said 'no'). This raises two questions: first, why did the Korean War finally come to an end, and second, why did it take so long to agree on the armistice?

a) Why did the Korean War come to an end?
i) Why the United States wanted peace
The United States wanted peace because:

- The financial burden of the war was great. In 1953, the Secretary of the Treasury told Truman's successor President Eisenhower that the expenditure was damaging US government finances.
- The war had cost many American lives, and the American public had turned against what was frequently referred to as 'Truman's War'. In an autumn 1951 poll, a majority agreed that the Korean War was 'an utterly useless war'.
- There was pressure from America's allies and from **non-aligned nations** to end the military stalemate.
- From May 1951, Communist accusations that the United States was using bacteriological warfare in Korea were damaging America's international reputation. Historians are divided over the truth of the accusation. Reputable historians such as Cumings have shown that the use of chemical warfare was seriously considered: huge stockpiles of sarin nerve gas were

Key term

**Non-aligned
nations**
Countries that
remained neutral in
the Cold War.

being prepared for use in the war. In 1976, the head of the CIA admitted that the Army Bacteriological Warfare Laboratories at Fort Detrick in Maryland had been commissioned in early 1952 to develop bacteriological agents and delivery systems.

- Some feared that if the conflict continued, the USSR might join in the fighting and the Korean War could escalate into a Third World War.
- The JCS emphasised that the United States should not be pinned down by the Korean conflict, as trouble could erupt in Europe (Germany was always particularly volatile). If that were to happen, American forces would be overstretched and unable to meet the Communist threat there. In May 1951, General Omar Bradley, chairman of the JCS, told Congress that China was not the greatest threat faced by the United States, and that an escalated clash with China would be 'the wrong war, at the wrong place, at the wrong time, and with the wrong enemy'. In the same congressional hearings, Secretary of Defence George Marshall expressed his belief that the United States should not escalate the war in order to win it, but must accept that the containment of Communism necessitated a limited war strategy.

ii) Why the other combatants wanted peace
The other combatants wanted peace because:

- China needed to concentrate on its domestic problems. Its economy was suffering. Hundreds of thousands of soldiers were dying. Also, China was anxious lest the conflict escalate. Historians disagree over whether President Eisenhower's threat to use nuclear weapons contributed to the Chinese decision to seek peace.
- The Soviet desire for peace was partly due to the death of Stalin in March 1953, which caused a struggle for power amongst his likely successors. They were keen to have peace for several reasons. They wanted to concentrate on the succession, and to decrease the risk of general war. They also hoped to create tensions between the United States and its less belligerent allies.
- North Korea was suffering food shortages, and Kim was increasingly anxious to end the conflict, because he was clearly not going to attain reunification.

iii) How peace was achieved
The change in personnel in both the USSR (with the death of Stalin in March 1953) and United States (with the accession of Eisenhower to the presidency in January 1953) made it easier to achieve peace. The new leaders had neither started nor sustained their nation's involvement in the war. So, their prestige was not at stake in the way that their predecessors' prestige had been. Also, Eisenhower was a military hero and the American public trusted his judgement in matters of war. The new president effectively 'bought off' Syngman Rhee by offering him financial aid and a

promise to defend him if South Korea were attacked. Finally, the new president and many other Americans were convinced that Eisenhower's threats about using atomic weapons helped persuade the Chinese to sign the armistice.

Much credit was due to the backroom talks at the UN between the US Soviet specialist George Kennan and the Soviet ambassador to the UN, Jacob Malik. Their talks, away from the public posturings characteristic of many peace negotiations, did important ground work for the eventual armistice.

b) Why it had taken so long to arrange the armistice?

In June 1951, both the Americans and the Chinese issued public statements about the desirability of ending the conflict, but the Chinese suggested laying down arms and then talking, while the Americans, fearing that China would use such a pause to prepare for another offensive, said agreement on armistice terms had to precede the cessation of hostilities. Thus, from the start, both sides were anxious not to give the other any advantage.

There was a great preoccupation with saving face. When UN negotiator Vice Admiral C. Turner Joy put a UN flag on the table on the first day (10 July 1951) of the negotiations, the North Korean representative quickly put up a larger North Korean flag. The talks were initially located in North Korean/Chinese-held territory, at Kaesong, and the Chinese made sure that while they sat on high upholstered chairs, the UN negotiators were given smaller, wooden seats. After a few weeks, the talks were moved to Panmunjom, midway between the front lines.

After a bitter war, it is usually difficult to get the participants to agree on peace. Ridgway could hardly bear to talk to the Chinese, and cabled the JCS:

> To sit down with these men and deal with them as representatives of an enlightened and civilised people is to deride one's own dignity and to invite the disaster their treachery will inevitably bring upon us … [Our delegates should] employ such language and methods as these treacherous savages cannot fail to understand, and understanding, respect.

Defectors
There were 21,805 Chinese and North Korean POWs who did not want to be repatriated, and 23 Americans and one Briton who defected to Communism.

In the negotiations, according to the historian Peter Lowe, the Americans were simplistic, the Communists were inflexible and Syngman Rhee ('Our goal is unification') was obstructive, and their combined characteristics slowed down the process. Rhee's behaviour was such that the US considered replacing him.

Truman played a major part in delaying the peace, because he refused to allow Communist POWs to be returned to China. Truman insisted that the POWs were Communists who wanted to defect to the 'Free World', but many were actually South Koreans who had joined the Communists either voluntarily or at gunpoint. Others were Chinese Nationalists trapped in China at the end of the Chinese civil war. The Chinese pointed out that under international law, POWs had to be repatriated.

Some historians attribute Truman's inflexibility on the POWs to
principle and humanitarian motives. Others say he sought a
propaganda victory in the Cold War. It seems unlikely that he
sought domestic political advantage in his stubborn stance, as few
Americans cared about the POWs. Indeed, such was the
impatience to end the war, that more than half of Americans were
willing to use the atomic bomb.

Summary diagram: The signing of the armistice in 1953

Why peace?	Why so long?
• Expensive (lives and money) • American public anti-war • UN countries tired of war • Conflict could escalate • JCS 'Europe-firsters' • Eisenhower's nuclear threat? • Stalin died, Soviets busy • Public trusted Eisenhower • Eisenhower 'bought off' Rhee • Kennan/Malik talks • New US president, less 'face'	• Neither side wanted to give the other any advantage • Saving face • Bitterness • US simplistic • Communists inflexible } Lowe • Rhee obstructive • Truman and POWs

5 | The Results and Significance of the Korean War: The Impact on American Society and Politics

Key question
How did the Korean War impact on American society and politics?

There were over 30,000 American deaths in Korea: to
contemporaries, this now 'forgotten war' was immensely
important and significant, both in domestic politics and in the
wider Cold War context.

a) McCarthyism
The Korean War intensified the McCarthyite hysteria that the
senator's rabid anti-Communism had generated since February
1950 (see page 21). Schools had atomic attack drills, in which
children were trained to hide under desks in the event of a Soviet
bomb being dropped on them. Sales of backyard bomb shelters
increased. Communists were banned from employment as
teachers or civil servants. Free speech was badly affected as left-
wingers and suspected Communists were persecuted. For
example, black entertainer Paul Robeson, who spoke out in favour
of the USSR, had his passport confiscated in 1950.

b) The American economy
The war had a great impact on the American economy. It cost the
United States $67 billion, and subsequently billions more were
spent on rebuilding South Korea. The increased defence
expenditure boosted the gross national product, but also
generated inflation.

c) Truman's presidency

The Korean War greatly damaged Truman's presidency. After the war caused inflation, over half a million steelworkers struck for better wages in April 1952. In response, Truman seized the steel mills, which led to a constitutional crisis. Truman was humiliated when the Supreme Court ruled that his actions were unconstitutional.

Truman's failure to obtain a congressional declaration of war helped to saddle him with all the blame for 'Truman's War', and, according to the historian Patterson, rendered him 'virtually powerless' either to control Congress or to effectively lead the country. It made him decide against standing for re-election in 1952, as it had caused his popularity ratings to plummet. The war helped to ensure the 1952 victory of the Republican Dwight D. Eisenhower, who had promised to bring peace: 'I shall go to Korea'. The American people, tired of Truman, felt that Eisenhower, already a popular military hero from the Second World War, could be trusted to bring an acceptable peace in Korea, where his son was fighting.

d) Waging war in a democracy

The Korean War demonstrated the difficulties of waging war in the American democracy. Feeling threatened by McCarthy and the Republicans and still stung by accusations of having 'lost' China, Truman had entered the war partly because he was anxious about the Democratic Party's performance in the forthcoming congressional mid-term elections. After Inchon, Truman's decision to cross the 38th parallel was partly taken because the American public thirsted for revenge on the aggressor. Then, when the Chinese entered the war and the US did badly, public pressure made Truman's successor get the United States out of the war. Thus public opinion shaped the outbreak and the course of the war. This was particularly evident in the case of the Truman administration's dealings with MacArthur, who might well have been sacked long before April 1951 had it not been for his popularity with the American people.

e) African Americans

One highly desirable outcome of the Korean War was a speeding up of the desegregation of the army ordered by President Truman in 1948. At this time, most African Americans in the southern United States were not allowed to vote or to sit in the same schools or restaurants as white Americans, but under the pressure of war, the US forces in Korea were integrated. Short of manpower and slowed up by having to run a black and a white army, both the army top brass and ordinary soldiers realised that segregation hurt them. 'We didn't do it to improve the social situation', said the deputy army chief of staff. 'It was merely a matter of getting the best out of the military personnel that was available to us.'

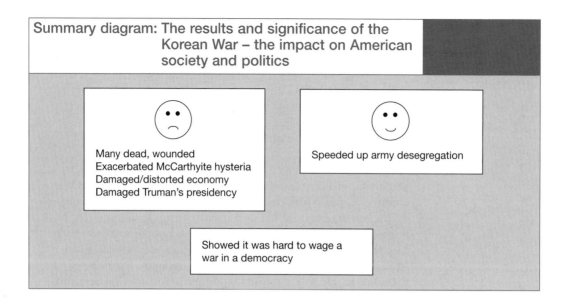

Summary diagram: The results and significance of the Korean War – the impact on American society and politics

Many dead, wounded
Exacerbated McCarthyite hysteria
Damaged/distorted economy
Damaged Truman's presidency

Speeded up army desegregation

Showed it was hard to wage a war in a democracy

6 | The Results and Significance of the Korean War: The Impact on US Foreign Policy

Key question
How did the Korean War impact upon US foreign policy?

a) Containment worked

Containment (see page 34) could be said to have worked. The United States had gone to war to save South Korea from Communism and to restore the *status quo* in the Korean peninsula. In that, the United States succeeded. The United States had been seen as willing and able to halt Communist expansion, and had 'saved' South Korea and also ensured Japanese security. The Korean War speeded up Japan's development into a reliable and invaluable US ally (see pages 23–4).

> **Korea and the Japanese economic miracle**
> Nissan and Toyota produced and repaired trucks for the Americans during the Korean War, and soon grew into industrial giants on the world stage. The whole Japanese economy benefited greatly from the war, as the US relied heavily on Japanese products and facilities.

b) American prestige and credibility

In some ways, the Korean War helped American prestige and credibility. The United States had held the line against the Communists, and restored the *status quo*. However, the United States had failed in its attempt to reunify the peninsula. General Matt Clark said:

> I gained the unenviable distinction of being the first United States Army Commander in history to sign an armistice without victory.

c) Sino-American relations

The Korean War greatly damaged Sino-American relations, and it would be more than two decades before the two nations finally exchanged ambassadors. In the fighting after the Chinese entry into the Korean War, it was China that impressed the world. In the military stalemate from 1951 to 1953, the Chinese troops had effectively held the Americans to a draw. As well as standing up to the world's leading power, the new China could be argued to have outfaced General MacArthur, who had unsuccessfully advocated a more aggressive American policy towards China.

d) MacArthur's dismissal

The dismissal of General Douglas MacArthur was significant in three ways. Firstly, it signalled Truman's commitment to his doctrine of containment of Communism, which necessitated only limited war. Truman rejected MacArthur's desire to enter into a full-scale war with China, which might well have led to a Third World War. Secondly, Truman was asserting the constitutional principle of civilian control over the military. Thirdly, the sacking signalled that Western Europe remained vital to US security, as JCS chairman Omar Bradley attested before Congress in May 1951. Bradley, in a clear attack on MacArthur and other Republican 'Asia-firsters', denied that China was the greatest threat to the United States. For Bradley and for other Europe-firsters, Russia was the greatest enemy and Europe the greatest prize. However, it can reasonably be argued that the Korean War had shifted the storm centre of the Cold War from Europe to Asia.

e) The arms race and US alliances

The Korean War was important in escalating the arms race between the United States and the USSR. It prompted a massive US and Soviet military build-up. Truman ordered a speeding up of the US hydrogen bomb programme, aiming to give America a weapon with even greater destructive power than that of the atomic bombs dropped on Japan. Furthermore, the Korean War inspired the United States to strengthen **NATO**, the new defensive Western military alliance masterminded by the US in 1949. In the building up of NATO, the US began the remilitarisation of West Germany. The Korean War dramatically changed the US relationship with Germany and Japan. Two nations that only a few years before had been America's bloody enemies now became close allies. The war also affected the US relationship with South Korea and Taiwan.

Key term

NATO
The North Atlantic Treaty Organisation was an anti-Communist Western military alliance established by the United States in 1949.

f) Undemocratic allies

The American historian James Matray has emphasised that, while the United States believed and claimed that it fought for democracy in the Cold War, the Korean War left it wedded to two odious regimes in Asia, those of Chiang Kai-shek in Taiwan and Syngman Rhee in South Korea.

g) The United Nations

One of Truman's declared aims in entering the Korean War was to support the United Nations, and it could be argued that the UN had worked. Sixteen nations had sent military aid, and many others had sent food or medics. Many countries were involved in Korea, and 17,000 UN soldiers died there. Truman called the war a 'UN police action'. However, there are many arguments that suggest that this was not a UN but a US war. Over 90 per cent of the 'UN' forces were American and South Korean. The UN had requested that MacArthur communicate directly with the UN, but Truman rejected that.

Furthermore, the US took important decisions without reference to its UN allies who often disapproved of American decisions and actions. Britain, for example, disliked the US re-injecting itself into the Chinese civil war (see pages 33–5), was very anxious about the US decision to cross the 38th parallel, and was angry and unhappy when the US talked of using atomic weaponry in Korea. Some historians emphasise the non-stop tensions that arose between the US and its allies over unilateral US actions during the Korean War. For example, several US allies criticised the May 1953 American bombing of North Korean dams and irrigation systems, because these actions affected civilians.

h) A Cold War turning point

James Matray sees the Korean War as significant in that it constituted the critical turning point in the whole Cold War, with:

- the massive increase in US defence expenditure and commitment to NATO
- the poisoning of Sino-American relations
- the cementing of the relationship with the 'odious' regimes of Syngman Rhee and Chiang Kai-shek.

Matray sees the 'main legacy' as being that the 'United States thereafter pursued a foreign policy of global intervention and paid an enormous price in death, destruction, and damaged reputation'. This was particularly the case in relation to Vietnam.

i) Vietnam

The Korean War proved so unpopular in United States that it might have been expected to have taught subsequent presidents to keep US troops out of the jungles of mainland Asia. However, while Eisenhower apparently learned this lesson, Kennedy and Johnson did not. It was during the Korean War that the United States first became involved in Vietnam: convinced by events in Korea that Communism was on the march, Truman increased financial aid to the French because they too were fighting Communism.

Summary diagram: The results and significance of the Korean War – the impact on US foreign policy

- Credibility/prestige damaged when crossed 38th parallel
- Damaged Sino-American relations
- Encouraged US involvement in Vietnam
- Escalated arms race
- US wedded to Rhee and Chiang

- Containment worked?
- *Status quo* in Korea restored
- Japan 'saved' and prospered
- Civilian control over military established (ultimately)
- Showed UN worked?
- Helped democracy?

- Turning point in Cold War
- Shifted storm centre of Cold War to Asia

Study Guide: AS Questions

In the style of Edexcel

To what extent was the USA's involvement in Korea in the years 1950–3 successful? (30 marks)

> *Exam tips*
>
> *The cross-references are intended to take you straight to the material that will help you to answer the question.*
>
> This question asks you to assess the USA's achievements and failures in order to come to a judgement about 'successful'. It is important that you develop a balanced argument and come to an overall conclusion. You will have no more than 40 minutes to answer this question.
>
> You will not have time to develop more than four or five points, so it is also important to be selective as you plan your answer. Be clear before you start what criteria you are going to use ultimately to measure 'success'. A good starting point would be the USA's own aims. Do not waste time scene-setting in your introduction. Get on with the essay purposefully, indicating what criteria you will use to assess success.
>
> What were the successes? You could consider evidence of:
>
> - Support for the UN's role (page 72).
> - The restoration of the original border at the 38th parallel (page 70).
> - Containment of Communism (page 70).
> - The development of Japan as a US ally (page 70).

And the failures or weakness? You could consider:

- The extent to which the conflict was perceived as America's war, rather than a UN mission (page 72).
- The damage to US prestige and credibility resulting from the eventual failure of the push into the North (page 70).
- The huge cost to the USA in personnel and the financial burden (page 68).
- The enhancement of Communist China's position on the world stage (page 71).

What overall conclusion you come to will depend on what weight you give to the points on both sides. Bearing in mind that the USA's key aim was the containment of Communism, on which side does the weight of evidence lie in your view?

In the style of OCR

(a) **Study Sources A and C.**
Compare these sources as evidence for the American view of the policy of containment at that time.

(b) **Study all of the sources.**
Use your own knowledge to assess how far the sources support the interpretation that MacArthur and Truman had different policy aims in Korea.

Source A

Dean Acheson, speaking to the Senate Foreign Relations Committee, 12 January 1950. The US Secretary of State explains how the Truman Administration will approach the Communist threat across Southeast Asia and the Pacific.

The line Japan–Okinawa–Philippines is our first line of defence and on this line the US has impregnable defence. In Southeast Asia, including Burma, India, Siam [Thailand], Indochina and Indonesia, about the most we can do is encourage them and give them some aid. It is a mistake, I think, in considering Pacific and Far East problems to become obsessed with military considerations. Important as they are, there are other problems that are not capable of solution through military means. These other problems arise out of the susceptibility of many areas and countries in the Pacific area to subversion and penetration.

Source B

From: 'US courses of action with respect to Korea', a report to the National Security Council, 1 September 1950. The US Administration decides its policy on operations in northern Korea.

As UN forces drive back those of North Korea and approach the 38th Parallel, the decisions taken by the US and other UN members, and by the Kremlin, will determine whether hostilities are confined to Korea or spread so that the danger of a third world war is greatly increased.

Only if no action has been taken by the Soviet Union or the Chinese Communists to reoccupy Northern Korea before UN forces reach the 38th could UN forces undertake ground operations north of the 38th without a substantial risk of general war. Our action in crossing the Parallel would create a situation to which the Soviet Union would be almost certain to react. While the risk of Soviet or Chinese Communist intervention might not be lessened if only Republic of Korea forces conducted operations north of the 38th, the risk of general hostilities would be reduced. In no circumstances should other UN forces be used in the northeastern province bordering the Soviet Union or in the area along the Manchurian border.

UN forces have a legal basis to operate north of the 38th to compel withdrawal of North Korean forces behind this line or to defeat these forces. The UN commander should be authorised to conduct operations north of the 38th of destroying the North Korean forces, provided that there has been no entry into North Korea by major Soviet or Chinese Communist forces or any announcement of intended entry.

Source C

General MacArthur to Congressman Joseph Martin, 20 March 1951. Nine months into the war, MacArthur sums up the situation for the Republican Minority Leader in the House of Representatives.

My views and recommendations with respect to the situation created by Red China's entry into war against us in Korea have been submitted to Washington in most complete detail. Generally these views are well known and clearly understood, as they follow the conventional pattern of meeting force with maximum counterforce.

It seems strangely difficult for some to realise that here in Asia is where the Communist conspirators have elected to make their play for global conquest, and that we have joined the issue thus raised on the battlefield; that here we fight Europe's war with arms while the diplomats there still fight it with words; that if we lose the war to Communism in Asia the fall of Europe is inevitable, win it and Europe most probably would avoid war and yet preserve freedom. As you pointed out, we must win. There is no substitute for victory.

Source D

From: Fourth International, *published in June 1951.*
An anti-Stalinist Communist magazine analyses the reasons for MacArthur's dismissal.

The Senate hearings have revealed that, so far as the main practical aspects of foreign policy and military strategy in the Far East are concerned, the differences between MacArthur and the administration are small. General Marshall has come out as strongly for keeping Formosa [Taiwan] out of China's hands as the partisans of MacArthur could have desired. Their whole argument boils down to the question: Is the bombing of Manchuria and the naval blockade of China's coast advisable at present? It appears that what the Pentagon and the White House objected to in MacArthur's policy was not so much its essence as its timing. MacArthur, as General Bradley put it, wanted 'the wrong war, with the wrong enemy, in the wrong place, at the wrong time'.

Source E

From: Robert Smith, MacArthur in Korea: The Naked Emperor, *published in 1982. A modern historian analyses MacArthur's actions in March 1951.*

The investigation of the Senate Joint Committee into MacArthur's dismissal noted the shock to national pride. That was true, but it was not deserved. Crudely, deliberately, with complete understanding of what would ensue, MacArthur undertook to sabotage Truman's effort, in March 1951, to open peace negotiations with the Chinese. No one not blinded by hero worship could overlook the arrogance and contempt with which MacArthur deliberately flouted Truman's directive by issuing an ultimatum to China.

Exam tips

The cross-references are intended to take you straight to the material that will help you to answer the questions.

(a) Compare the content of both sources but also compare matters like their authorship, date and typicality. This is vital because the question asks for comparison 'as evidence for …'. Take serious note of the introductions and attributions – they point you in the right direction.

At first sight, Sources A and C seem to offer contrasting views. What is going on here? Be clear that containment was Truman's own policy – the Truman Doctrine was perhaps the key pronouncement of US Cold War policy. What is being debated here is what containment should mean in this part of the world. Source A comes from a politician second only to the president; Source C from the commanding soldier. Explain that what we have is an argument at the highest level about the direction of US policy:

- Acheson (Source A) had recently been appointed as Secretary of State and was working up the framework in which containment would operate. He is setting clear limits, and excludes Korea from the zone where the US will act.
- MacArthur (Source C) takes the opposite line, arguing the US must fight aggressively in Korea and take on China.

Ask why they are so different. Point out the very different times when each spoke/wrote: Source A dates from six months before the Korean War began. That said, MacArthur was more hawkish than Acheson. You might end by noting that Truman rejected MacArthur's 'iron fist' line and sacked him.

(b) There is no 'right' answer. Your job is to weight the evidence and give a clear judgement on the question so that you actually answer it. Make sure you consider every source, judging them against each other and your own knowledge to decide how far they confirm or undermine the interpretation in the question.

Keep your focus on the aims of MacArthur and Truman in 1951. The sources offer differing views so group them according where they stand on the matter:

- The modern historian (Source E) agrees: MacArthur deliberately disobeyed the president, aiming to sabotage his plan to make peace with China.
- Against that, Source D argues that Truman and MacArthur essentially wanted the same thing. Source D is an unusual source in offering contemporary commentary from a Communist perspective which is anti-Stalinist.
- The other three sources lock together. Sources A and B are also political sources, setting out Truman's careful Cold War policy and the limits it set. Against that line, Source C (MacArthur) pushes for a different policy because he says victory or defeat in the Cold War itself depends on what happens in Korea.

The question tells you to use your own knowledge to test how far the sources support the interpretation.

Truman and MacArthur were indeed both anti-Communist Cold War warriors so Source D's claim should not be dismissed outright. Given that Source A dates from so long before, is it relevant? Yes, because it gives context to Source B, showing Truman would not wage unlimited war or risk direct conflict with China or Russia. Read in that context, MacArthur's line (Source C) is very different: all-out war is essential.

What do you know to help you to decide between them? In support of the claim, you could mention:

- MacArthur's aggressive ideas (for example, his wish to cross the Yalu River and to use atomic weapons – pages 53 and 59) that run contrary to Truman's Cold War policy in Sources A and B.
- That the 1951 US Senate Committee investigation found against MacArthur and backed (more or less) Truman's decision to sack him for disobedience (page 64).
- That MacArthur had a reputation for disobedience (Roosevelt called him one of the most dangerous men in America).

Against the claim, you could argue:

- MacArthur was the victim of Truman's Administration. They wanted a limited war of position and saw that MacArthur (who preferred a war of movement) was not the general to deliver that. Washington wanted MacArthur out and chose to see differences of opinion as fundamental disagreements on high policy.

- That line could be developed to ask how far the sacking was politically motivated since MacArthur had strong links to the Right of the Republican Party.
- That could take you on to the question of 'who controls the military?' which was hotly debated in 1950–1. Truman's strike against MacArthur was a direct move to keep control firmly in civilian hands.
- Perhaps Source D is not entirely wrong. MacArthur was demanding all-out war on China. As General Bradley told Congress (quoted in Source D), MacArthur's strategy would 'involve us in the wrong war, with the wrong enemy, in the wrong place, at the wrong time'.

4

Vietnam and Foreigners Before 1953

POINTS TO CONSIDER

There are three particularly controversial questions regarding American involvement in Vietnam: 1) Why did the United States get involved? 2) Which president(s) bore most responsibility for that involvement? 3) Why did the United States fail there? This chapter helps to answer those questions, through covering the following:

- Ho Chi Minh and Vietnamese nationalism
- The United States and Vietnam, 1941–5
- The reasons for early American involvement in Vietnam
- The extent to which Truman committed the USA in Vietnam

Key dates

1887		Indochina (Vietnam, Cambodia and Laos) under French domination
1929		Ho Chi Minh established Indochinese Communist Party
1939–45		Second World War
1941		Japan completed conquest of French Indochina
		Ho Chi Minh returned to Vietnam
		Vietnam Independence League (Vietminh) established
1941–5		USA at war with Japan
1945	April	President Roosevelt died; Truman became president
	September	Ho Chi Minh declared Vietnamese independence
1945–9		Start of Cold War between USA and USSR
1945–6		Outbreak of Franco-Vietminh War
1949	October	China became Communist
1950	January	USSR and China recognised Ho's Democratic Republic of Vietnam
	February	Start of 'McCarthyism'
	May	Truman gave France money to fight Communism in Vietnam

1 | Ho Chi Minh and Vietnamese Nationalism

Two of the most important reasons why the Americans were to fail in Vietnam were (a) Vietnamese nationalism and (b) the leadership of Ho Chi Minh (1890–1969).

a) Vietnamese nationalism before 1900

The vast majority of nineteenth-century Vietnamese people were peasant farmers producing rice on fertile river deltas. The growing of rice was a communal activity carried out by the people of each village. Their community spirit and nationalism had been vital in fending off frequent Chinese attempts to conquer Vietnam. During centuries of struggle against its giant neighbour China, little Vietnam had generally been successful: the Vietnamese had perfected guerrilla warfare techniques and harassed the Chinese into confusion and exhaustion.

During the late nineteenth century, the French began attacking Vietnam. By 1887 the countries subsequently known as Vietnam, Cambodia and Laos were under the control of the French, who referred to them collectively as **Indochina**. However, Vietnamese nationalists such as Ho Chi Minh dreamed of independence.

b) The shaping of a Vietnamese leader

From 1911 to 1930, Ho Chi Minh travelled abroad in order to help to prepare himself for the eventual struggle for Vietnamese independence. When in France, he mixed with political radicals who discussed the Communist revolution currently convulsing Russia. Ho discovered that he shared many Communist beliefs (especially opposition to the **colonialist** white nations that dominated Asians and Africans), although he said later, 'It was patriotism and not Communism that originally inspired me.'

In 1919, US President Woodrow Wilson was in France masterminding the peace settlement at the end of the First World War. Ho was impressed by Wilson's emphasis on the right to **self-determination** and by the words of the American Declaration of Independence (1776), which said that all men were created equal and entitled to a say in who governed them. Although Wilson ignored Ho's petition for democratic reforms in Vietnam, Ho never ceased to call on the Western democracies such as America and France to live up to their declared principles.

In 1924 Ho went to Moscow, where he found the Soviet leadership disappointingly uninterested in Vietnam. Then he visited China and began to organise Vietnamese students in China into a revolutionary league. 'I have become a professional revolutionary', he said in 1927. Back home, Vietnamese nationalists clashed with their French colonialist oppressors, so Ho decided that the time would soon be ripe for a Vietnamese revolution. He therefore established the Indochinese Communist Party in Hong Kong in 1929. Throughout the 1930s, Ho's

Key question
Who and what had inspired Vietnamese nationalism?

Indochina (Vietnam, Cambodia and Laos) under French domination: 1887

Key date: Ho Chi Minh established Indochinese Communist Party: 1929

Key dates

Key question
Who and what shaped and inspired Ho Chi Minh's nationalism and Communism?

Indochina
The countries now known as Vietnam, Cambodia and Laos.

Colonialist
Also known as Imperialist. Believer in the acceptability of one country making a colony out of another country.

Self-determination
When the people have the right to decide how they will be governed.

Key terms

Mandarin
A high-ranking
civil servant.

Profile: Ho Chi Minh 1890–1969

1890	– Born to a Vietnamese nationalist of the **mandarin** class in central Vietnam
1911–41	– Travelled to observe other countries
1941	– Returned to Vietnam and established League for the Independence of Vietnam (Vietminh) to combat Japanese occupation of Vietnam
1945	– Declared newly independent Democratic Republic of Vietnam (DRV)
1945–6	– Unsuccessful negotiations with the French. Increased Franco-Vietminh military clashes (the First Indochina War or the Franco-Vietminh War)
1950	– DRV recognised by USSR and People's Republic of China
1950–3	– Most of Vietnamese countryside under Vietminh control
1954	– French decisively defeated at Dienbienphu. Geneva Accords 'temporarily' divided Vietnam (with Ho's Vietminh dominant in the North, and Bao Dai in the South), and promised elections in a reunified Vietnam in 1956
1959	– Communist guerrillas (Vietcong) caused increased problems for Ngo Dinh Diem, ruler of South Vietnam. Ho increasingly in the background, but his followers dominated the North Vietnamese government in Hanoi. As 'Uncle Ho', he was increasingly the symbol of nationalism and national unity
1969	– Died

Ho Chi Minh was one of the most influential Communist leaders of the twentieth century. He was the prime mover in the establishment of the unusually nationalistic Communist Party of Vietnam, which he led for three decades. He led the Vietnamese people to victory over the Japanese and the French, and then towards victory over the United States.

In an age when alternative Vietnamese leaders ruined their nationalist credentials by association with foreign powers, Ho Chi Minh's main appeal lay in his patriotism. Significantly, in the 1920s and 1930s, other Communists criticised him as too nationalistic.

He was willing to dilute or even ignore Communist ideology in order to maximise support. He successfully cultivated the 'common touch'. In the 1950s, American observers reported that the bulk of the population supported 'Uncle Ho', as he called himself. He was to be seen everywhere – villages, rice fields, meetings and the battlefront. As he never married and paid little attention to his blood relations, he really seemed like 'uncle' Ho to many of his fellow countrymen.

A Vietnamese nationalist cartoon from the early 1930s showed peasants driving out French colonial troops. The peasants shout 'Wipe out the gang of imperialists, mandarins, capitalists and big landlords!'

writings were smuggled into Vietnam while he continued travelling, carefully observing Communism in China and the Soviet Union, and mentally preparing himself for the struggle for Vietnamese independence. His great opportunity came in the Second World War.

c) The Vietnamese nationalists' search for leadership

One of the main reasons why Ho Chi Minh was a popular leader was because of the dearth of appealing alternatives. One such unappealing alternative was the Vietnamese Emperor Bao Dai, whose association with the French compared unfavourably with Ho's patriotism. During the Second World War (1939–45) Bao Dai exchanged French domination for Japanese domination. The outbreak of war in Europe had distracted European colonial powers such as France, enabling the expansionist Japanese to take over southern Indochina in 1941.

Exasperated by Bao Dai's collaboration with foreign imperialists, many Vietnamese nationalists looked to Ho Chi Minh to provide effective leadership. In early 1941 Ho finally returned to his native land. He told other nationalists that all Vietnamese should unite to fight both the Japanese and their

Key question
How did Ho Chi Minh gain popularity in Vietnam?

Key dates

Second World War: 1939–45

Japan completed conquest of French Indochina; Ho Chi Minh returned to Vietnam: 1941

Vietnam Independence League (Vietminh) established: 1941

French Indochina.

Key term

Vietminh
Ho's Vietnamese nationalist followers were known as the Vietminh after 1941.

French collaborators in Indochina. Ho and his friends called their movement the Vietnam Independence League, more commonly known as the **Vietminh**. The Vietminh were both nationalists and Communists. With a programme of more equal distribution of wealth and power and freedom from the French and Japanese, the Vietminh appealed to many Vietnamese people.

Summary diagram: Ho Chi Minh and Vietnamese nationalism

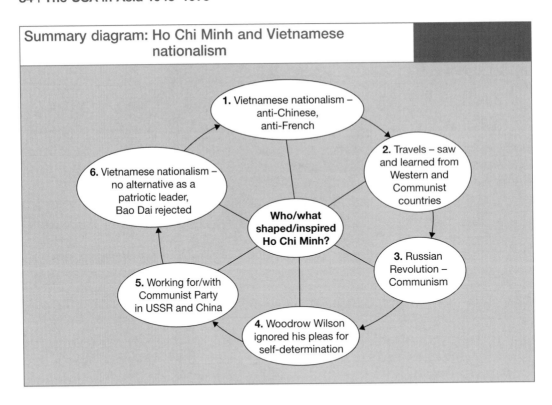

2 | The United States and Vietnam, 1941–5

a) American ideas about Vietnam, 1941–5

Like the Vietnamese, the United States was at war with Japan (1941–5). During the war, **President Roosevelt** was uncertain about what to advocate for French Indochina after Japan was defeated. Preoccupied with winning the war, he told a colleague on 1 January 1945, 'I still do not want to get mixed up in any Indochina decision. Action at this time is premature.' The experts in his State Department offered him conflicting advice: the Far East division criticised French rule and claimed that unless France allowed self-government in Indochina there would be bloodshed and unrest there for years; the European specialists were pro-French, seeing France as an ally in Europe, and they urged the president to refrain from any policy towards Indochina that might alienate the French.

b) Ho's early relations with the Americans
i) Ho and the Americans in the Second World War

One of the main reasons the Americans got involved in Vietnam was their dislike of Ho Chi Minh, but their early relationship was promising. Impressed by the military and economic might of the United States, Ho hoped that he could gain American support for Vietnamese independence. Ho's Vietminh co-operated with the Americans in the fight against the Japanese, and the Americans admired them.

Key question
What did the United States envisage for post-war Vietnam?

Franklin Roosevelt 1882–1945
US president 1933–45. In his fourth and final term he gave some thought to the best post-war government for Vietnam, but made no practical impact on that country.

Key figure

Key question
Was US hostility to Ho Chi Minh inevitable?

USA at war with Japan: 1941–5

Key date

ii) Ho and Truman

In April 1945 Roosevelt died in office and was succeeded by Vice-President Harry Truman (see his profile on page 19). Truman sided with the European specialists in the State Department. He assured the French that America recognised their pre-eminent position in Indochina, but expressed his hope that they would grant more self-government to the Vietnamese. Ho was privately cynical about the Americans:

> They are only interested in replacing the French … They want to reorganise our economy in order to control it. They are capitalists to the core. All that counts for them is business.

iii) Ho's declaration of independence

Ho flattered the Americans, enlisting their aid in drafting the speech he made before hundreds of thousands of his fellow countrymen on 2 September 1945 after the Japanese surrender in the Second World War. In that speech Ho declared the independence of the Democratic Republic of Vietnam. He began by quoting from the American Declaration of Independence and from President Roosevelt, who had repeatedly said that he wanted 'to see sovereign rights and self-government restored to those who have been forcibly deprived of them'.

iv) The United States and the return of the French

The French chose to ignore Ho's declaration of independence in September 1945. Anxious to compensate for their humiliation during the Second World War and to retain wealthy southern Vietnam, they were determined not to give up their old colony. Within days of Ho's declaration, some Vietminh clashed with French soldiers, which some consider the outbreak of the first Vietnam War. Fighting between Ho's Vietminh and the French escalated as increasing numbers of French troops were transported to Indochina by the British, who sympathised with France's desire to retain its empire. America went along with this because, in the developing Cold War context, Truman did not want to alienate the French.

Between October 1945 and February 1946 eight friendly messages from Ho to Washington went unanswered. Due to ever-increasing American anti-Communism, the US had stopped co-operating with Ho, even though the USSR still recognised French rule over Vietnam.

Summary diagram: The United States and Vietnam, 1941–5

```
                          ┌──────────────┐
                          │  Roosevelt   │
                          └──────────────┘
              ┌──────────────────┼──────────────────┐
              ▼                   ▼                  ▼
    ┌──────────────────┐  ┌──────────────┐  ┌──────────────────┐
    │ State Department │  │ No Indochina │  │ State Department │
    │ Far Eastern      │  │ decision yet │  │ European         │
    │ experts –        │  └──────────────┘  │ experts –        │
    │ get French out   │         │          │ keep France      │
    └──────────────────┘         ▼          │ friendly         │
                          ┌──────────────┐  └──────────────────┘
                          │   Truman     │
                          └──────────────┘
                                 │
                                 ▼
                          ┌──────────────┐
                          │ Let French   │
                          │ back         │
                          └──────────────┘
```

3 | The Reasons for the Early American Involvement in Vietnam

Key question
Why did Truman get involved in Vietnam?

President	Dates	Chapters
US presidents in the era of American involvement in Vietnam		
Harry Truman	1945–53	4
Dwight Eisenhower	1953–61	5
John Kennedy	1961–3	6
Lyndon Johnson	1963–9	7–9
Richard Nixon	1969–73	10

American intelligence agents in Hanoi reported to Truman in September 1945 that the traditionally nationalistic Vietnamese were 'determined to maintain their independence even at the cost of their lives'. However, the Truman administration helped to restore French rule, because of the Soviet and Chinese Communist threat, McCarthyism, the Korean War and the desire to support France.

a) The Soviet threat

We have seen (pages 18 and 20) how after the Second World War, Americans believed that Communism threatened international free trade and the democratic ideals which were important to American well-being and security. By 1947 the Truman administration felt that Ho was probably Stalin's puppet, so when the French appealed for aid, cleverly maintaining that Ho was part of a worldwide Communist conspiracy orchestrated by Moscow and likely to lead to Soviet domination everywhere, Truman slowly came to the conclusion that he must help them.

In 1948, some State Department specialists pointed out that Ho had made friendly gestures to America and that the Vietnamese Communists were *not* subservient to Moscow, but the

Outbreak of Franco-Vietminh War: 1945–6

Key date

China became
Communist: October
1949

USSR and China
recognised Ho's
Democratic Republic
of Vietnam: January
1950

Start of
'McCarthyism':
February 1950

Truman gave France
money to fight
Communism in
Vietnam: May 1950

general atmosphere in early Cold War America was not conducive
to such subtleties of analysis. In 1949 Secretary of State Dean
Acheson said that it was 'irrelevant' to ask whether Ho was 'as
much nationalist as Commie [Communist]' for 'all Stalinists in
colonial areas are nationalists'. This American conviction that
what was at stake in Vietnam was the expansion of Communism
(rather than a Vietnamese war for independence) would
eventually embroil America in a bloody war there.

b) US hostility to Communist China

Under attack from the Republicans for having 'lost' China (see
page 5), Truman's anxiety about further Communist expansion in
Asia was fuelled by the JCS contention that the world balance of
power was at stake in Southeast Asia, an area full of strategically
vital materials (such as rubber), where American allies such as
Japan and Australia might be vulnerable to Communist attack.
Truman's anxiety increased when Ho (having failed to obtain
American recognition in exchange for a promise of neutrality in
the Cold War) persuaded China and the Soviets to recognise his
Democratic Republic of Vietnam in January 1950. In the next
month, convinced that the Communists were now on the march
in Asia, the United States finally recognised the supposedly
independent 'Associated State of Vietnam' that had been set up by
the French in 1949.

c) The McCarthy hysteria and the Korean War

As we have seen (page 21), amidst the accusations that Truman
had 'lost' China, Senator Joseph McCarthy began whipping many
Americans into an anti-Communist frenzy in February 1950. After
the June 1950 North Korean attack on South Korea and the
influx of Chinese troops into Korea after October 1950 (see
Chapters 1 and 2), American fears of Chinese expansionism were
confirmed. In this situation and atmosphere it is not surprising
that the Truman administration decided that Indochina must not
be allowed to fall into Communist hands.

d) US support for its NATO ally

Even before the Korean War, the Truman administration
concluded that the French were invaluable allies against
Communism in both Indochina and Europe, and therefore
deserving of American assistance. Acheson and Truman were very
conscious that France was important to the stability of the
Western alliance in Europe and to NATO (see pages 19 and 71).
When France linked Franco-American co-operation in Europe
with American aid in Indochina, it served to confirm the US
belief that they must become more involved in that region. In
May 1950, Truman offered $10 million to support the French
military effort, and established a US Military Assistance Advisory
Group (MAAG) in Saigon. Although at this stage there were only
15 American military officers in MAAG, by the end of 1950, the
US had given France $100 million, along with aircraft, patrol
boats, napalm bombs and ground combat machinery.

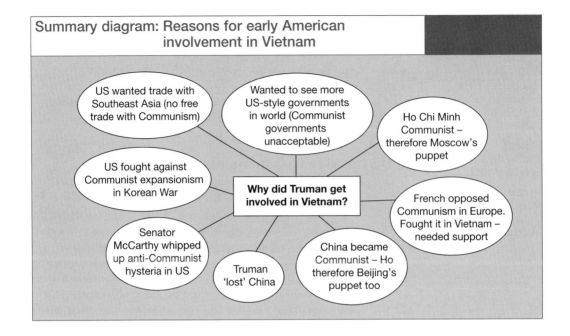

Summary diagram: Reasons for early American involvement in Vietnam

4 | 'These Situations … Have a Way of Snowballing'

By the end of Truman's presidency, the Americans were more convinced than the French of the importance of Vietnam in the global struggle against Communism, and America was paying nearly 80 per cent of the French bill for Indochina. Truman had given over $2 billion to the French war effort and $50 million for economic and technical aid to the Vietnamese people.

Franco-American relations were not always smooth. French unwillingness to grant any real independence to Vietnam caused anxiety within the Truman administration. Some feared that France and America were being distracted from the more important issue of European defence against Communism by this involvement in Indochina. One State Department Far East specialist admitted that 'the trouble is that none of us knows enough about Indochina'.

A Defence Department official warned in November 1950 that America was becoming dangerously and deeply involved:

> we are gradually increasing our stake in the outcome of the struggle … we are dangerously close to the point of being so deeply committed that we may find ourselves completely committed even to direct intervention. These situations, unfortunately, have a way of snowballing.

Key question
To what extent had Truman committed the USA in Vietnam?

5 | Key Debates on the Truman Years

As the United States did not consider Vietnam important before the Second World War, historians are interested in why the region became so important after the Second World War.

a) A key debate: why did Truman become involved in Vietnam?

It was the Cold War context that made little Vietnam important to the United States: State Department official Dean Rusk (see page 119) knew at the time that 'this is part of an international war'. 'Had American leaders not thought that all international events were connected to the Cold War there would have been no American war in Vietnam' (Schulzinger, 1997). Historians disagree about the causes of the Cold War and about Truman's motivation in Vietnam. There are three main schools of thought.

i) Orthodox interpretations

Orthodox historians of the Cold War see the United States resisting Communist aggression and expansion in Vietnam. Orthodox historians, such as Herring (1979) and Schulzinger (1997), considered Truman's involvement in Vietnam to be part of his containment strategy. Having told the American public in his Truman Doctrine speech of 1947 that the world was divided into two very different spheres, and indicated that some kind of conflict was inevitable, there was great public pressure (Blum, 1982) on Truman to continue to hold the line against any Communist advance.

Some historians (such as Shaplen, 1966) emphasise that as part of the containment policy, the Truman administration felt it had to support its ally, France, in the French struggle to retain Indochina, as a strong France was essential to help contain Communism in Europe. However, Leffler (1997) insists that the Truman administration's policy was, 'not determined by the imperative of their European policy ... but by their conviction that the West could not afford to lose Indochina'. While Leffler sees Truman motivated primarily by the desire for security for the United States, he criticises Truman for exaggerating the Soviet threat and the failure to see that the nationalistic Ho Chi Minh was a very different leader from the Soviet Union's puppet rulers of Eastern Europe.

ii) Revisionist interpretations

Revisionist historians (see page 27) emphasise the United States' desire to shape the world in its own image. Revisionists emphasise the economic motivation behind US foreign policy, and criticise it as aggressive and acquisitive. For example, Kolko (1985) says that it was the markets and raw materials of Southeast Asia that motivated Roosevelt then Truman's interest in Vietnam, and that the United States aimed, 'to create an integrated, essentially capitalist world framework out of the chaos of the Second World War and the remnants of the colonial system'. Vietnam became important because a Communist, nationalist revolution there posed a threat to this global capitalist system. If this revolution succeeded, others might follow. Some historians, such as Schaller (1985), stressed that the United States did not want those markets simply for itself, but wanted its important

Key term

Orthodox historians
American historians who see the United States as resisting Communist aggression in the Cold War.

trading partners France, Britain and Japan to have continued access to those markets.

iii) Post-revisionist interpretations

Post-revisionist historians (see page 27) recognise that both the USA and the USSR were ambitious and aggressive, with security concerns and frequent mutual misunderstandings. Historians such as Anderson (2005) recognise that there were many factors involved in Truman's involvement in Vietnam. By the end of Truman's presidency, says Anderson, '**geopolitical** strategy, economics, domestic US politics, and cultural arrogance shaped the growing American involvement in Vietnam'.

b) A key debate: to what extent had Truman committed the United States in Vietnam?

'The Vietnam war was not an American war' during the Truman years, according to Anderson (2005). Although a Vietminh victory would constitute 'an unacceptable strategic gain' for the Communist world, says Anderson, American dislike of French colonialism 'restrained US involvement. US policy decisions had defined Indochina as strategically important, but those decisions had not yet committed the United States to the Vietnam War.'

While Anderson apparently exonerates Truman from blame for what became a highly unpopular American involvement, Herring felt the Vietnam involvement was the virtually inevitable result of Harry Truman's containment policy. 'It was the mind set of the Truman administration which ultimately led to that tragic and misguided war', agreed Byrnes (2000).

> **Geopolitical**
> Political positions governed by the United States' geographical location in the world.
>
> *Key term*

Some key books in the debates

D. Anderson, *The Vietnam War* (New York, 2005).
R.M. Blum, *Drawing the Line: The Origins of the American Containment Policy in East Asia* (New York, 1982).
M. Byrnes, *The Truman Years* (London, 2000).
G. Herring, *America's Longest War* (New York, 1979).
G. Kolko, *Anatomy of a War* (New York, 1985).
M. Leffler, *A Preponderance of Power: National Security, the Truman Administration, and the Cold War* (Stanford, 1997).
M. Schaller, *The American Occupation of Japan: The Origins of the Cold War in Asia* (New York, 1985).
R.D. Schulzinger, *A Time for War: The United States and Vietnam, 1941–75* (New York, 1997).
R. Shaplen, *The Lost Revolution: The United States in Vietnam, 1946–68* (New York, 1966).

---

5 Eisenhower and Two Vietnams

POINTS TO CONSIDER

A century of French involvement in Indochina ended in 1954 at a conference held at Geneva in Switzerland. A divided Vietnam emerged from this conference. Truman's successor, President Eisenhower, became the sponsor of the southern part of Vietnam, while Ho Chi Minh led the north. This chapter looks at:
- Ho, Giap and the French failure in Indochina
- The debate over American intervention in Dienbienphu
- The Geneva Conference on Indochina, 1954
- Two Vietnams and two leaders
- The wisdom of Eisenhower's policy
- The extent to which Eisenhower committed the USA in Vietnam

Key dates

1954	Spring	Eisenhower decided against US intervention to help French at Dienbienphu
	April	Eisenhower's domino theory
	May	French defeated at Dienbienphu
		International conference discussed French Indochina at Geneva
	July	Geneva Accords: Vietnam 'temporarily' divided
	September	Establishment of Southeast Asia Treaty Organisation (SEATO)
	November	Eisenhower sent General Collins to help/assess Diem
1955	May	Diem decisively defeated religious sects in South Vietnam
	October	Diem held 'fair' elections in South Vietnam
1956		Ho Chi Minh's government brutally suppressed revolts in North
1960		Communist disruption of South Vietnam had dramatically increased
		Second Indochina War or Vietnam War began

1 | Ho, Giap and the French Failure in Indochina

Key question
Why was France unable to keep control of Vietnam?

Eisenhower inherited Truman's commitment to the French and continued to finance their military effort. However, the French continued to lose ground, because of Bao Dai's unpopularity, Ho's popularity, Giap's brilliance, Vietnamese ingenuity and French arrogance.

a) Bao Dai's unpopularity and Ho's popularity

The French puppet emperor, Bao Dai (see page 82), was never popular in Vietnam. In late 1951 a US official said his government 'has no appeal whatsoever to the masses'. In sharp contrast, Ho was seen by many Vietnamese as a patriot who cared about the ordinary people of Vietnam (see page 81). His fairer redistribution of land and educational and health care programmes helped to win over the Vietnamese peasantry.

b) Vietnamese rebel strengths

Although the French had more men and materials, Ho's Vietminh proved elusive and determined. 'You can kill ten of my men for every one I kill of yours', Ho told one Frenchman, 'but even at those odds, you will lose and I will win'. Vietminh guerrilla tactics utilised the physical geography of the country. The Vietminh would make surprise attacks then retreat to western Vietnam's jungle and mountains, which were enveloped by monsoon mist for half the year. 'If only the Vietnamese would face us in a set battle', lamented one French officer, 'how we should crush them'. The Chinese supplied Ho with weapons and also, most important of all, the Vietminh fought for an inspiring cause, a free and more **egalitarian** Vietnam. Vietnamese rebel strengths were such that the French, despite all their apparent advantages, found it very difficult to win the war.

Egalitarian
In this context, a Vietnam in which people had greater social, economic and political equality.

Key term

c) Vo Nguyen Giap

The brilliant Vietminh military commander, Vo Nguyen Giap, was of great importance in the defeat of the French. Giap's father, sister, and, later, his wife, were 'subversives' who were killed by the French. From the age of 13, Giap was on the French list of revolutionary nationalists. He joined the Indochinese Communist Party in 1937, believing that the Communist emphasis on co-operation and sharing fitted in with Vietnamese traditions and was therefore appropriate for Vietnam.

From 1944, Giap commanded the Vietnamese Liberation Army or Vietminh (see page 83), which initially numbered around 5000. In November 1946 the Vietminh officially declared war on the French. Giap improved military training and set out plans for revolutionary war. He would start with guerrilla warfare to wear down the enemy, then slowly move to set-piece battles as his army grew stronger. Like Ho, Giap paid great attention to winning over the ordinary people.

Diplomatic
In international relations, 'diplomacy' means relations between nations; a diplomat represents his or her nation abroad; nations that fully recognise each other have diplomatic relations.

Mao's 1949 triumph (see page 5) transformed the situation. Mao gave Giap and Ho **diplomatic** recognition, more armaments, advice, and sanctuary in China if Vietnamese soldiers were in trouble.

By 1952 Giap commanded over a quarter of a million regular soldiers and a militia nearing two million. Each army division was supported by 40,000 porters carrying rice or ammunition along jungle trails and over mountain passes. Many porters were women, the so-called 'long-haired army', whom the Vietminh found to be more effective than the male porters. Giap's soldiers willingly suffered for their country and their freedom, marching over mountains and through jungles, often with insufficient food. Units held self-criticism sessions, during which errors were admitted and forgiven. Giap's soldiers followed his rules when dealing with civilians: be polite; be fair; return everything borrowed; do not bully; do not fraternise with women; try not to cause damage and if you do, pay for it.

The French inability to win in Vietnam owed much to Giap's fanatical determination to defeat them, and to the way he trained, deployed and inspired his army. Chinese aid was also important. It then took a crucial battle to make the French give up.

Profile: General Giap c. 1911–

c. 1911	– Born to an anti-colonialist scholar-gentry family in North Vietnam
1920s	– Educated at University of Hanoi, became a history teacher
1926	– Joined Communist movement
1930	– Arrested by French for supporting student strikes
Mid-1930s	– Joined Indochinese Communist Party. Read books on guerrilla tactics; decided slow, patient 'people's war' was best
1945	– Minister of the Interior in Ho Chi Minh's new Democratic Republic of Vietnam
1954	– Defeated French at decisive battle of Dienbienphu, which brought French colonialist regime to an end. Became deputy prime minister of North Vietnam
1960s	– Vital work in defeating American forces supporting anti-Communist regime in South Vietnam
1973	– United States' departure from Vietnam owed much to Giap
1976–80	– Defence Minister of newly united Communist Vietnam
1982	– Retired from government

Giap was important in that his military strategy and tactics played a vital role in defeating first the French and then the United States, which brought about an independent Communist Vietnam.

d) Dienbienphu (1954)

While Ho and Giap went from strength to strength, the French had problems. They tried what they called 'yellowing' their army (enlisting native Vietnamese) but did not trust these new recruits and gave them little responsibility. In France itself, many people were beginning to lose heart and interest in Indochina, which gave great importance to the great military struggle between the French and the Vietminh at **Dienbienphu**.

In 1954, hoping to put pressure on the Communists in nearby Laos, the French built a fortress at Dienbienphu in the hope of drawing the Vietminh into a set-piece battle. Both the French and the Americans thought that Dienbienphu could be held indefinitely. Both failed to anticipate that thousands of peasant volunteers would dismantle heavy, long-range guns, take them piece by piece up into the surrounding hills, successfully camouflage them until they were ready to be fired, and bombard the fortress from the surrounding high ground.

French defeated at Dienbienphu: May 1954

Key date

Dienbienphu
Site of decisive Vietminh military victory over France in 1954.

Key term

Ho Chi Minh (centre) and Vo Nguyen Giap (on Ho's far left) plan the attack on Dienbienphu.

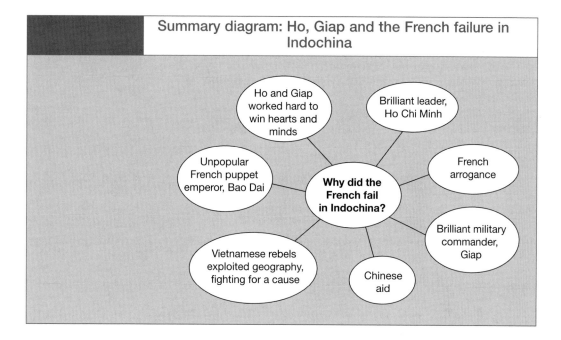

Summary diagram: Ho, Giap and the French failure in Indochina

Key question
To what extent was Eisenhower committed to helping the French in Vietnam before Dienbienphu?

2 | Dienbienphu: The Debate over American Intervention

a) Eisenhower and the French before Dienbienphu

Not long before the showdown at Dienbienphu, Eisenhower had given the French $385 million worth of armaments for an offensive against the Vietminh, but many questions were being asked within the Eisenhower administration about the extent to which America should be involved in Vietnam:

- Was Southeast Asia vital to US security?
- If Southeast Asia was vital to US security, should America get involved in Indochina?
- If America did get involved in Indochina, should that involvement take the form of financial aid to the French, US military advisers assisting the French, US air and/or sea support for the French, or the sending of US ground troops to Indochina?
- Did the US have enough troops to make a difference in Indochina?
- Was victory possible in Indochina in conjunction with the French or if America were there alone?
- Was America willing to risk a clash with China over intervention in Indochina?
- How much was America willing to do without allied (including UN) support?

Like most people in his administration, Eisenhower considered Southeast Asia vital to US security. However, he was more moderate than many in his views on what America should do

> ## Profile: Dwight D. Eisenhower 1890–1969
>
> | | |
> |---|---|
> | 1890 | – Born to a poor family in Texas; moved to Kansas |
> | 1917–18 | – Distinguished service in First World War |
> | 1942–5 | – Supreme Commander of US troops in Europe in Second World War |
> | 1945–8 | – Army Chief of Staff |
> | 1950 | – Truman appointed him Supreme Commander of NATO |
> | 1952 | – Elected president (Republican); main campaign promises included ending the Korean War and '**rollback**' |
> | 1953 | – Ended Korean War; refused to speak out against McCarthyism |
> | 1954 | – Rejected Geneva Accords and helped to establish 'independent' state of South Vietnam. Set up Southeast Asia Treaty Organisation (SEATO) |
> | 1956 | – Re-elected president |
> | 1961 | – Retired to Pennsylvania |
> | 1969 | – Died |
>
> Eisenhower was important in ending the Korean War and his importance in the Vietnam War is that he continued and increased American involvement there. Initially, he continued Truman's policy of helping the French to fight Communism in Vietnam. As the French withdrew, he helped to set up the South Vietnamese state, in defiance of the Geneva Accords (see pages 99 and 101). American prestige was thereby committed to the maintenance of South Vietnam. However, he only sent in military advisers to help South Vietnam, not combat troops.

Key term

Rollback
The Eisenhower administration verbally rejected President Truman's containment of Communism and advocated pushing back Communism in places where it was already established.

there. He considered it easier and cheaper to pay other countries to help defend America: Communism threatened America and the French were fighting Communism, so it was better to pay the French to fight Communism than to send American boys to do it. However, early in 1954 Eisenhower responded to French pleas for extra help by sending US bombers accompanied by 200 American technicians. He told Congress that he disliked putting them in danger but that 'we must not lose Asia'.

By March, the situation at Dienbienphu was beginning to look hopeless, so France requested a US air strike against the Vietminh in order to strengthen the French negotiating position at Geneva. Eisenhower gave the request serious consideration. Meanwhile, throughout the weeks of struggle at Dienbienphu, American schoolchildren prayed for the French to defeat the atheist Communists.

b) Arguments for American intervention at Dienbienphu

Eisenhower was concerned about Vietnam and Dienbienphu for several reasons:

Key question
What were the American arguments for helping the French at Dienbienphu?

Key dates

Eisenhower's domino theory: April 1954

Eisenhower decided against US intervention to help French at Dienbienphu: spring 1954

- French strength was being drained away in Vietnam and Eisenhower wanted France to be a strong NATO member to help defend Western Europe against the Soviet threat.
- The French threatened to be unhelpful about European defence arrangements and to get out of Indochina unless America aided them there.
- In the presidential election campaign, Eisenhower had rejected Truman's policy of containment of Communism and had advocated liberation of Communist countries ('rollback'). As yet he had not 'liberated' a single soul from Communism.
- Eisenhower knew that Truman's popularity had suffered greatly because he had 'lost' China and he did not want the Democrats to say he had 'lost' Vietnam.
- In a March 1954 speech, Eisenhower's Secretary of State John Foster Dulles said the administration feared Chinese influence and aggression in Indochina.
- Most important of all, Eisenhower felt that the loss of Vietnam to Communism would affect the global balance of power: if the US allowed Vietnam to fall to Communism, other Southeast Asian countries would follow. At a press conference in April 1954, Eisenhower articulated his 'domino theory'. He said Vietnam was vitally important to America, because if it fell to Communism, neighbouring countries might follow like dominoes, which would mean the loss of raw materials and millions of people to the Communist world.

Eisenhower privately said that 'in certain areas at least we cannot afford to let Moscow gain another bit of territory'. He briefly toyed with the idea of a lightning American air strike at Dienbienphu – in unmarked planes because 'we would have to deny it for ever'.

Key question
What were the American arguments against helping the French at Dienbienphu?

c) Arguments against American intervention

Not every influential American agreed that something should be done about Vietnam:

- Some disliked the domino theory, doubting whether the loss of a relatively small country to Communism would cause the loss of others.
- Some of the military and the Secretary of Defence felt that Indochina was 'devoid of decisive military objectives' and that any US intervention there would be pointless, 'a serious diversion of limited US capabilities'.
- One vice-admiral insisted that 'partial' involvement through air and sea forces alone would be a delusion. 'One cannot go over Niagara Falls in a barrel only slightly', he said.
- While he was commander of NATO, Eisenhower had said that 'no military victory is possible in that kind of [jungle] theatre'. In the early 1960s, he wrote, 'the jungles of Indochina would have swallowed up division after division of US troops'. He pointed out the dangerous possibility that the US could find itself fighting Communists everywhere and felt he could not

put US troops on the Asian mainland again just a year after he had gained massive popularity by getting them out of Korea.

- Even if Eisenhower had wanted to send US troops, there were none readily available. His **'new look'** defence policy emphasised nuclear weaponry at the expense of manpower.
- Many Americans were uncertain about the wisdom of being too closely entangled with the French, whom Eisenhower privately described as 'a hopeless, helpless mass of protoplasm'! The French themselves disliked the American conditions for involvement. France did not want to grant total independence to Vietnam and then carry on fighting there under a US commander.
- Eisenhower subsequently wrote that 'the strongest reason of all' for America to stay out was the United States' unique tradition of anti-colonialism, which enhanced its reputation in the Cold War world. He recognised the danger of replacing French colonialism with American colonialism.
- Perhaps more importantly, Eisenhower and Dulles tried but failed to get the British support that Congress required before they would approve American military intervention. Prime Minister Churchill said the struggle was not winnable and might trigger the Third World War. Ironically, one unenthusiastic senator was Lyndon Johnson, who said, 'We want no more Koreas, with the United States furnishing more than 90 per cent of the manpower.'

Key term

'New look' Republican policy emphasising nuclear weaponry rather than conventional forces for defence.

Faced with all this uncertainty, Eisenhower decided against direct American intervention in Vietnam, which doomed the French to defeat at Dienbienphu and ensured that the French government and people were ready to give up and get out of Indochina.

Summary diagram: Dienbienphu – the debate over American intervention

Arguments for and against US intervention at Dienbienphu

For	Against
• Eisenhower had continued to invest money/honour in Vietnam	• US could get out and say, 'The French lost it'
• Communism had to be stopped – and Eisenhower had talked of 'rollback' and 'dominoes'	• Losing a small country full of peasants to Communism would not greatly affect the balance of power • Only just out of unpopular Korean War
• Good to let French soldiers do the fighting against Communism	• The French were 'hopeless' • Few conventional forces ('new look') • Congress and Britain said 'No'
• France's help needed in NATO – have to support France in Vietnam	• Impossible to win in Vietnam with French imperialists • Might lead to a Third World War with China

3 | The Geneva Conference on Indochina, 1954

Key question
Why was the 1954
Geneva conference
held?

a) Reasons for the International Conference at Geneva in 1954

While the French and Vietminh battled at Dienbienphu, an international conference was called to discuss Indochina. In France many were tiring of the struggle and/or were aware of worldwide expectation that the war ought to be brought to an end. An armistice had finally ended three years of bitter fighting in Korea, so the time seemed ripe to try to end the fighting in French Indochina. Stalin had died and the new Soviet leaders wanted to show that they were keen to decrease Cold War tension. Communist China favoured negotiations because it wanted to forestall American involvement in Indochina and it judged that participation in the peace talks would gain it increased international recognition and respectability.

Not everyone was enthusiastic about negotiations. The Eisenhower administration feared that in their eagerness to get out of Vietnam the French might concede too much to the Communists. Ho Chi Minh and the Vietnamese Communists were clearly winning the struggle for Vietnam and saw nothing to be gained from talking, while Bao Dai's new prime minister Ngo Dinh Diem did not want to negotiate with the French or Ho, because he feared and distrusted both of them.

The Chinese and Russians put great pressure on Ho to negotiate, but even before he said 'yes', the Soviets had agreed to a conference. Talks on the future of French Indochina were to begin on 8 May 1954 at Geneva. In the meantime the struggle for Dienbienphu continued.

Key dates
International
conference discussed
French Indochina at
Geneva: May 1954

Geneva Accords:
Vietnam 'temporarily'
divided: July 1954

Key term
Geneva Accords
Agreements
reached at Geneva
in 1954 by France,
China, Ho Chi
Minh and the
USSR, that Vietnam
should be
temporarily
divided, with
national elections
held in 1956.

Key question
What did the
participants hope to
gain from the Geneva
conference?

b) The Geneva conference (1954)

On 7 May 1954 the victorious Vietminh raised their red flag over Dienbienphu. The next day delegations representing France, Bao Dai, the Vietminh, Cambodia, Laos, the United States, the Soviet Union, the People's Republic of China and Great Britain assembled in Geneva to discuss ending the war in Indochina. Each delegation had different aims. For example, while Ho's Vietminh and Bao Dai sought Vietnamese independence, the French hoped to retain some influence in Indochina. America sought to contain Communism in Southeast Asia and to avoid elections in Vietnam, knowing that Ho Chi Minh would win. America rejected the idea of Communists in the government of Vietnam, and hoped for a united non-Communist Vietnam.

Key question
What was agreed at
Geneva in 1954?

c) The Geneva Accords (1954)

In the **Geneva Accords**, the Vietminh, in effect represented by China's premier, Zhou Enlai, agreed with France that:

- There would be Communist rule in the north of Vietnam while Bao Dai and his new prime minister, Diem, would govern the south. Ho's Vietminh would have to give up the territory which they occupied south of the 17th parallel (the line of partition

Redrawing the map at the Geneva Conference (1954).

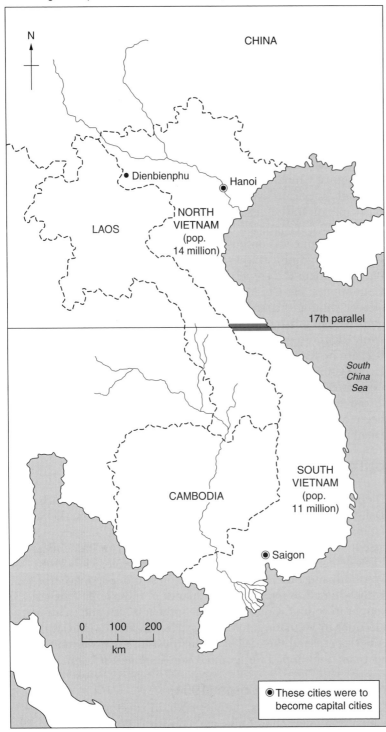

French Indochina consisted of what Americans would come to know as Vietnam, Laos and Cambodia. At Geneva, Vietnam was temporarily (supposedly) divided along the 17th parallel into a Communist North (under Ho) and a non-Communist South (under Bao Dai and Diem). Elections would (supposedly) be held in 1956 to reunite the country. Laos and Cambodia gained independence.

between what would soon become North and South Vietnam was fixed at the latitude of 17 degrees north of the Equator, known as the 17th parallel). There would be a 10-km Demilitarised Zone (DMZ) above that parallel.

- The French forces would withdraw from the north and Ho's Vietminh forces from the south. There would be a truce between them.
- There would be democratic elections for a single Vietnamese government in 1956, when Vietnam would be reunified.
- Neither the northern nor the southern Vietnamese were to make any military alliances with foreign powers, nor were they to allow foreign military bases in their territories. The French would remain in the south only in order to help prepare for the elections in 1956.

Other than the ceasefire, no documents were signed.

Key question
What was the significance of the Geneva Accords?

d) The significance of the Geneva Accords

The Geneva Accords were significant in several ways. The negotiations had shown Ho Chi Minh that Communist China and the Soviet Union were not uncompromisingly supportive of his Democratic Republic of Vietnam. In order to gain the settlement that they wanted, they made Ho accept a settlement that forced the Vietminh to retreat behind the 17th parallel. Ho agreed, because he believed that the agreement that there would be nationwide elections in 1956 would be respected and knew that as the most popular Vietnamese national figure he was virtually certain to win (Eisenhower wrote in his 1963 memoirs that Ho would have won 80 per cent of the vote in a fair election). Also, Ho needed Chinese and Soviet aid, and he needed the time for consolidation in the north that peace would give him. The United States was significantly slow to pick up and/or exploit those divisions within the Communist world. (Dulles knew there were Sino-Soviet tensions yet did not use them to advantage at Geneva.)

The ceasefire in Vietnam was between the French and the Vietminh – not between the Vietminh and any South Vietnamese government. New premier Diem of South Vietnam rejected the agreements as they put half of Vietnam under Communist control. He rightly predicted that 'another more deadly war' lay ahead. Unwilling to recognise Communist control of the northern half of Vietnam, the Eisenhower administration agreed to respect, but would not sign, the Geneva agreements, saying 'the United States has not itself been a party to or bound by the decisions taken', and warning that America would view 'any renewal of aggression' with 'grave concern'. America chose to misinterpret the temporary ceasefire line of the 17th parallel as a permanent division between two states, a northern one which was Communist and a southern one which was not. The Geneva settlement and Vietnam had become victims of the Cold War.

Summary diagram: The Geneva conference on Indochina, 1954

	What did they want?	What did they get?
USA	No Communist gains	Half of Vietnam was not Communist, half was
USSR	Decreased Cold War tension	Settlement that did not last
China	Keep US out. Gain international recognition	Recognition, but US stayed in Southeast Asia
France	Respite. Retain some influence in Indochina	Got out. Hardly retained any influence
Ho Chi Minh	Control over as much of Vietnam as possible	Got half of Vietnam
Diem	Control over as much of Vietnam as possible	Got half of Vietnam, but soon lost it
UK	Peace in Southeast Asia. Halt spread of Communism	Uneasy, temporary peace. Communism not halted

4 | Two Vietnams and Two Leaders

After the Geneva conference, Ho and the Communists governed North Vietnam (from Hanoi) while Diem governed South Vietnam (from Saigon). Like all Vietnamese nationalists, Ho and Diem would have preferred a united Vietnam. One great question was whether either of them had the necessary skill and support to bring about national unification.

a) Ngo Dinh Diem – background

Diem came from a Catholic, mandarin family, and he successfully continued the family tradition of government service until he clashed with his French masters in 1933. A nationalist, he resented French unwillingness to give the Vietnamese any real power. In 1950 Diem went to the US, where he met and impressed prominent American Catholics such as Senators John Kennedy and Mike Mansfield.

Key question
Did Diem have the ability, power and support to unite Vietnam?

Mansfield is an important figure in the history of the US involvement in Vietnam. He illustrates the importance of the role of Congress, American ignorance of Vietnam, and finally, how there was influential opposition to the involvement during the 1960s. Mansfield knew virtually nothing about Vietnam ('I do not know too much about the Indochina situation. I do not think that anyone does'). However, Mansfield played a vitally important part in the continued support of Diem after 1955, as his congressional colleagues considered him to be their Indochina specialist.

Profile: Ngo Dinh Diem 1901–63

1901	–	Born into a noble Vietnamese Catholic family in central Vietnam
1933	–	Minister of the Interior to Emperor Bao Dai; resigned because of French domination
1933–45	–	Lived quietly in Hue
1945	–	Captured by Communist forces; declined to join Ho Chi Minh's government and went into exile
1954	–	Returned at Bao Dai's request to be prime minister of US-backed government in South Vietnam
1955	–	Defeated Bao Dai in government-controlled referendum; made himself president of newly declared Republic of South Vietnam
1956	–	Refused to carry out Geneva Accords' planned nationwide elections; increasingly autocratic
1963	–	Persecution of Buddhist majority led United States to withdraw support and collude in his assassination by his army generals

Diem was important in that many influential Americans perceived him as the only non-Communist who was anywhere near capable of running Vietnam. While he frequently showed considerable political cunning, his US-supported South Vietnamese government was always unpopular. The fact that there was no clear alternative non-Communist leader suggests that South Vietnam was not a viable state.

Key dates

Establishment of Southeast Asia Treaty Organisation (SEATO): September 1954

Eisenhower sent General Collins to help/assess Diem: November 1954

Diem decisively defeated religious sects in South Vietnam: May 1955

Key terms

SEATO
Defensive alliance between USA, Britain, France, Australia, New Zealand and Pakistan, 1954.

Protocol
In this context, an agreement between signatory nations.

In 1954, Bao Dai thought that the American contacts might make Diem useful, so in 1954 he made Diem his prime minister. By that time the vast majority of Vietnamese nationalists with leadership qualities were Vietminh. Any non-Communist nationalists with potential had been killed by the French or the Vietminh, or had given up political activities. Diem thus slid into a leadership vacuum.

b) Diem and American 'nation building'
i) Diem and the Americans in 1954
Eisenhower felt that Ho had triumphed at Geneva and that the United States had to do something to 'restore its prestige in the Far East'. Dulles therefore quickly masterminded the Southeast Asia Treaty Organisation (**SEATO**), which combined America, Britain, France, Australia, New Zealand and Pakistan in a defensive alliance. SEATO members agreed to protect South Vietnam, Cambodia and Laos under a separate **protocol** – a transparent American device to circumvent the Geneva agreement, which had said that the Vietnamese must not enter into foreign alliances or allow foreign troops on their soil.

The Geneva agreements were similarly ignored in that the French were supposed to stay in South Vietnam to enforce the ceasefire until the nationwide elections were held in July 1956.

However, Diem, whom the French prime minister described as incapable and mad, rejected the idea of nationwide elections because he knew Ho would win. Soon after Geneva, Diem had decided to turn his back on the French and to rely instead on the Americans, who quickly pledged him their support. When the French finally left in April 1956, Dulles said 'We have a clean base there now, without the taint of [French] colonialism'. He referred to Dienbienphu as 'a blessing in disguise'.

Diem and his American patrons agreed that the Communist menace must be halted and that one way to do this was to build a stable, non-Communist South Vietnamese state. In November 1954, Eisenhower sent his Second World War associate General 'Lightning Joe' Collins to implement a 'crash programme' to maintain Diem's regime. Collins urged **land reform** as Saigon's main priority, but Truman's MAAG (see page 87), with its emphasis on military solutions rather than social and economic reform, dominated US assistance to Diem.

ii) American doubts about Diem

The Americans were not entirely happy with their new South Vietnamese allies. According to Vice-president Richard Nixon, the problem was that 'the [South] Vietnamese lacked the ability to conduct a war by themselves or govern themselves'. Dulles admitted that America supported Diem 'because we knew of no one better': he was simply the best of a bad bunch. The JCS were unenthusiastic about involvement with Diem, believing that his government was unstable. Although Dulles contended that helping Diem to train his army would make his government stable, General Collins reported that Diem's regime was hopeless. The Eisenhower administration nearly withdrew their support, but in the spring of 1955 Diem's effective action against Bao Dai and other non-Communist opponents halted them.

iii) Diem's defeat of Bao Dai

In October 1955, Diem held an election in South Vietnam, now clearly a separate state. Those voting for Bao Dai were punished: some were held down to have pepper sauce poured into their nostrils. Diem claimed 98.2 per cent of the vote, rejecting an American adviser's proposals that 60 or 70 per cent was a more credible figure. Out of 450,000 registered voters in Saigon, Diem claimed that 605,025 had voted for him! Through a combination of force, fraud and friendship with America, Diem appeared to have made himself undisputed leader of the new state of South Vietnam. There was no real rival: Bao Dai remained in France and had refused to contest the election.

iv) MAAG and the Catholic migration south

The Eisenhower administration now increased aid to Diem. MAAG gave him hundreds of millions of dollars and advice on politics, land reform and covert operations against the Vietminh. America had helped to transport around a million Vietnamese

The South Vietnamese presidential family in 1963. Diem is second from the right.

President Ngo Dinh Diem (front left) with Donald Quarles, Deputy Secretary of Defence, reviewing a guard of honour outside the Pentagon in honour of the president's visit, 16 May 1957.

from the north to the south. Most of the refugees were middle-class, educated and Catholic. They were (initially) supportive of Diem, but their arrival made Diem even less popular among the predominantly Buddhist southerners.

v) The nature of Diem's regime
Diem visited America in 1957, when Eisenhower praised him as the 'miracle man' of Asia. Unfortunately, Diem's belief in his own infallibility and rectitude was so strengthened by such words that when Americans advised him that his repressive and unpopular administration needed to reform to survive, Diem dug his heels in and did nothing. His government had become a family operation and while Diem himself lived frugally, his family squabbled amongst themselves in their struggle to get rich.

Diem favoured his fellow Catholics from the north and the wealthy landowner class. He never appealed to the ordinary people as Ho did. Like the Americans who supported him, Diem failed to comprehend how the Vietminh ideas about greater economic equality could win so many peasant hearts. Diem disliked meeting his people and only reluctantly toured South Vietnam at the behest of his American patrons who rightly feared that unlike 'Uncle Ho' he lacked the common touch.

c) Support for Ho and Communism
i) Ho's ruthlessness
In many ways Ho's regime in the North was as unpleasant as that of Diem in the South. Ho's Communists liquidated thousands of landlords and opponents, and even loyal Vietminh by mistake. In 1956 Ho's soldiers (**People's Army of Vietnam** or PAVN) had to put down a revolt: 6000 peasants were killed or deported. Subsequently Ho and Giap admitted having wrongfully resorted to terror. On the other hand, Ho's egalitarian regime, free from apparent foreign domination, often won the hearts of the people in a way that Diem's never did.

ii) Ho's popularity
Joseph Alsop, one of the few Americans who had toured rural South Vietnam when it was still occupied by the Vietminh, wrote about his 1954 travels for the *New Yorker* magazine in 1955:

> I would like to be able to report – I had hoped to be able to report – that ... I saw ... signs of misery and oppression ... But it was not so ... the Vietminh could not possibly have carried on the resistance for one year, let alone nine years, without the people's strong, united support.

Many southerners remained quietly loyal to Ho after Vietnam was divided in 1954, although others disliked both Diem and the Communists.

Key question
Did Ho Chi Minh have the ability, power and support to unite Vietnam?

Key date
Ho Chi Minh's government brutally suppressed revolts in North: 1956

Key term
People's Army of Vietnam
Formal name of Ho's North Vietnamese Army by 1956.

Key dates

Communist disruption of South Vietnam had dramatically increased: 1960

Second Indochina War or Vietnam War began: 1960

Key terms

National Liberation Front
From 1960, Ho's southern supporters gave themselves this name.

Vietcong
After 1960, Diem called the National Liberation Front 'Vietcong' (Vietnamese Communists or VC).

People's Liberation Armed Forces
The name which Ho's southern supporters called their forces after 1960.

Agrovilles
New and well-defended villages set up by Diem's regime to keep Communists out.

ARVN
Diem's Army of the Republic of Vietnam.

iii) Communist activism in South Vietnam

Before 1959 Ho had discouraged supporters in the South from attacking Diem's regime. Hanoi wanted to be seen to be abiding by the Geneva agreements and was bitterly divided about whether consolidation in the North should take priority over liberation of the South. This gave Diem the opportunity to arrest and execute many southern Communist activists, whose numbers dropped from around 10,000 in 1955 to nearer 2000 by 1959. That forced the South's Communists into open revolt. By 1960 Hanoi had decided to give liberation equal priority to consolidation.

From 1960 Ho's southern supporters called themselves the **National Liberation Front** (NLF), but Diem called them **Vietcong** (Vietnamese Communists or VC). Like the Vietminh in 1945, the NLF emphasised national independence rather than social revolution and contained non-Communists. The NLF organised itself into the **People's Liberation Armed Forces** (PLAF). The second Indochina War or Vietnam War had begun.

Diem responded to the rising levels of violence and disruption by relocating peasants to army-protected villages called **agrovilles**. The peasants hated forced, expensive removals from their homes, lands and sacred ancestral tombs. Dissatisfaction with the regime of 'American Diem' was ever-increasing. In 1960, 18 prominent Vietnamese nationalists petitioned Diem for moderate reform, but he became even more repressive in response. The US ambassador recommended that Diem introduce political and social reform rather than concentrate on the use of military force, but MAAG disagreed.

d) Diem's situation in 1961

By 1961 Diem had received around $7 billion from the Eisenhower administration. 'We bet pretty heavily on him', said Eisenhower. Senator Kennedy described Diem as 'our offspring'. One exasperated US official in Saigon described Diem as 'a puppet who pulled his own strings – and ours as well'. While many knowledgeable Americans warned from the first that the struggle could not be won with Diem in power, others disagreed. Diem's American supporters were often those who saw the conflict in Vietnam in simple military terms, believing that Diem's battles were against unpopular Communists and could be won simply by pouring in more military aid and money. The problem was that the Communists had a fair amount of popular support in South Vietnam and that Diem had to deal with so much non-Communist opposition. Even his army (the Army of the Republic of Vietnam or **ARVN**) contained opponents, some of whom unsuccessfully rebelled against him in 1960. By 1961 America was supporting a very unpopular regime in South Vietnam.

Summary diagram: Two Vietnams and two leaders

Diem	Ho
Massively dependent on US aid	Some help from China and USSR
Unpopular with ordinary people	Popular with ordinary people
Unwilling to redistribute landed wealth	Willing to redistribute landed wealth
Lacked appealing personality	Charismatic, common touch
No supporters in North	Many supporters in South
Both nationalistic	
Both ruthless with opponents	

5 | Assessment of Eisenhower's Policy

a) Eisenhower and the commitment question

While campaigning for the presidency, Eisenhower had
emphasised the importance of liberating people from
Communism. By those self-imposed standards he had failed.
North Vietnam became a Communist state during his presidency.
However, historians generally consider his Vietnam policy to have
been a success. They tend to judge presidents by the extent to
which they got America committed. Eisenhower did not send
thousands of American troops to Vietnam as Johnson did, so
Eisenhower is judged to have been relatively successful in dealing
with Vietnam.

Eisenhower inherited a limited involvement in Vietnam.
Truman had financially aided the French in their struggle to
retain influence in Vietnam. All members of the Eisenhower
administration agreed that Vietnam was important in the Cold
War and some (including Vice-president Nixon and, possibly,
Dulles) were even willing to use atomic bombs to help the French
there, but Eisenhower said:

> You boys must be crazy. We can't use those awful things against
> Asians for the second time in less than 10 years. My God.

Eisenhower deserves credit for rejecting the atomic option. He
recognised that the use of atomic bombs would probably lead to
conflict with the Soviets and China. Nonetheless, Eisenhower's
administration made Vietnam even more important than
Truman's had.

Key question
To what extent was
Eisenhower
responsible for the
US involvement in
Vietnam?

Some historians praise Eisenhower for refusing to send Americans into combat in Vietnam. His memoirs suggest that he realised this was militarily and politically unwise. However, it must be remembered that Eisenhower gave a great deal of support to the French attempts at a military solution. Furthermore, it was probably only congressional leaders and the reluctance of his British allies that stopped him increasing direct American involvement during the struggle for Dienbienphu. In defiance of the Geneva Accords, Eisenhower effectively made the United States the guarantor of an independent state of South Vietnam and committed the US to the defence of a particularly unpopular leader in Diem. He gave Diem $7 billion worth of aid and 1500 American advisers, nearly half of whom were military. Once such a commitment was undertaken, it was arguable that America had incurred an obligation to see it through. From that point it would prove to be but a short step to putting American soldiers into Vietnam.

Significantly, no one in the Eisenhower administration was urging reconsideration of the commitment to Vietnam, simply arguing about its nature. Ambassador Eldridge Durbrow urged political reform, to make South Vietnam a democracy, but the State Department and Dulles favoured concentration upon a strong government in Saigon to combat Communism.

b) Questions to think about

In order to come to conclusions about Eisenhower's responsibility for the American involvement in Vietnam, several questions need to be answered. Could any American president be seen to ignore any 'threat' from Communism in the Cold War era? When one president had committed American foreign policy in a certain direction was it feasible for another to reverse it? Once America had greatly aided the anti-Communists in South Vietnam could it legitimately then just dump them? Those who would answer 'no' to any of those questions would seem to suggest that Eisenhower was right, and that what was right would inevitably lead to American involvement in Vietnam.

However, much depends on the sort of questions one asks. Was Communism really such a threat to America? Was Vietnam going Communist really going to affect the course of the Cold War? Did America have any right to intervene in what was in effect an internal debate about what kind of government Vietnam should have? Negative answers to these questions would suggest that Eisenhower was mistaken in his policies. On the other hand, many Americans agreed with him, raising final questions. Can any president transcend the prejudices and preoccupations of his time? And if he does, will he and his party get re-elected?

6 | Key Debates

a) Why did the United States get involved and remain in Vietnam?

Once several presidents were involved in trying and failing to defend Communism in Vietnam, it was clear that the United States was stuck in a very difficult situation. As successive presidents got more and more involved, Halberstam (1964) published *The Making of a Quagmire*, from which the so-called '**quagmire theory**' of US involvement developed. According to this theory, because of their ignorance of the Vietnamese people and situation, and their overconfidence in American power and ideals, US leaders let the United States get gradually trapped in an expensive commitment in an unimportant area, unable to exit without losing credibility. In the early 1970s, Halberstam and Fitzgerald wrote critically of US arrogance and ignorance of the appeal of Communism in Vietnam.

An alternative theory, the '**stalemate theory**', emerged in the 1970s. First Daniel (1972) then Gelb and Betts (1979) claimed that the United States held to the commitment and even escalated in order not to win but to avoid being seen to lose by the American voters.

Many historians, whether implicitly or explicitly, argue that the commitment made to Vietnam by the previous president(s) made it harder for each president's successor(s) to exit without the US and the president(s) losing face. This is the '**commitment trap**' interpretation.

By the early 1980s, the 'flawed containment' (Divine, 1988) historians combined the quagmire interpretation with the global containment viewpoint, which said that in trying to halt Communism, the United States got bogged down in a no-win situation.

Key terms

Quagmire theory Belief that the US got slowly and increasingly trapped in Vietnam, due to ignorance, overconfidence and credibility concerns.

Stalemate theory Belief that the US continued to fight an unwinnable war in Vietnam, simply to avoid being seen to be defeated.

Commitment trap The theory that each president after Truman was bound to continue the US involvement in Vietnam.

b) Should Eisenhower be blamed for increased American involvement in the Vietnam War?

Some historians absolve Eisenhower of responsibility for the American war in Vietnam. 'Eisenhower revisionists' such as Ambrose (1984) point out his statesmanship in not getting entangled in Dienbienphu. Gardner and Anderson (2005), on the other hand, contend that John Foster Dulles welcomed the end of French neocolonialism after Dienbienphu and gladly took the opportunity effectively to replace it. Short (1989) blames years of conflict in Vietnam on the US refusal to accept the Geneva Accords, while some historians criticise the Eisenhower administration either for its unwillingness to look beyond the Christian Diem in Vietnam or for its failure to consider promising non-Communist politicians in Southeast Asia (Kaiser, 2000 and Nashel, 2005). Anderson (1991 and 2005) rejected those who claimed that Eisenhower's decision not to help the French at Dienbienphu shows his statesmanship, claiming that Eisenhower tried hard to get Congressional and British support for that aid. Anderson emphasises that both Eisenhower and Dulles continued to see Vietnam as vital in the Cold War context, and concludes that 'Eisenhower left Kennedy a policy of unequivocal support for Diem that had kept the domino from falling, but had not produced a self-sufficient nation in the South'. Anderson concluded that, 'the Eisenhower administration trapped itself and its successors into a commitment to the survival of its own counterfeit creation', that is, the non-viable South Vietnamese state.

c) Were US actions legal?

Historians debate the legality of the US position in relation to the Geneva Accords. LaFaber (1989), for example, claimed that 'US officials used this supposed collective security pact [SEATO] to justify the unilateral American commitment to Vietnam'. Weinstein (1967) criticised the United States for supporting Diem's refusal to consult with North Vietnam on the elections, which freed North Vietnam to defy the Accords too. Defenders of the Eisenhower administration said that Saigon was not obliged to hold the elections as Bao Dai's representatives at Geneva had not signed the relevant parts of the Geneva Accords. They claimed that no country should be bound to an agreement made by a past colonial oppressor (France) and that free elections were impossible in the Communist North.

A second 'legal' issue concerns the outbreak of the second Indochina War or Vietnam War around 1960. Kahin and Lewis (1969), in a popular textbook, said that the initiative came from southern dissidents, driven to desperation by Diem's repression. Here, the blame for the war lay with Saigon, not Hanoi. The significance of this interpretation is that it rejected the claim of successive US administrations and other historians (for example, Pike, 1966) that this war was not a civil war, but an invasion from the North. Duiker (1998) rejected both 'extreme views', saying that what broke out at the end of the 1950s was 'an insurgent movement inspired by local conditions in the South but guided and directed from Hanoi'.

d) A no-win Cold War situation?

Naturally, American historians write America-centred histories of the conflict, although some try to place American decision-making in a more international context (Logevall, 2001), often emphasising the contemporary viewpoint of other nations. For example, the British rejected the 'falling dominoes' theory, convinced that what happened in Vietnam would have no impact on British Malaya. Logevall gives a balanced argument, both critical of the Eisenhower administration but also recognising that:

> making a stand in the Southern parts of Vietnam was not an illogical move in 1954, given the globalisation of the Cold War, given the domestic political realities, and most of all perhaps, given that the costs seemed reasonable – a few thousand American advisers on the ground, a few hundred million dollars in aid.

This would help to explain Dulles' candid assessment that the chances of success for the creation of the South Vietnamese state were only 10 per cent. The Eisenhower administration, says Duiker, 'went into the Diem experiment with its eyes wide open'.

Some key books in the debates
S. Ambrose, *Eisenhower: The President* (New York, 1984).
D. Anderson, *Trapped by Success: The Eisenhower Administration and Vietnam* (New York, 1991) and *The Vietnam War* (New York, 2005).
R. Divine, 'Vietnam reconsidered', *Diplomatic History* (1988).
W. Duiker, *US Containment Policy and the Conflict in Indochina* (Stanford, 1994) and *Sacred War* (New York, 1995).
D. Ellsberg, *Papers on the War* (New York, 1972).
F. Fitzgerald, *Fire in the Lake* (Boston, 1972).
L. Gardner, *Approaching Vietnam* (New York, 1988).
L. Gelb and R. Betts, *The Irony of Vietnam* (Washington DC, 1979).
D. Halberstam, *The Making of a Quagmire* (New York, 1964).
S. Jacobs, *America's Miracle Man in Vietnam* (Duke, 2004).
G. Kahin and J. Lewis, *The United States in Vietnam* (New York, 1969).
D. Kaiser, *An American Tragedy* (Harvard, 2000).
W. LaFaber, *The American Age* (New York, 1989).
F. Logevall, *The Origins of the Vietnam War* (London, 2001).
D. Pike, *Viet Cong* (Cambridge, Massachusetts, 1966).
A. Short, *The Origins of the Vietnam War* (London, 1989).

Study Guide: AS Question

In the style of Edexcel

How far do you agree that Eisenhower showed good judgement in his handling of the question of Vietnam?

Exam tips

The cross-references are intended to take you straight to the material that will help you to answer the question.

Avoid any temptation to describe or narrate a history of developments in the Vietnam question over this period. Your answer will be effectively organised if you first clarify what decisions or judgements Eisenhower had to make and then assess the consequences of those decisions.

Eisenhower's aim was the containment of Communism. He faced pressure to be more interventionist in Vietnam in support of that aim and he was also alive to the dangers of direct involvement. Did he follow a well-judged policy which did just enough to 'keep the domino from falling' or did his decisions nevertheless result in a 'commitment trap' for himself and his successors?

Did he do just enough to keep the domino from falling?
You could consider that, while he failed to prevent North Vietnam from becoming Communist (was that ever a realistic possibly?), he:

- rejected the atomic option and the associated possibility of open conflict with the USSR and China (page 108)
- undermined the elements of the Geneva Accords which would assist the unification of Vietnam (pages 100–1 and 109)
- actively promoted and supported the Diem regime while avoiding direct military involvement (pages 103–6 and 107–9).

Were his decisions well judged?
On the one hand, a non-Communist regime was established in South Vietnam. On the other hand, to explore whether Eisenhower deepened a 'commitment trap' you should consider evidence of:

- the USA's increased involvement in Vietnam – financial assistance and the role of 'advisors' (page 109)
- the implications of the unpopularity of the Diem regime (pages 104–6, 107 and 109).

In coming to your judgement, be careful not to be too influenced by hindsight. Bear in mind the options open to Eisenhower at the time and whether there was a practical political option to reject intervention in Vietnam. You could note that a key weakness of the USA's position by 1960 was that it was committed to propping up an unpopular dictatorial regime in South Vietnam. Was the decision to install the Diem regime well judged? Were different options open to Eisenhower's administration?

There is not an expected answer to this question. It is debated by historians, and you have been given the opportunity to show your understanding of the arguments for and against the proposition. However, you must make clear what your overall conclusion is – and make sure it is in line with the argument in your answer and the weight you have given to the evidence you have deployed.

6 'Vietnam is the Place' – The Kennedy Crusade (1961–3)

POINTS TO CONSIDER

During the presidency of John Fitzgerald Kennedy (1961–3), American involvement in Vietnam dramatically increased. This chapter invites consideration of the following questions:

- Why did Kennedy continue the American commitment to Vietnam?
- Had Kennedy lived longer, would he have got out of Vietnam?
- Was it Kennedy's (as opposed to Johnson's) war?
- Were Kennedy's Vietnam policies wise?

This chapter examines these questions through sections on:

- Kennedy's early ideas about Vietnam
- The president and his advisers
- Cuba, Laos and Vietnam
- Kennedy and Diem
- Assessments of Kennedy

Key dates

1960		Kennedy advocated greater Cold War activism during presidential election campaign
1961	January	Kennedy became president
	April	Kennedy humiliated by failure to overthrow Castro in Cuba (Bay of Pigs)
	May	De Gaulle warned Kennedy of Vietnamese quagmire
1962		12,000 American advisers in Vietnam Strategic hamlets programme
	February	Kennedy created MACV
	May	McNamara said US winning the war
1963	January	Vietcong defeated ARVN and Americans at Battle of Ap Bac
	Spring	Anti-Diem protests by Buddhists
	September	Kennedy said the South Vietnamese had to win the war themselves, but that it would be a mistake for the USA to get out
	November	Diem assassinated; Kennedy assassinated

1 | Introduction: Kennedy's War?

While Vietnam was a minor side-show in the Cold War for Truman and Eisenhower, it became far more important during the Kennedy presidency, although it was only under President Johnson that Vietnam became a national obsession.

There can be no doubt that the Kennedy presidency saw an increased commitment to South Vietnam. However, since Kennedy's death there has been considerable debate over his policy. The debate has been affected by the knowledge that during the presidency of his successor, the Vietnam War became highly controversial and unpopular. Kennedy's supporters have been inclined to argue that the Vietnam War was 'Johnson's War' and that just before his assassination Kennedy was planning to get America out. The Johnson administration was much criticised for its apparent lack of understanding of Vietnam and for reliance on military solutions to the problems there. However, the study of the Kennedy administration's policies reveals similar failures of perception as well as a massive increase in the American commitment in Vietnam. These issues are sometimes forgotten by those who concentrate upon Johnson's presidency in isolation.

Key question
Was it 'Kennedy's War'? Or 'Johnson's War'?

2 | Kennedy's Early Ideas about Vietnam

By the time Kennedy became president in January 1961, his ideas on Vietnam had already been shaped and demonstrated. Kennedy's Catholic family loathed Communism. As a young, Democratic **Congressman**, Kennedy agreed with President Truman that the expansion of Communism must be 'contained' by America, but attacked him for 'losing' China in 1949 (see page 5).

Like most Americans, Kennedy believed in Eisenhower's domino theory, but criticised Eisenhower for allowing the rise of Communism in the newly emergent nations of the **Third World**, which Kennedy considered to be the new Cold War battleground. Like Eisenhower, Kennedy rejected the idea of nationwide Vietnamese elections, because Ho would win.

In a 1956 speech to the American Friends of Vietnam, Kennedy reiterated the domino theory, calling South Vietnam the 'cornerstone of the free world in Southeast Asia'. He said other countries such as India, Japan, the Philippines, Laos and Cambodia would be threatened if Vietnam became Communist. He called Vietnam 'a proving ground for democracy in Asia' and 'a test of American responsibility and determination in Asia'. He said the 'relentless' Chinese had to be stopped, for the sake of US security.

Kennedy criticised Eisenhower for losing the initiative in foreign policy and during his 1960 presidential election campaign Kennedy said that the country needed a president 'to get America moving again'. His campaign **rhetoric** was militantly anti-Communist. He described the Communist ideology as 'unceasing in its drive for world domination'.

Key question
Did Kennedy's pre-presidential career and beliefs make greater involvement in Vietnam inevitable?

Key dates

Kennedy advocated greater Cold War activism during presidential election campaign: 1960

Kennedy became president: January 1961

Key terms

Congressman
Member of the House of Representatives, where he or she votes on laws.

Third World
Cold War-era name for developing nations.

Rhetoric
Stylised speech, designed to impress and persuade.

President Kennedy explaining the situation in Vietnam.

So, although most Americans were unaware of events in Vietnam when Kennedy became president, his background suggested that he might be even more interested in and committed to Vietnam than his predecessors.

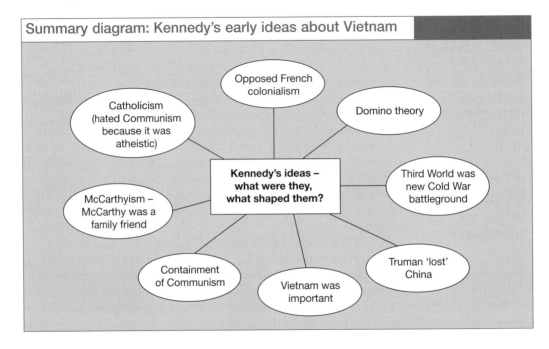

Summary diagram: Kennedy's early ideas about Vietnam

Opposed French colonialism

Domino theory

Catholicism (hated Communism because it was atheistic)

Kennedy's ideas – what were they, what shaped them?

Third World was new Cold War battleground

McCarthyism – McCarthy was a family friend

Containment of Communism

Vietnam was important

Truman 'lost' China

Key question
Who and what
shaped Kennedy's
Vietnam policy?

3 | The President and his Advisers

The interests, emphases and characters of President Kennedy and his chosen advisers shaped US policy towards Vietnam.

a) Kennedy – the impatient crusader in the Third World

i) Campaign rhetoric

In some ways Kennedy was a prisoner of his own Cold War campaign rhetoric – designed to win votes, it served to limit his foreign policy options once in the White House. Having made much of the need for a more dynamic foreign policy, Kennedy was duty-bound to increase defence expenditure and foreign involvement.

ii) Youth, inexperience and 'a time for greatness'

Kennedy was particularly sensitive about references to his youth and inexperience and this made him keen to be assertive in foreign affairs. At a 1961 White House luncheon, a newspaper editor challenged Kennedy:

> We can annihilate Russia and should make that clear to the Soviet government … you and your Administration are weak sisters … [America needs] a man on horseback … Many people in Texas and the Southwest think that you are riding [your daughter] Caroline's tricycle.

A red-faced Kennedy who retorted 'I'm just as tough as you are' was clearly a president who thought he had much to prove. He was well aware that the nation was more likely to rally around a narrowly elected president during a time of national crisis. His campaign slogan had been 'a time for greatness' and in his book *Profiles of Courage* (1954) Kennedy had said that 'great crises make great men'.

iii) Third World insurgency

Just before Kennedy's inauguration the Soviet leader had forecast the ultimate triumph of Communism through wars of national liberation in Third World countries such as Vietnam, for which he promised Soviet aid. Kennedy's conviction that the Third World was likely to be the main future arena of the struggle between the US and the Soviet Union, coupled with Eisenhower's warning that the Republican Party would attack 'any retreat in Southeast Asia', suggested that Kennedy was likely to make a stand in Vietnam.

iv) Advisers

Kennedy's eagerness to get things moving made him impatient with the State Department, so when he sought advice on foreign affairs he looked to close friends such as Secretary of Defence Robert McNamara. Kennedy was thus influenced by the Defence

---

Profile: John Fitzgerald Kennedy 1917–63

1917	– Born to a wealthy, Irish Catholic, Democrat family in Boston, Massachusetts
1940	– Graduated from Harvard; wrote the bestselling *Why England Slept*, which criticised British unpreparedness for war
1941–43	– Second World War hero
1947–53	– Served three terms in the House of Representatives; criticised Truman administration for 'losing' China
1952	– Successful senatorial campaign against popular incumbent, Republican Henry Cabot Lodge Jr; Senator until 1960
1953	– Ambivalent towards family friend and fanatical anti-Communist Senator Joseph McCarthy – 'Half my people in Massachusetts look upon McCarthy as a hero'
Late 1950s	– Served on Senate Foreign Relations Committee; advocated massive aid to emerging Third World nations
1960	– Campaigned for president, with Lyndon Johnson as running mate; campaign characterised by Cold War rhetoric and Kennedy family glamour; narrowly elected
1961	– Embarrassed by Bay of Pigs fiasco; Khrushchev seemed to bully/dominate Kennedy at the Vienna summit
1962	– Made Khrushchev back down over the Cuban Missiles Crisis
1963	– Signed nuclear test ban treaty Assassinated

John F. Kennedy is important in the Cold War context in that his presidency was full of crises, for which he and/or Soviet leader Khrushchev clearly bore some blame. In many speeches, Kennedy advocated greater US militancy in the Cold War. He is important in the Vietnam context in that he dramatically increased US involvement there.

Department, which was naturally inclined to see problems in terms of military solutions (unlike the State Department and its diplomatic experts).

b) Secretary of Defence Robert McNamara – the statistics man

Key question
Why was McNamara important?

Secretary of Defence McNamara's background was in business. Dynamic, tough-talking, persuasive, competent and down-to-earth, McNamara was the only cabinet member to become part of the charmed social circle around the president. McNamara's powerful personality, coupled with Secretary of State Dean Rusk's deliberately colourless public persona, meant that his power within the cabinet was inevitably greater. Enormous influence and judgemental lapses on the part of McNamara proved unfortunate with regard to Vietnam. Like Rusk, McNamara was a great believer in the US commitment to Vietnam, but his solutions to the problems in that faraway land were always military – an emphasis which proved unhelpful.

A *New York Times* reporter commended his efficiency but found cause for concern in his total conviction that he was always right, his lack of historical knowledge and his tendency to try to reduce problems to statistics by eliminating the human factor. With regard to Vietnam, as McNamara subsequently admitted, these weaknesses were to prove disastrous. Trained in the importance of statistics, McNamara tended to look at numbers of weapons and men, while forgetting that poorly armed people will sometimes fight to the death for their independence. 'We were kidding ourselves into thinking that we were making well-informed decisions', said one McNamara deputy years later. Unfortunately, President Lyndon Johnson retained McNamara as Secretary of Defence until early 1968.

c) Secretary of State Dean Rusk – the quiet professional

Like McNamara, Rusk was a hard-line **Cold Warrior**. Always a keen student of international relations, he worked in the Truman State Department in the Second World War. He believed that the appeasement of aggressors had led to that war and was determined to oppose what he considered to be Communist aggression. He had had a considerable influence on America's Vietnam policy since the late 1940s.

Kennedy said that he wanted to dominate foreign policy personally, so the self-effacing Rusk seemed a good choice as Secretary of State. However, after their first meeting, Rusk told a friend, 'Kennedy and I simply found it impossible to communicate. He didn't understand me and I didn't understand him.' This seems to have been an accurate summary of their working relationship.

Like McNamara, Rusk believed in American involvement in Vietnam, but as the fighting continued there, he felt it was the preserve of the Defence Department rather than the State Department.

Here then was an explosive situation: a crusading president keen to be assertive and to make a name for himself, who felt that the Third World and probably Southeast Asia was the next great Cold War arena; a president who listened to those more likely to put the emphasis on the military battles than on the battles for the hearts and minds of the people. It is easy to see how all this would lead to increasing US military involvement in Vietnam.

Key question
Why was Rusk important?

Key term

Cold Warrior
One who wanted the US to wage the Cold War with even more vigour.

Profile: Robert McNamara 1916–2009

1916	–	Born in San Francisco, California
1939	–	Master's degree from Harvard Business School; joined Harvard faculty
1941–5	–	Developed logistical systems for bomber raids and statistical systems for monitoring ground troops and supplies during the Second World War
1940s–50s	–	One of the Ford Motor Company's dynamic young 'Whiz Kids' hired to revitalise the company; successful cost-accounting methods
1960	–	President of Ford
1961–8	–	Secretary of Defence in Kennedy then Johnson administration. Advocated 'flexible response', including **counter-insurgency** techniques
1962	–	Visited South Vietnam; optimistic about US success there; staunch advocate of increased involvement
1964	–	Visited South Vietnam, publicly optimistic about US success there
1966	–	Visited South Vietnam, publicly optimistic, but privately questioned US involvement
1967	–	Openly tried for peace negotiations with Hanoi; publicly opposed bombing of North Vietnam
1968 February	–	Left Defence to become President of the World Bank (1968–73), where he was sympathetic to Third World nations
1995	–	Wrote *In Retrospect: The Tragedy and Lessons of Vietnam*, in which he described mistaken assumptions of US foreign policy but managed to avoid putting too much blame on himself
2009	–	Died

> **Key term**
>
> **Counter-insurgency** Style of warfare geared to dealing with guerrillas.

McNamara is vitally important in the history of US involvement in Vietnam. As Secretary of Defence, he greatly encouraged first President Kennedy then President Johnson to send US ground troops to Vietnam, and also advocated large-scale bombing. Having played perhaps the major role in getting thousands of US troops into the war, he then changed his mind, and declared that the US had got it all wrong.

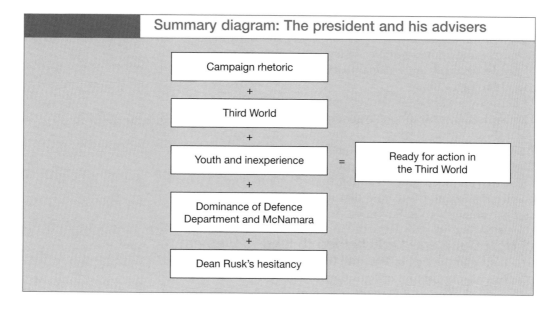

Summary diagram: The president and his advisers

Campaign rhetoric

+

Third World

+

Youth and inexperience = Ready for action in the Third World

+

Dominance of Defence Department and McNamara

+

Dean Rusk's hesitancy

Key question
How do problems in Cuba and Laos help us to understand why Kennedy continued and increased the American involvement in Vietnam?

4 | Cuba, Laos and Vietnam

a) Cuba and Vietnam

In his first week in office Kennedy privately declared that the major problem areas of the Third World were the Congo, Cuba, Laos and Vietnam, the last being 'the worst we've got'.

In Cuba, as in Vietnam, Kennedy felt bound to support an enterprise to which his predecessor had committed America and which took the form of military opposition to a popular nationalist leader who was also a Communist. Fidel Castro, like Ho, had a radical reform programme which many considered appropriate for a Third World country and it was by no means inevitable that he would be the tool of Moscow or Beijing. Despite a few warning voices within the administration, the Kennedy administration sponsored an unsuccessful anti-Communist invasion at the Bay of Pigs in Cuba in 1961.

Key date
Kennedy humiliated by failure to overthrow Castro in Cuba (Bay of Pigs): April 1961

There was dissent within the Kennedy administration over Cuba as over Vietnam. Some talked of 'adventurism' in Cuba and said intervention would 'compromise our moral position in the world', but what social psychologists call '**group-think**' proved triumphant. In both Cuba and Vietnam the Kennedy administration's policy and actions were neither systematically thought out nor exhaustively discussed by all who might have contributed valuable ideas.

Key term
'**Group-think**'
When the herd instinct halts independent thought or disagreement.

This Bay of Pigs failure naturally had an impact on US policy towards other Third World countries, including Laos.

b) Laos and Vietnam

Of the three countries (Vietnam, Cambodia and Laos) that had emerged from French Indochina, it was Laos that occupied Kennedy most in the early days of his presidency. He feared a Soviet-backed Communist triumph there. The State Department, the CIA, the JCS and his close advisers favoured US military intervention, but Kennedy was held back by the Bay of Pigs failure, by the limited number of few soldiers and aircraft available, and by congressional fears that intervention might lead to a clash with China.

Kennedy nevertheless sent US military advisers to assist the Laotian leader, an unpopular general whom he described as a 'total shit'. During 1961–2, Laos was apparently 'neutralised': the USA and USSR agreed that it would be governed by a coalition. However, Laotian Communists proved uncooperative and Ho's Vietcong continued to use Laotian trails to get to South Vietnam, confirming Kennedy's feeling that the Communists must be stopped somewhere in Southeast Asia.

c) How Cuba and Laos helped to lead to Vietnam

The failure of the Bay of Pigs and the 'draw' consequent on the supposed neutralisation of Laos meant that outright victories had to be won elsewhere. 'There are just so many concessions that one can make to the Communists in one year and survive politically', Kennedy told a friend after the Bay of Pigs. 'We just can't have another defeat in Vietnam.' He confided to a *New York Times* reporter, 'Now we have a problem in making our power credible, and Vietnam is the place.' One insider has suggested that **hawks** within the administration would only accept neutrality in Laos in return for an activist policy in Vietnam.

Vietnam was more suitable for US intervention than Laos in several ways. It had a long coastline where US naval supremacy could be brought to bear. Diem seemed to many Americans to have South Vietnam under control and democracy seemed to have a good chance of working there. Given that the US was already committed to help South Vietnam before Kennedy's presidency, a US departure would result in a loss of face and would 'undermine the credibility of American commitments everywhere', as Rusk and McNamara told Kennedy. They pointed out domestic political considerations: there would be 'bitter' divisions amongst the American public if Kennedy got out of Vietnam, 'extreme elements' would make political capital out of the retreat, and Kennedy did not want to be accused of 'losing' Vietnam in the way that Truman had 'lost' China.

Key term

Hawks
Militant Cold Warriors in the USA; those at the other end of the spectrum were known as doves.

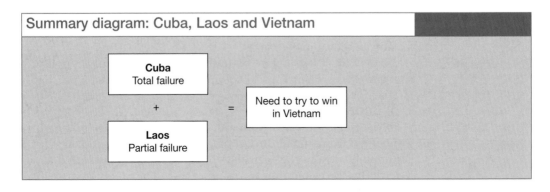

Summary diagram: Cuba, Laos and Vietnam

5 | Kennedy and Diem

When he became president, Kennedy had several options in relation to Vietnam. Exiting Vietnam did not seem to be one of them: the JCS warned Kennedy that, 'any reversal of US policy could have disastrous effects, not only on our relationship with South Vietnam, but with the rest of our Asian and other allies as well'. The negotiations option was never really seriously considered and/or pursued. Kennedy sanctioned unofficial peace talks in the summer of 1962 but Hanoi's position was that America must get out before any meaningful negotiations could take place, so that was the end of that. Prior to autumn 1963, the administration only really considered two options: it could either concentrate on the military effort against the Communists, or concentrate on reform there in order to win the hearts and minds of the Vietnamese people.

a) Military solutions
i) Increased military involvement

At Kennedy's accession, there were 800 American military advisers in South Vietnam. Kennedy immediately stepped up the financial aid to Diem to enable him to increase his army. Diem's quarter of a million soldiers still could not wipe out the Vietcong, so the JCS and the National Security Council recommended putting US ground troops in, but Kennedy preferred to increase the number of advisers there. By October 1961, there were 2000 US military advisers, and in 1962, 12,000. Increasing quantities of American weaponry flooded into South Vietnam. The US provided helicopters and pilot 'advisers'. Although Kennedy publicly denied it, these pilots were actively involved in the war. They transported troops, undertook reconnaissance missions and provided fire support for ARVN units. Kennedy authorised the use of defoliants. Sprayed from American helicopters, the defoliants stripped the trees and enabled better aerial observation. Meanwhile, on the ground, more and more American advisers accompanied ARVN units.

In order to co-ordinate this increased US military involvement, the Kennedy administration created the **Military Assistance Command, Vietnam** (MACV), which replaced MAAG (see page 87). However, the South Vietnamese army, ARVN, continued to lose ground. Their weakness was exposed in the battle of Ap Bac in January 1963.

ii) The battle of Ap Bac (January 1963)
Course of events

In January 1963, a Vietcong force was located in **Ap Bac**, not far from Saigon. Two thousand ARVN troops, accompanied by 113 American armoured personnel carriers, American-operated helicopters and bombers, and American advisers, went to surround Ap Bac. They did not know that there were as many as 350 guerrillas there.

Key question
Did Kennedy's military solution to the Vietnam problem work?

Key dates

12,000 American advisers in Vietnam: 1962

Kennedy created MACV: February 1962

Key terms

Military Assistance Command, Vietnam
MACV was created by Kennedy to co-ordinate US efforts in South Vietnam in February 1962.

Ap Bac
An important battle, the first major clash between the Vietcong and ARVN, in which American advisers and materials played a big part.

The ARVN troops refused to attack the Vietcong at Ap Bac. Five US helicopters and three pilots were lost and the ARVN troops refused to mount a rescue mission.

Reasons for the US/ARVN failure
The US/ARVN effort had failed because:

- The strength and preparedness of the Vietcong had been unexpected.
- According to the Americans, the ARVN's General Cao was unwilling to fight.
- Diem was unwilling to listen to American advice on the deployment of his troops: he feared losing too many men and preferred to use his best CIA-trained soldiers to keep himself in power.
- The Americans had not helped in that they had delayed the attack by a day to enable American helicopter pilots to sleep off the excesses of New Year's Eve.

The results/significance of the battle of Ap Bac
Ap Bac was significant because it drew unprecedented attention in the US, where the South Vietnamese performance was unfavourably reviewed. Also, it showed that Diem was probably militarily incapable of winning the war.

Thus, by early 1963, it was clear that, despite ever-increasing US military aid, Diem was not winning the war against the Communists. American officials estimated that Saigon controlled 49 per cent of the population, the Vietcong 9 per cent, with the rest in dispute.

iii) Differing viewpoints
Throughout his presidency, Kennedy received conflicting advice about Vietnam.

1961
When Kennedy visited France in May, President de Gaulle warned him:

> the more you become involved out there against Communism, the more the Communists will appear as the champions of national independence ... You will sink step by step into a bottomless military and political quagmire, however much you spend in men and money.

In October, Kennedy sent his friend General Maxwell Taylor to evaluate the military situation. Taylor recommended sending in American ground troops. The JCS, NSC and McNamara all agreed with the recommendation, even, said McNamara, if it meant Soviet and Chinese intervention (a prospect that frightened Dean Rusk).

Key dates

Vietcong defeated ARVN and Americans at Battle of Ap Bac: January 1963

De Gaulle warned Kennedy of Vietnamese quagmire: May 1961

McNamara said US winning the war: May 1962

In November, Kennedy sent another trusted friend, Kenneth Galbraith, to Saigon to assess the situation. Galbraith criticised the administration's diagnosis that this was a military rather than a political problem, called Diem a loser, said the Americans looked like the French colonialists, and expressed incredulity that anyone in Kennedy's administration could claim that Vietnam was strategically important. Galbraith feared that increased US involvement could only end in defeat and humiliation.

1962

When McNamara visited Vietnam in May, he declared that 'every quantitative measurement we have shows we are winning the war', but this was a very dubious assertion. Meanwhile, Under-Secretary of State George Ball warned that 'we'll have 300,000 men in the paddies and jungles' within five years. 'George, you're crazier than hell', said the president. 'That just isn't going to happen.'

In November, Kennedy sent Senator Mike Mansfield to report on Vietnam. Mansfield's report was critical of Diem and the increasing American involvement. Kennedy was displeased. 'You expect me to believe this?' 'Yes. You sent me', replied Mansfield. 'This isn't what my people are telling me', said Kennedy. Subsequent reports were a mixture of pessimistic references to Diem and the optimistic belief that American firepower must win eventually and that the VC could not afford to continue the struggle in the face of it.

These warnings and uncertainties made Kennedy cautious. He worried that American power might become overextended. He felt that the Vietnamese situation was very complex, that this was not a clear-cut case of Communist aggression as Korea had supposedly been (see page 15). He doubted that Congress and America's SEATO allies (see page 104) would be tempted to intervene in an obscure war so far away with so many guerrilla opponents, where millions had been spent for years without success. While he accepted that Diem needed a great deal more aid and advisers, Kennedy was as yet unwilling to send in US ground troops, saying that once they were there, there would soon be demands for more.

Key date
Strategic hamlets programme: 1962

Key question
Was reform a feasible option?

Key term
Strategic hamlets
Fortified villages in South Vietnam, similar to agrovilles.

b) The reform option

The Kennedy administration frequently advised Diem that one of the best ways to defeat the Communists was to introduce greater political, social and economic equality to South Vietnam. Diem ignored most of the advice. One of his 'reforms' was introduced in 1962, and was a disaster. From early 1962, Diem adopted the policy of '**strategic hamlets**', fortified villages in which the Vietnamese peasants would hopefully be isolated from the Vietcong. Unfortunately the Vietcong frequently joined the other residents and played on their discontent at having to pay for and to build the stockades. This prompted an American observer to note that the Saigon regime's officials, 'haven't the faintest idea what makes peasants tick'.

The strategic hamlets scheme was run by Diem's highly unpopular brother Ngo Dinh Nhu, who ignored US advice when establishing them, so that within a year the Vietcong captured thousands of US weapons from hamlets foolishly set up too far from Saigon. American journalist Stanley Karnow felt that Nhu was 'approaching madness' by this time. Concerned only with increasing his own power, Nhu ignored the social, economic and political reforms that the US suggested he introduce in the hamlets. This led to increased opposition to the Diem/US regime. Many years later it was revealed that Nhu's deputy in this business was a Communist who did his best to sabotage the scheme.

c) Debate and division in Diem's Vietnam
i) 1962

Key question
Why did Americans turn against Diem?

During 1962 there was slowly increasing criticism of Diem's military and political ineptitude in the American press, despite Kennedy administration attempts to pressurise the *New York Times* into a change of viewpoint. As yet the American press was not questioning the wisdom of involvement in Vietnam, just the tactics pursued and the results attained.

ii) Early 1963

By the spring of 1963 relations between Diem and the US were very tense. Diem resented US 'advice' and seemed to be considering a settlement with Hanoi which would get the Americans out, while Kennedy told a journalist friend that:

> we don't have a prayer of staying in Vietnam ... These people hate us. They are going to throw our asses out ... But I can't give up a piece of territory like that to the Communists and then get the American people to re-elect me.

iii) Catholics versus Buddhists

It is possible that their mutual Catholicism had played a part in Kennedy's support of Diem. However, Catholics were a minority in South Vietnam and in spring 1963 there was trouble.

Anti-Diem protests by Buddhists: Spring 1963
Key date

The Diem regime allowed the flying of Catholic flags in honour of Diem's brother (an archbishop in the Catholic church), but banned flags for the celebration of Buddha's birthday. When 10,000 Buddhists protested, Diem sent in soldiers. Seven Buddhists were killed.

In June, a 73-year-old Buddhist priest set himself alight in protest. His flesh burned away leaving only his heart, which became an object of worship to the Buddhist majority. This dramatic protest made headlines in America. Other such deaths followed and Nhu's unpopular wife ('No Nhus is good news', joked one American reporter) made things worse by flippant references to barbecues.

Kennedy was shocked at the front-page newspaper pictures of the Buddhist martyrs. 'How could this have happened?' he asked. 'Who are these people? Why didn't we know about them before?'

A Buddhist priest burns himself to death in protest against Diem's religious policies.

Possibly Kennedy was simply trying to deflect blame from himself here, but if he really did not know of the Catholic–Buddhist tension, he had been lax in doing his homework on a country to which he had sent several thousand Americans.

By August, Diem appeared to be waging religious war on the Buddhist majority. Neither the military option nor the reform option was working. Kennedy felt it was time to replace Ambassador Frederick Nolting, who knew little about Asia, with Henry Cabot Lodge II, who knew a little more. Under Lodge, the US chose a third and more ruthless option, getting rid of Diem.

d) The new ambassador

Key question
What was Lodge's role?

A January 1963 State Department report had said the US lacked vision and planning in its Vietnam policy, and recommended the appointment of a 'strong' ambassador to Vietnam to co-ordinate the military and 'nation-building' efforts there. Lodge was a patriot, a Second World War military hero, and an experienced and ambitious Republican politician with a particular interest in foreign affairs. His relations with the press were always good, which was important to Kennedy, because the American press was attacking US support of Diem.

Key term

Bipartisan
When both Republicans and Democrats cooperate.

On the other hand, Lodge was not ideal for the co-ordinating role envisaged by the State Department. He lacked practice in team-work and administration. Kennedy probably chose him because he represented the **bipartisan** approach to Vietnam, although one White House insider said the president was keen to deflate a pompous old rival and therefore approved the appointment 'because the idea of getting Lodge mixed up in such a hopeless mess as Vietnam was irresistible'.

Rusk told Lodge in June 1963 that Vietnam had become a great burden to the president, taking up more of the president's time than any other issue. Rusk urged Lodge to be 'tough', to 'act as a catalyst' and not to 'refer many detailed questions to Washington'. Lodge certainly obliged.

e) Washington, Lodge and the overthrow of Diem
i) Lodge's arrival, August 1963

Key question
What was the US role in Diem's overthrow?

Lodge believed that the United States had to help South Vietnam, and that effective help required the removal of Diem. An anti-Diem group in the Kennedy administration got the president, preoccupied with the forthcoming civil rights March on Washington, to agree that Diem must be got rid of unless he instituted dramatic changes. There had been no real discussion about this, to the anger of McNamara and other influential men: 'My God', said the president, 'my government's coming apart'.

In the absence of firm leadership from Washington, Ambassador Lodge acquired an unusual amount of control of US policy in Vietnam. He turned Congress and American public opinion against Diem and Nhu, through press 'leaks' on their activities, and was happy to learn of an ARVN plot against Nhu.

ii) Administration disunity

Kennedy's disunited administration rejected both the option of using US combat troops and the idea of a total withdrawal. In September interviews, Kennedy criticised the Saigon regime and said the US could send advisers, 'but they have to win it – the people of Vietnam – against the Communists'. He acknowledged that Diem needed to change his policies and personnel, but said it would be a mistake for the United States to get out Vietnam, reiterating the domino theory and warning of the influence of expansionist China in Vietnam.

In September, Kennedy sent more observers, including McNamara and Taylor, to Vietnam. Their reports on American military activity were optimistic, but those on Diem's regime were pessimistic. By this time Nhu was negotiating with Hanoi, confirming the American conviction that he and Diem had to go. President Kennedy said there needed to be a change in the Saigon government, because of the 'harm which Diem's political actions are causing to the effort against Vietcong'. Bobby Kennedy, the president's brother, floated the idea that perhaps 'now was the time to get out of Vietnam entirely', but there was no one in the administration willing to take up the challenge to look at the problem afresh.

Key date
Kennedy said the South Vietnamese had to win the war themselves, but that it would be a mistake for the USA to get out: September 1963

iii) The coup

Key term

Coup
A *coup d'état* is the illegal overthrow of a government, usually by violent and/or revolutionary means.

The ARVN plotters were assured that they would have America's tacit support in their **coup**, which occurred on 2 November 1963. Lodge gave vital encouragement but publicly denied any US involvement.

It was perhaps naive to think there could be a coup but no assassinations. When Diem and Nhu were found dead, Lodge said triumphantly, 'Every Vietnamese has a grin on his face today', but Kennedy heard the news 'with a look of shock and dismay'. We might never know for certain whether Kennedy tacitly approved the idea of assassinating his Vietnamese friend Diem (or his Cuban enemy Castro, against whom the CIA frequently plotted). It seems possible that he did.

Key date

Diem assassinated; Kennedy assassinated: November 1963

Ironically Kennedy himself would meet the same fate as Diem within three weeks. 'The chickens have come home to roost', said Madame Nhu with grim satisfaction.

iv) The situation at Kennedy's death

At the moment of Kennedy's death there were nearly 17,000 American 'advisers' in Vietnam. The increase in the number of American advisers in Vietnam during Kennedy's presidency is the most convincing argument that Kennedy would not have 'got the United States out of Vietnam', although he was talking of a thorough review of America's Vietnam policy just before he died and some of his intimates insist he would have got America out of Vietnam. Kennedy told one senator friend, 'I can't [get out] until 1965 – after I'm re-elected.'

However, Rusk, Johnson and Bobby Kennedy were among those who said he had no plans to get out. Indeed, Bobby, who knew him best, said that, effectively, his brother had no plans at all! Kennedy's biographer James Giglio describes Kennedy's Vietnam policy as a shambles at the time of his death.

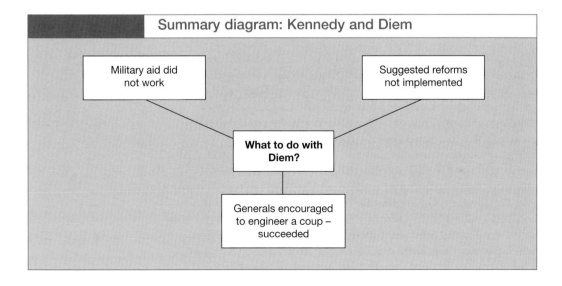

Summary diagram: Kennedy and Diem

Military aid did not work

Suggested reforms not implemented

What to do with Diem?

Generals encouraged to engineer a coup – succeeded

6 | Conclusions

Kennedy's belief that little Vietnam was so important seems ludicrous to us, although in the contemporary Cold War context many other Americans agreed with him. It could be argued that, following the route sketched out by his predecessors, Kennedy had interpreted events in Vietnam within a Cold War context which did not really apply. Ho Chi Minh was neither a Moscow nor a Beijing puppet and it could be argued that Kennedy had invested Vietnam with a Cold War importance that it did not really merit. Despite his frequent uncertainty about the wisdom of US involvement, he had increased his country's commitment to an unpopular regime that he then helped to overthrow in the final weeks of his life. General Westmoreland subsequently attributed enormous significance to the American role in the demise of Diem. It 'morally locked us in Vietnam'. By encouraging a change of government in South Vietnam, Kennedy greatly increased America's obligation to subsequent Saigon governments, which he himself recognised in a cable to Lodge on 6 November 1963. The Kennedy administration claimed to be promoting democracy in South Vietnam but had supported a dictator and then a military clique. Kennedy had passed a poisoned chalice to his successor.

7 | Key Debates
a) Why Kennedy increased the American commitment

Historians differ in trying to explain why Kennedy increased the American commitment to South Vietnam. Orthodox historians (for example, Smith, 1984–90) argue that Moscow/Beijing support of Hanoi gave Kennedy little choice. In the Cold War era, he simply had to resist Communism.

Revisionists are critical of Kennedy's motives. For example, McCormick (1989) and Hearden (1991) claim that he was sustaining America's overseas empire. Duiker (1994) and Berman (1982) accused Kennedy of exaggerating the strategic importance of Vietnam and emphasised domestic political calculations.

Kaiser (2000) is generally sympathetic to Kennedy, emphasising how he long resisted great pressure from his military and civilian advisers to get involved in a war in Southeast Asia, whether Vietnam or Laos. That great pressure naturally contributed greatly to the increased American commitment.

Many historians believe that as Truman and Eisenhower had committed the US to involvement in Vietnam, Kennedy was caught in the 'commitment trap' (see page 110). Kennedy himself told President de Gaulle that he had inherited the possibly unwisely created SEATO from Eisenhower and that it would look bad if the United States dumped SEATO. In 1976, Jonathan Schell pointed out that a crucial change from the Eisenhower administration to the Kennedy administration was that the 'territorial domino theory' became the 'psychological domino theory' or the 'doctrine of credibility'. It was not so much the territorial loss as the psychological loss that would be crucial if Vietnam fell – not so much that other territories would become Communist, but that the world would see that the United States lacked the determination to prevail.

b) The assassination of Diem

Historians differ over the significance of the assassination of Diem. Some historians (for example, Hammer, 1987) and contemporaries (for example, Lyndon Johnson and Richard Nixon) cite US collusion in the coup against Diem as the US government's greatest mistake and probably the single most important cause of the full-scale American involvement in the war. On the other hand, Kaiser (2000) claims that the greatest responsibility for the overthrow of Diem lay with Diem himself, as he had managed to alienate all his supporters, whether South Vietnamese or American. Kaiser also emphasised how Rusk and in particular McNamara urged continued support of Diem to the very end.

c) What if Kennedy had lived?

Counterfactual history asks 'what if' a particular event had not happened. It is currently highly fashionable and much debated. Because Kennedy's assassination cut short his presidency, there is inevitably much counterfactual speculation on 'what might have happened if Kennedy had lived'.

History as written by Kennedy's old friends and associates, such as Arthur Schlesinger Jr, claims that Kennedy would have got out of Vietnam. This exonerates Kennedy (and his friends and associates) from any blame for what turned out to be a highly unpopular and unsuccessful war. Much depends on which Kennedy pronouncements and/or actions one concentrates on. Persuaded by Kennedy's expressed doubts about involvement, William Rust and John Newman contend that, had he lived, Kennedy would have withdrawn American military advisers. Freedman (2000) studied Kennedy's Vietnam policies in the context of Kennedy's response to crises in Berlin, Cuba and Laos, and concludes that Kennedy would not have escalated the US involvement in Vietnam. Freedman's well-substantiated arguments are in themselves quite persuasive, although, significantly, Freedman makes little mention of Kennedy's dramatic increase in the number of advisers sent to Vietnam.

Concentrating on the scale of Kennedy's escalation of the involvement, Bassett and Pelz (1989) doubt that Kennedy intended to withdraw. 'There had been no official American reassessment of the strategic value of Vietnam. The commitment, in fact, was stronger than ever', said Anderson (2005); thousands more advisers had been sent in and Kennedy had 'embraced the war both in private and in public, making it more difficult for his successor to walk away from it'. Fredrik Logevall (2001) emphasises that 'public outrage' in the US at Diem's refusal to reform and mistreatment of Buddhists gave Kennedy 'a plausible excuse for disengaging the United States from Vietnam' – had he wanted to do so.

Some key books in the debates

L.J. Bassett and S.E. Pelz, in T.G. Paterson (editor), *Kennedy's Quest for Victory* (New York, 1989).

W.J. Duiker, *US Containment Policy and the Conflict in Indochina* (Stanford, 1994).

L. Freedman, *Kennedy's Wars* (Oxford, 2000).

E.J. Hammer, *A Death in November: America in Vietnam*, 1963 (New York, 1987).

P.J. Hearden, *The Tragedy of Vietnam* (New York, 1991).

D. Kaiser, *American Tragedy: Kennedy, Johnson, and the Origins of the Vietnam War* (Harvard, 2000).

F. Logevall, *The Origins of the Vietnam War* (Longman, 2001).

T.J. McCormick, *America's Half-Century: US Foreign Policy in the Cold War* (Baltimore, 1989).

J.M. Newman, *JFK in Vietnam* (New York, 1992).

W.J. Rust, *Kennedy in Vietnam* (New York, 1985).

J. Schell, *Time of Illusion* (New York, 1976).

R.B. Smith, *An International History of the Vietnam War*, 3 vols (New York, 1984–90).

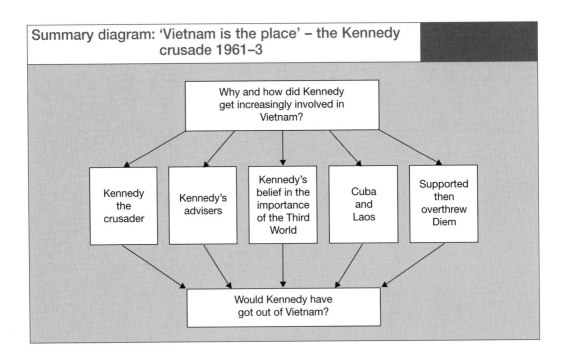

Summary diagram: 'Vietnam is the place' – the Kennedy crusade 1961–3

Study Guide: AS Questions

In the style of AQA

(a) Explain why the Vietcong were able to win popular support in South Vietnam between 1956 and 1963.　　　　(12 marks)

(b) 'Kennedy chose to increase American commitment to South Vietnam because he wanted to maintain the USA's status as a super-power.' Explain why you agree or disagree with this statement.　　　　(24 marks)

Exam tips

The cross-references are intended to take you straight to the material that will help you to answer the questions.

(a) To answer this question you will need to provide a range of factors and prioritise between these. There are a number of reasons to assess:

- The appeal of Communism (pages 83 and 92).
- Ho Chi Minh's nationalism and patriotism (pages 83, 92 and 106).
- The military effectiveness of the Communists, and the ineffectiveness of ARVN (pages 92–4 and 123–4).
- The refusal of Diem to introduce meaningful political and economic reform (page 125).
- The corruption and unpopular policies and personnel in Diem's government (for example, the Nhus, agrovilles, strategic hamlets, the persecution of Buddhists and the favouring of Catholics; pages 104–6, 107 and 125–7).
- The association of the Diem regime with the United States, which offended Vietnamese nationalism (page 106).

Structure your answer carefully and try to offer a logical and well-supported conclusion that emphasises what you consider to be the main factor or factors.

(b) Clearly it would be wrong to suggest there was only one reason for the increase in US involvement in Vietnam under Kennedy and this question is effectively asking you to evaluate a range of reasons and to assess whether the desire for superpower status was the most important or overriding factor. Historians are divided on the issue (see pages 130–1), so there is really no right or wrong answer. Your response should be as convincing as you can make it, given the evidence available to you, but do try to offer some sort of judgement. You will probably want to consider Kennedy's early ideas about Vietnam (summarised on page 115); his own character and youth when he became president (page 117); his advisers (pages 117–20); the influence of Cuba (pages 121–2); and his relationship with Diem (pages 123–9). As well as the broad internal and external pressures on Kennedy, you should assess the importance of ideological (the domino theory, pages 97 and 115), economic (Southeast Asia contained minerals and other important economic resources), and strategic considerations (referring, for example, to the debate over Laos). Your answer should be analytical, leading to a balanced and convincing conclusion.

7 'Johnson's War'?

POINTS TO CONSIDER

Although President Johnson's real preoccupation was social reform (building a 'Great Society') in the United States, he sent nearly a million American soldiers to Vietnam and became the president most associated with and hated for what he called 'that bitch of a war'.

This chapter covers what is probably the major question facing anyone studying American involvement in Vietnam: was it 'Johnson's War'? This question is investigated in sections on:

- Why Johnson continued US involvement in the war
- How Johnson was able to escalate the war
- Why Johnson escalated the American involvement in Vietnam
- Johnson's doubts
- Was it 'Johnson's War'?

Key dates

1963	November	Kennedy assassinated; Johnson became president
	December	Increased numbers of PAVN regulars sent to South Vietnam
1964	March	South Vietnamese situation 'very disturbing' (Taylor and McNamara); Johnson publicly confident, privately uncertain
	August	Gulf of Tonkin incident and resolution
	November	US presidential election Working Group recommended escalation
	December 24	Vietcong attacked Saigon bar full of US officers
1965	February	Vietcong attacked huge US airbase near Pleiku
	March	'Rolling Thunder' began First American ground troops landed in Vietnam

		First anti-war protests in American universities
	May	Congress voted $700 million for war in Vietnam
	June	Ky became leader of South Vietnam
	July	Johnson announced sending 50,000 more troops to South Vietnam
	October	Johnson asked 'Where are we going?'
	December	Over 200,000 US troops in Vietnam
	December	Polls showed most Americans pro-escalation
1968		535,000 US troops in South Vietnam

Key question
Did the US world-view make Johnson's continuation of the war inevitable?

1 | Why Johnson Continued US Involvement in the War

a) A man of his time

Johnson aroused much hostile criticism for 'his' war, but he was a typical American of his time in his patriotism, anti-Communism and misunderstanding of foreigners.

i) Patriotism

Johnson was intensely patriotic and proud of US military prowess. As a senator he always voted to build up the armed forces. America had always been victorious in wars. Defeat by what he called 'that damn little pissant country', 'that raggedy-ass little fourth-rate' Vietnam was inconceivable.

ii) Ideology, security and national honour

Like many Americans, Johnson genuinely believed his country fought for world freedom as well as American security in two world wars, in Korea and in Vietnam. Like many of his generation, he abhorred the idea of appeasing an enemy: 'If you let a bully come into your front yard one day, the next day he'll be up on your porch, and the day after that he'll rape your wife in your own bed.' As vice-president, Johnson firmly believed that America should fight Communist 'aggressors' in Southeast Asia whatever the cost. Like Kennedy and Eisenhower, Johnson believed that Vietnam was a 'domino': if it fell to Communism the countries around it would rapidly follow suit. He felt that it was a question of national honour for the United States to continue its commitment to its South Vietnamese ally and to stick by SEATO (see page 104).

iii) Misunderstanding foreigners

Like many Americans, Johnson found it quite difficult to understand foreign affairs and foreigners. 'The trouble with

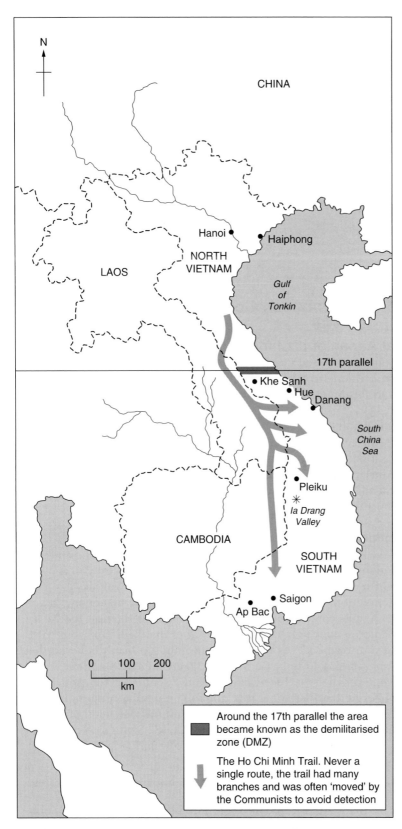

Important places in the American era in Vietnam (c. 1956–73).

Profile: Lyndon Baines Johnson 1908–73

1908	– Born into poor Texas ranching family
1920s	– Trained and worked as a teacher
1930s	– Worked in government; ran successfully for House of Representatives
1948	– Elected senator
1960	– Joined Democratic ticket as Kennedy's vice-presidential candidate
1963 November	– Kennedy assassinated, Johnson became president
1964 November	– Elected president, in landslide victory
1965	– Sent first American ground troops to Vietnam; increasingly unpopular
1968 March	– Said would not stand for presidency again, and would request peace talks
1969 January	– Returned to Texas ranch
1973	– Died

In the context of the Vietnam War, Johnson is usually considered to be the most important president. It was he who sent in tens of thousands of American ground troops, for which he became (and remains) exceptionally unpopular.

foreigners is that they're not like the folks you were reared with', he said, only half jokingly. He felt that Ho Chi Minh was another Hitler and should be treated accordingly.

Key question
Did Kennedy's assassination make Johnson's continuation of the war inevitable?

b) The impact of Kennedy's assassination

Did Johnson's patriotism, anti-Communism and misunderstanding of foreigners make it inevitable that he would continue American involvement in Vietnam? Perhaps not. He knew that a long war would probably lose the support of Congress and the public. He knew the weaknesses of the Saigon government: in 1961 he said that Diem must reform and fight his own war. He knew that only China and the USSR would benefit if America got 'bogged down chasing guerrillas' over Asiatic rice fields and jungles. Nevertheless, he continued the American involvement. One major reason was the Kennedy legacy.

Johnson resented the younger and less experienced man being president. Amidst the sorrow that Johnson felt at Kennedy's assassination in November 1963, there was also joy at attaining the presidency. Guilt feelings contributed to his determination to stand by all Kennedy had done and those who had helped Kennedy to do it. 'I swore to myself that I would carry on', Johnson subsequently explained. 'I would continue for my partner who had gone down ahead of me … When I took over, I often felt as if President Kennedy were sitting there in the room looking at me.' Two days after Kennedy's assassination, the new president told Ambassador Lodge he was not going to 'lose Vietnam … Tell those generals in Saigon that Lyndon Johnson intends to stand by

Key date
Kennedy assassinated; Johnson became president: November 1963

our word'. 'My first major decision on Vietnam had been to reaffirm President Kennedy's policies', Johnson said later.

The tragic circumstances of Johnson's accession to power thus caused him to make a vital decision with little apparent debate and discussion. Emotionally and constitutionally, the new president felt that he had to continue the policies of his properly elected predecessor.

There is a case for calling Vietnam 'Kennedy's War'. Kennedy had increased American involvement in Vietnam. As vice-president, Johnson had opposed American support for the coup against Diem, realising that it dramatically increased American obligation to subsequent Saigon regimes. However, Kennedy's death ensured that Johnson would not repudiate his predecessor's Vietnam policy. Knowing he had no real **popular mandate**, the new president hesitated to abandon any Kennedy commitment or Kennedy officials. The retention of Kennedy's advisers helped to ensure continued involvement in Vietnam.

Popular mandate Clear evidence that a political leader has the majority of the people behind him and his policies.

Key term

c) Johnson and his advisers

In order to decide whether Vietnam was 'Johnson's War', his relationship with his advisers must be investigated. Did they share responsibility for the war?

Key question
Did Johnson's advisers make his continuation of the war inevitable?

i) Kennedy's men

Johnson's freedom of action and thought were inevitably circumscribed because in the circumstances of his accession to power he was tied to Kennedy's men. Johnson's retention of Kennedy men such as McNamara and Rusk meant that no fresh ideas emerged on the Vietnam problem. Rusk was obsessive about continuing the struggle in Southeast Asia. He believed that withdrawal would cause loss of faith in America's commitment to oppose Communist aggression and lead to a Third World War.

McNamara was so important in making policy that some called Vietnam 'McNamara's War'. In his memoirs (1995) McNamara

---

Warning voices

There were some warning voices. The influential Democratic Senate majority leader, Mike Mansfield, kept asking Johnson pertinent questions:

- Why should a democracy like the US support military governments in Saigon?
- Did the people of South Vietnam really want a crusade against Communism?
- What US interest was at stake in little Vietnam?

Johnson did not want this kind of discussion. 'The president expects that all senior officers of the government will move energetically to insure the full unity of support for … US policy in Vietnam', said a secret memorandum of November 1963.

criticised both himself and Johnson's other civilian and military advisers for an inability to ask the searching and relevant questions that needed to be asked at every stage of US involvement in Vietnam. McNamara lamented the administration's lack of historical knowledge and understanding of matters such as Sino-Vietnamese rivalry (due to McCarthyism, China experts were sacked from the State Department because their praise of Mao's military achievements was perceived as pro-Communism) (see page 21).

Although the CIA was gloomy about the situation in Vietnam, many in the administration believed that America would somehow triumph. The Kennedy men remaining in the State and Defence Departments and the White House wanted to save face. No one wanted to admit past errors. No one seemed to want real debate.

ii) Advice from the military

In wartime, the beliefs and advice of the military were inevitably influential. Like Kennedy, Johnson found some military men scary, especially air force chief Curtis LeMay, who wanted to 'bomb Vietnam back into the Stone Age'. However, Johnson inherited involvement in a war and as **commander-in-chief** felt duty-bound to listen to the generals. As Vietnam was the only war the generals had, they wanted to continue with it and indeed intensify it in order to win.

iii) The first president to lose a war

Johnson's personal political ambition reinforced what the generals were advising. He repeatedly said he did not want to be the first president to lose a war, especially to the Communists.

Johnson's military and civilian advisers and his own beliefs and ambitions thus guided him towards the continuation of the commitment to Vietnam, even though the situation there was deteriorating.

d) Early debates, doubts and decisions

i) The situation in Vietnam, 1963–4

From December 1963 Hanoi sent increasing numbers of People's Army of North Vietnam (PAVN) regulars south, which greatly strengthened the VC. Diem's successor, General 'Big' Minh, retreated to his tennis court and his garden where he raised orchids. He was soon deposed. Minh's successors were even less impressive. The strategic hamlets programme was clearly a failure and the Vietcong impressively countered US air power with ever-increasing supplies of Soviet and Chinese weaponry. It was estimated that the Communists controlled around half of South Vietnam. General Maxwell Taylor and McNamara visited Saigon and in March 1964 described the situation as 'very disturbing'. The South Vietnamese were generally apathetic and unwilling to fight. Prime Minister Khanh begged for more US aid.

Key term

Commander-in-chief
Under the US constitution, the president commands the US armed forces.

Key question
Was Vietnam being 'reassessed' by the Johnson administration in 1963–4?

Key dates

Increased numbers of PAVN regulars sent to South Vietnam: December 1963

South Vietnamese situation 'very disturbing' (Taylor and McNamara); Johnson publicly confident, privately uncertain: March 1964

ii) The debate on what to do next

Taylor, Rusk, McNamara and the JCS favoured escalation and direct action against North Vietnam. LeMay said North Vietnam should be bombed because 'we are swatting flies [in South Vietnam] when we should be going after the manure pile [North Vietnam]'. Johnson felt the war needed to be won quickly before Congress demanded American withdrawal. Early in the Johnson presidency Vietnam was supposedly being 'reassessed' every day, but what was being reassessed by the Johnson administration was not *whether* American involvement should continue but *how* it should continue.

iii) Public confidence, private doubts

On 20 April, Johnson publicly declared that America was 'in this battle as long as South Vietnam wants our support' in its fight for freedom, but his private doubts were revealed in May 1964 conversations:

> I don't think the people of the country know much about Vietnam, and I think they care a hell of a lot less. We tell [Moscow, Beijing and Hanoi] … that we'll get out of there [Vietnam] … if they will just quit raiding their neighbours. And they say 'Screw you'. All the senators are all saying 'Let's move, let's go into the North.' They'd impeach a president that would run out, wouldn't they? … I stayed awake last night thinking of this thing … It looks to me like we're getting into another Korea … I don't think that we can fight them 10,000 miles away from home … I don't think it's worth fighting for. And I don't think that we can get out. It's just the biggest damned mess … What the hell is Vietnam worth to me? … What is it worth to this country? … Of course if you start running from the Communists, they may just chase you into your own kitchen … This is a terrible thing we're getting ready to do.

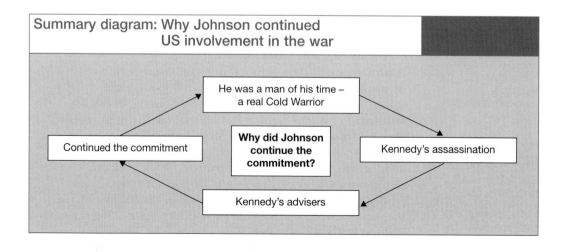

Summary diagram: Why Johnson continued US involvement in the war

2 | How Johnson was Able to Escalate the War

By July 1964, 200 Americans had died in Vietnam, and Johnson had added 2500 men to the US forces there, but South Vietnam's war against the Communists was still not going well.

Johnson thought that if the time came for escalation of American involvement in Vietnam, he would need congressional and public support. He believed that he obtained the former with the Gulf of Tonkin resolution, and the latter in the presidential election of November 1964.

a) August 1964 – the Gulf of Tonkin resolution
i) Sabotage and spying in the North

For a decade the CIA had been secretly sending South Vietnamese teams on sabotage missions to the North. In the first half of 1964 South Vietnamese gunboats raided North Vietnam's coast and Johnson approved covert American operations. American ships such as the *Maddox* went on espionage missions in the North's coastal waters.

ii) The Gulf of Tonkin incident

Johnson claimed that the North Vietnamese made two unprovoked attacks on the *Maddox* and the *Turner Joy* in the Gulf of Tonkin. On 4 August 1964 he asked for congressional support for avenging the attacks.

iii) The Gulf of Tonkin resolution

Believing that the lives of innocent American sailors had been jeopardised by the North Vietnamese, Congress willingly passed the Gulf of Tonkin resolution. The resolution gave the president the power to wage war in Vietnam: as Johnson said, it was 'like grandma's night-shirt – it covered everything'. The resolution said North Vietnamese naval units had violated international law: so, for the sake of world peace and American security, and because of SEATO obligations, the president was authorised to 'take all necessary steps' to help South Vietnam defend its freedom. The resolution would expire when the president believed that the situation in Southeast Asia was safe or when Congress decided to terminate it.

A few senators led by Mansfield were unconvinced that America was acting correctly. One bitterly pointed out that they had no choice but to support the president when he said there was a crisis. Another said 'all Vietnam is not worth the life of a single American boy', but no one listened. The Senate had been two-thirds empty for the debate on the resolution, which it passed 88 to 2.

iv) Who was to blame for the escalation?

Should Congress be blamed for giving Johnson the power to escalate the war? Johnson and McNamara were not totally open with them:

- over the covert raids (American naval missions were provocative)
- about the incident (there are many doubts surrounding the second North Vietnamese 'attack'. 'Hell', the president admitted years later, 'for all I know, our navy was shooting at whales out there')
- about the implementation of the resolution (did the administration wait for and even create the incident in order to ensure the passage of the resolution that they had prepared back in June 1964?).

In Johnson's defence, it was difficult to know exactly what had happened in the Gulf of Tonkin, and if there had been an attack, Americans would have expected him to respond. Also, it would have been irresponsible not to have had a resolution ready for an emergency.

Many believe that political calculations played a big part in Johnson's actions. During the summer of 1964, the Republican presidential candidate Barry Goldwater was accusing Johnson of being 'soft on Communism', so the president wanted to appear firm. Did Johnson exploit events both to intensify US military involvement in Vietnam and to win over the American public in an election year? While Johnson was trying to decide whether there had been a second attack, the press reported the supposed incident and Johnson felt trapped, fearing that if he did nothing his Republican opponent in the presidential election would call him a coward.

v) Results and significance of the Gulf of Tonkin resolution

The results and significance of the passage of the resolution were vitally important. With the resolution, Johnson appeared to have the nation behind him. Now the war could really be taken to the North: American aircraft bombed North Vietnam for the first time. This escalation made Johnson look tough. His public approval rating rose from 42 to 72 per cent, helping him to win the presidential election. Ominously, American prestige was even more firmly committed to defending South Vietnam. Should another escalatory step seem necessary it would be even easier. The resolution and the presidential election suggested a nation united behind its president in his Vietnam policy.

b) The 1964 presidential election

During the election campaign the administration became aware that the voters were asking many questions about Vietnam:

- Why are we still there?
- Why are we there at all?
- Why haven't we trained the Vietnamese to do their own fighting?
- Why can't we win?
- Why can't it be a UN effort like Korea?
- Would it be so disastrous if we got out?

Key question
How did the 1964 presidential election impact upon US involvement in Vietnam?

US presidential
election: November
1964

Foreign policy issues are rarely decisive in American presidential elections, but they were probably more important than usual in 1964. The Republican candidate Barry Goldwater was prone to verbal gaffes. When he said that America ought to use all its strength to win in Vietnam, he was seen as a trigger-happy hawk. He was widely if wrongly perceived as recommending the use of atomic weapons on Hanoi, while Johnson was perceived as the peace candidate. Privately, Goldwater said that as Vietnam was 'a national burden' and the people were divided over both the legitimacy of US involvement and the conduct of the war, it was not in America's best interests to make the war a campaign issue. Johnson was greatly relieved. This meant that there was no great open debate on Vietnam.

Johnson knew that if left-wingers accused him of being a war-monger or if right-wingers accused him of being 'soft on Communism' he might not get re-elected. He therefore reassured the left by saying that he did not intend to do anything rash or have a major war. He made a promise that might have been crucial to his re-election: 'We are not going to send American boys away from home to do what Asian boys ought to be doing for themselves.' On the other hand, he reassured the right by saying 'America keeps her word'. At Christmas 1963 he had told the JCS that he did not want to lose South Vietnam or get America into a war before the election: 'Just let me get elected and then you can have your war.' He also gained votes by appearing tough over the Gulf of Tonkin incident.

Did Johnson plan to escalate once elected? Like Kennedy, Johnson hoped that Saigon would be able to win its own war. During the election campaign neither he nor his advisers knew for sure exactly what to do about Vietnam, but most were reluctantly concluding that escalation was the only answer. He concentrated first on winning the election. Having won, he believed that he had a popular mandate to do as he saw fit.

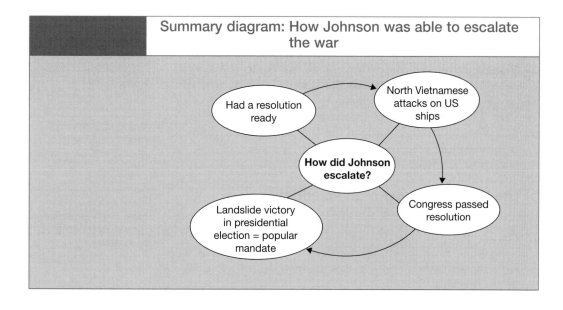

Summary diagram: How Johnson was able to escalate the war

3 | Why Did Johnson Escalate the American Involvement in Vietnam?

Key question
How did the performance of the Saigon government lead Johnson to escalate?

Some people believe that Johnson's personality made escalation inevitable. He could be combative, arrogant and overconfident. However, generalisations about Johnson's character are probably unhelpful. Sometimes there was fear and uncertainty behind his confident bluster. Privately and frequently he admitted that he did not know what to do about Vietnam. More often than not, he responded to advice and the pressure of events.

a) The incompetence of the Saigon government

Dates for South Vietnamese governments	
July 1954 to November 1963	– Diem
November 1963 to January 1964	– General Minh
January 1964 to February 1965	– General Khanh
February 1965 to June 1965	– Dr Quat
June 1965 to September 1967	– Air Vice-Marshal Ky
September 1967 to April 1975	– Thieu

One major cause of escalation was that the Saigon regime was obviously not winning the war. Ambassador Lodge (see pages 127–9) had had enough by late 1964. All he could suggest was that America should be prepared to run South Vietnam! In order to please the JCS, Johnson replaced him with General Maxwell Taylor. However, the situation demanded a real diplomat, not an impatient soldier. In December 1964 Taylor summoned the Saigon generals to the US embassy: 'Do all of you understand English? I told you all clearly at General Westmoreland's dinner that we Americans were tired of coups. Apparently I wasted my words … Now you have made a real mess. We cannot carry you forever if you do things like this.'

Back in Washington, Dean Rusk said, 'Somehow we must change the pace at which these people move, and I suspect that this can only be done with a pervasive intrusion of Americans into their affairs.'

So, the consensus among Johnson's advisers was that something must be done, especially when the Vietcong seemed able to strike at will at Americans in South Vietnam. In November 1964, 100 Vietcong had attacked and greatly damaged a US airbase near Saigon. The JCS demanded retaliatory air strikes on North Vietnam. These Vietcong attacks, which the Saigon regime seemed powerless to halt, nudged the Johnson administration towards escalation. It seemed necessary for the safety of Americans in Vietnam.

Working Group
A group of experts brought together by President Johnson to study Vietnam and make suggestions for future policies in autumn 1964.

Key term

Working Group recommended escalation: November 1964

Key date

b) The Working Group recommendations

Key question
How did the Working Group lead Johnson to escalate?

Johnson ordered a **Working Group** from the Defence Department, the State Department, the CIA and the JCS to study Vietnam and suggest policy options. The Working Group:

- said an independent and anti-Communist South Vietnam was vital to America

- reiterated the domino theory
- said that American 'national prestige, credibility, and honour' were at stake
- emphasised that escalation was necessary due to the weak Saigon government, which was 'close to a standstill' and 'plagued by confusion, apathy, and poor morale'
- suggested heavier bombing, to be halted only if North Vietnam would negotiate. US terms should be the continued existence of a non-Communist South Vietnamese government.

Thus, although Johnson is blamed for the escalation, most of those whom David Halberstam (see page 147) bitterly called 'the best and the brightest' were behind him. Johnson was commander-in-chief and his military and civilian experts were urging escalation in the interests of national security. Congress and the public seemed to be supportive.

Key question
Was there any opposition to Johnson's Vietnam policy?

Dissenting voices

An influential minority regretted that insignificant little Vietnam had taken on such disproportionate significance. George Ball (see page 125) wanted to concentrate on containing Communism in Europe. He warned Johnson that the more America got involved in Vietnam, the harder it would be to get out, and that the American public would not continue to support the war for long. Ball saw no point in bombing a country with a primarily agricultural economy, with industrial needs served by China and the USSR. Bombing the jungle in search of Vietcong would be like seeking needles in a haystack. He felt that American soldiers were ineffective in Asiatic jungles and an increasing American presence was no substitute for good government in Saigon. He feared that while perseverance proved America's reliability as an ally, it also suggested lack of judgement. He worried about worldwide reaction to a superpower bombing a tiny Asiatic state. Both he and Mansfield (see page 102) feared Chinese involvement.

Like Lodge before him, Ambassador Taylor warned that once American forces were committed, more would have to be sent in to protect them. He rightly forecast that white Americans would fight no better than the French in Asian jungles and that Americans would be unable to distinguish between a Vietcong and a friendly Vietnamese farmer. He feared that Americans would look like colonialists and conquerors and discredit any nationalist credentials of the Saigon regime.

Mansfield foresaw thousands of US soldiers going to Vietnam, thereby alienating Congress and world opinion. He rightly pointed out that sending in American ground troops was the way to keep Moscow and Beijing involved. Soviet-designed anti-aircraft defences were already bringing down many American planes.

c) Defending American bomber bases with 'Rolling Thunder'

In early 1965 Johnson took the first great escalatory step, when he began large-scale and continuous bombing in Vietnam.

The immediate trigger for the escalation in 1965 was concern over the security of US bomber bases and personnel. On Christmas Eve 1964 Vietcong (wearing South Vietnamese army uniforms bought on the black market) planted a bomb in a bar frequented by American officers. Not wanting any dramatic escalation at Christmas, Johnson did nothing, but in February 1965, the VC attacked a huge American camp near Pleiku. Eight Americans were killed and 100 were wounded. Johnson was furious: 'I've had enough of this'. The pressure from his advisers was great. Even Ball urged retaliation.

Johnson ordered massively increased air attacks on North Vietnam. America now moved beyond occasional air-raid reprisals to a limited air war against carefully selected parts of North Vietnam. Such was the intensity of the air strikes that by March they were known as '**Rolling Thunder**'. Sixty-seven per cent of Americans approved. Bombing the routes taking men and materials to the South would hopefully secure the position of Americans in South Vietnam, decrease infiltration from the North, demoralise Hanoi, and revitalise Saigon where there was some strong middle- and upper-class pressure for negotiations with Hanoi and an end to the bombing.

In February 1965 the *New York Times* said, 'It is time to call a spade a bloody shovel. This country is in an undeclared and unexplained war in Vietnam.' However, Johnson refused to declare war, because he feared extreme Cold Warriors would want to go all out, which would jeopardise the financing of the **Great Society** and lead to increased Soviet or Chinese involvement. 'Think about 200 million Chinese coming down those trails', said Johnson. 'No sir! I don't want to fight them.'

d) Defending American bomber bases with American troops

i) The reasons for sending in ground troops

In spring 1965 Johnson made his second great escalatory step when he sent large numbers of American **ground troops** to Vietnam, in response to a request from General Westmoreland. William Westmoreland had commanded the 16,000 US 'advisers' in Vietnam since June 1964. In spring 1965 he requested US marines be brought in to protect the vital US bomber base at Danang.

Westmoreland's request triggered the escalation. However, as has been seen (pages 135–45), there were many other reasons that help to explain Johnson's action.

ii) Ground troops arrive in Vietnam

The first 3500 marines landed at Danang beach on 8 March 1965, cheered by pretty Vietnamese girls in a welcome arranged by the US Navy. On 6 April 1965 Johnson approved an increase

Key question
Why did Johnson take the first great escalatory step?

Key dates

Vietcong attacked Saigon bar full of US officers: 24 December 1964

Vietcong attacked huge US airbase near Pleiku: February 1965

'Rolling Thunder' began: March 1965

Key terms

'Rolling Thunder'
Heavy, often non-stop US bombing of Vietnam.

Great Society
Johnson hoped to decrease American economic and racial inequality.

Ground troops
In March 1965, President Johnson sent the first few thousand regular soldiers (rather than just 'advisers') to Vietnam.

Key question
Why did Johnson take his second great escalatory step?

Key dates

First American ground troops landed in Vietnam: March 1965

Congress voted $700 million for war in Vietnam: May 1965

of over 18,000 American support forces to keep his soldiers supplied. He also sent in more marines. Privately, he said he wanted to avoid 'publicity' and 'minimise any appearance of sudden changes in policy'.

iii) Support for sending in ground troops

Many accuse Johnson of waging war without a declaration of war. Was it Johnson's undeclared war? Congress supportively granted $700 million for military operations in Vietnam in May 1965. Johnson told them that this was no routine grant: it was a vote to continue opposing Communism in Vietnam. The House of Representatives voted 408 to 7 and the Senate 88 to 3 in favour. As yet, the majority of American journalists were also hawks, even those like David Halberstam who later became bitterly anti-war. When Vietnam is called 'Johnson's War', this support from Congress and the press at the time of massive escalation should be remembered.

iv) Johnson's explanation of the escalation

In a speech in April 1965, Johnson summed up the reasons why the United States had to escalate its commitment to Vietnam:

- The US needed to fight if it wanted to live securely in a free world.
- North Vietnam, an aggressive nation that had attacked South Vietnam, needed to be opposed.
- North Vietnam was a puppet of the expansionist Communist powers, the USSR and China.
- The USSR and the People's Republic of China wanted to conquer all of Asia.
- Eisenhower and Kennedy had helped to build and defend South Vietnam: it would be dishonourable to abandon it.
- Abandonment of South Vietnam would cause all America's allies to doubt America's word and credibility.
- Appeasement could lead to a Third World War.

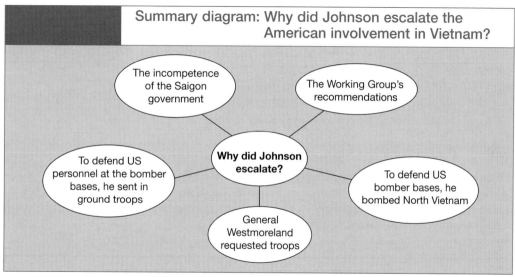

Summary diagram: Why did Johnson escalate the American involvement in Vietnam?

4 | 'Where Are We Going?'

a) Deterioration in Saigon

Johnson had hoped that the arrival of American troops would help to protect the bomber bases and improve the position of the Saigon regime. However, the situation in Vietnam continued to deteriorate.

In June 1965 the civilian government of Phan Huy Quat was overthrown by the military. General Thieu became head of state and Air Vice-Marshal Nguyen Cao Ky became prime minister – 'absolutely the bottom of the barrel', said one Johnson adviser.

Ky drank, gambled and womanised. He said Vietnam needed men like Hitler. Ky had been commander of South Vietnam's air force. He was a flamboyant figure, fond of purple jumpsuits, pearl-handled revolvers and dark sunglasses. Not surprisingly, under the incompetent, corrupt and unpopular Ky and Thieu, the Saigon government controlled less of South Vietnam and controlled it less effectively.

b) More American troops

In 1965 Ky's government was losing control of territory to the Vietcong who, according to Thieu, had 75 per cent of the countryside. As Taylor had feared, the more American troops poured in, the less the ARVN wanted to fight. As usual, Westmoreland demanded more American troops to prevent South Vietnam's collapse and to protect the American troops already there. In cabinet meetings throughout July, Johnson expressed

Key question
What was the immediate impact of the escalation?

Ky became leader of South Vietnam: June 1965

Johnson announced sending 50,000 more troops to South Vietnam: July 1965

Key dates

Profile: Nguyen Van Thieu 1923–2001

1923	– Born in Vietnam, son of a small landowner
1945	– Joined Vietminh, but switched sides and fought for the French colonialist regime
1956	– Served in Diem regime in South Vietnam
1963	– Played important part in successful coup against Diem
1965	– Became head of state in military government headed by Ky
1967	– Elected president under a new constitution; supported by USA
1971	– Re-elected without opposition
1973	– Felt betrayed by US in peace settlement with North Vietnam, after which US troops left South Vietnam
1975	– As Communist forces took over Saigon, resigned, and fled
2001	– Died in the USA

Thieu is perhaps as important as, and certainly similar to, Diem in the context of the US involvement in Vietnam. Like Diem, Thieu was incompetent, supported by the US in his several-year rule in South Vietnam, and dropped when it suited the Americans.

Wearing matching flight suits and scarves, Nguyen Cao Ky strolls hand-in-hand with his wife as they make an inspection tour of a battlefield.

Profile: Nguyen Cao Ky 1930–

1930	–	Born in northern Vietnam
1940s	–	Member of the French colonialist forces that opposed Vietnamese nationalists
1954	–	Joined South Vietnamese air force; Americans liked his bravado and anti-Communist attitude
1963	–	After Diem's death, became commander of South Vietnamese air force; with US help, built air force up to 10,000 men
1965 June	–	With Thieu and 'Big' Minh, led military coup against Premier Quat. Unpopular, due to authoritarianism
1967	–	Military leaders agreed Thieu should be president and Ky his vice-president
1975	–	When South Vietnam fell to Communism, fled to USA

Like Thieu, Ky was supported by the US when he was president of South Vietnam, lacked ability and was unpopular with his people.

doubts about the usefulness of sending more American troops. Nevertheless, on 28 July 1965, at noon when TV audiences were minimal, he announced that Westmoreland had asked for more men to meet mounting Communist aggression and that his needs would be met: 'We will stand in Vietnam'. The 75,000 troops in Vietnam would be increased to 125,000. Congressional leaders had given their assent the day before.

During 1965, polls and White House mail showed that:

- 70 per cent of the nation was behind Johnson
- 80 per cent believed in the domino theory
- 80 per cent favoured sending American soldiers to stop South Vietnam falling
- 47 per cent wanted Johnson to send in even more troops.

Clearly, Johnson was supported by the majority of Americans in his Vietnam policy. By the end of 1965 nearly 200,000 American soldiers were in Vietnam.

On the rare occasions that these American troops faced regular Communist soldiers (rather than guerrillas), they gave a very good account of themselves. In October 1965, for example, American troops defeated North Vietnamese regulars at the Battle of Ia Drang (see pages 168–9).

c) Doubts

As has been seen, not everyone was sure that this further escalation was the right answer. Protests had begun in the universities in March 1965 (see page 186). On hearing that a plane had been shot down, Johnson himself cried, 'Where are we going?' He confessed that hawkish General Curtis LeMay 'scares the hell out of me'.

A December 1965 bombing halt failed to persuade Hanoi to negotiate and a cabinet meeting showed the lack of consensus within the administration. George Ball thought the situation hopeless. Taylor and the CIA opposed sending more US troops. McNamara felt that military victory was unlikely. The JCS were divided over tactics. 'Tell me this', said Johnson to the JCS chairman, 'what will happen if we put in 100,000 more men and then two, three years later, you tell me we need 500,000 more? ... And what makes you think that Ho Chi Minh won't put in another 100, and match us every bit of the way?'

Johnson knew all the dangers. He was uncertain that America could win, but certain that it could not get out without irreparable damage to his own and his country's position. As American soldiers poured into Vietnam, the administration and military could not agree on what they should be doing there. Most, however, agreed that they *should* be there. This was not just 'Johnson's War'.

Key dates

First anti-war protests in American universities: 1965

Johnson asked, 'Where are we going?': October 1965

Over 200,000 American troops in Vietnam: December 1965

d) Escalation, 1965–8

Despite their doubts about the competence of the Ky/Thieu regime, General Westmoreland, the JCS and McNamara all agreed that the number of American troops in South Vietnam

War of attrition
Westmoreland
believed that US
numerical and
technological
superiority would
wear down the
Vietcong who must,
after losing a
certain number of
men, finally decide
to give up.

should be increased in the second half of 1965. McNamara did not claim that this would bring victory, but it would 'stave off defeat in the short run and offer a good chance of producing a favourable settlement in the longer run'.

Thus, by the end of 1965, around 200,000 American soldiers bore the burden of the fighting in South Vietnam, while US planes bombed both North Vietnam and South Vietnam. By the end of 1966, there were 385,000, and by early 1968, 535,000 American troops in South Vietnam. Westmoreland had initially believed that he could end the Communist insurgency within six months, but his strategy of a **war of attrition**, using technology and firepower, failed to wear down the enemy.

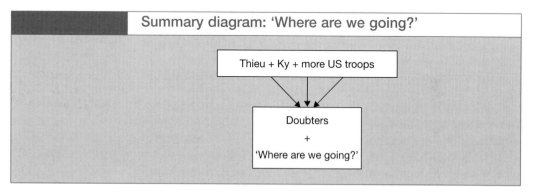

Summary diagram: 'Where are we going?'

Thieu + Ky + more US troops

Doubters
+
'Where are we going?'

5 | Was it 'Johnson's War'?

Key question
Who bore
responsibility for the
escalation of US
involvement?

In some ways it seemed as if it was 'Johnson's War'. He made the decision to continue Kennedy's commitment and then to escalate. He ordered each escalatory step, first 'Rolling Thunder', then the sending of increasing numbers of American troops.

On the other hand, others shared the responsibility. Johnson had inherited a strong commitment to South Vietnam from his predecessors with whose Cold War ideas he agreed. In the circumstances of his accession to the presidency, it would have been particularly difficult for him to disengage America from Vietnam, even had he been so inclined. He felt bound to continue Kennedy's policies and keep Kennedy's advisers.

When Johnson escalated American involvement in Vietnam dramatically, his military and civilian advisers shared responsibility for his policies. He always liked to claim that his responsibility had been shared with Congress and the public and there was a lot of truth in what he said: they *were* clearly supportive of his Vietnam policies early in his presidency. A December 1965 poll showed that a large majority of Americans favoured increasing American troops to 500,000 men. Johnson's biographer Vaughn Davis Bornet, while critical of the president's policies, reminds us that:

Poll showed most
Americans were pro-
escalation: December
1965

535,000 US troops in
South Vietnam: 1968

> If Vietnam did not ultimately go well, in a democratic republic like the United States one must look at the Congress and the people themselves, for three national elections were held during the Johnson years.

6 | Key Debates

No historians dispute that Johnson massively escalated the US commitment in Vietnam. However, there is great disagreement over the amount of control he had over the process, and why he escalated to such an extent.

a) How much control did Johnson have over the escalation process?

Some historians (for example, Burke and Greenstein, 1989) have contended that Lyndon Johnson dominated policy-making.

Herring (1979) admitted that Johnson's impatient character was not ideally suited to complex counter-insurgency warfare in Vietnam, but warned against overemphasis on the president's personality, describing Johnson as almost pathologically unable to make a decision, and cautious and reluctant in escalation. On that latter point, VanDeMark (1991) and Barrett (1993) agree.

Many historians are critical of Johnson's advisers and President Kennedy. McMaster accuses the JCS of dishonesty (1997). Kennard (1991) similarly accuses Kennedy and Maxwell Taylor. Di Leo (1991) blames George Ball's careerist ambitions for his ineffective challenges to Vietnam policy.

Yuen Foong Khong (1992) found Johnson and his advisers obsessed with lessons they thought they had learned from history, but Khong and others are convinced that the wrong lessons were learned: Ho Chi Minh was not Hitler. Universal ignorance of Vietnam was admitted by Robert McNamara in his memoirs (1995).

Historians agree that Johnson's domestic programme of social reform was his main interest, and Berman (1989) and Kearns (1976) emphasised that he felt he had to appear tough on foreign policy to stop conservatives defeating his domestic plans. There is considerable unanimity on this depiction of Lyndon Johnson as one who wanted to ensure the survival of South Vietnam, but who wanted to avoid a Third World War and the end of his Great Society dreams. Schmitz (2005) saw Johnson as a victim of the commitment trap (see page 110): 'All the logic and rationale of the Cold War and containment called for escalation.'

b) Did Johnson lie about the Gulf of Tonkin incident?

Sometimes, historical research can alter interpretations, and Anderson (2005) cites the Gulf of Tonkin incident as an excellent example. Early studies (for example, Windchy, 1971) based on congressional hearings and other public sources concluded that Johnson deceived Congress and the public about North Vietnamese attacks on US ships. However, Moise (1996) looked at declassified documents and found that the administration genuinely believed that there had been two attacks on American destroyers.

c) Are most historians' interpretations of Johnson's policies unsympathetic?

Many historians are highly unsympathetic to Johnson and his choices. Kahin (1986) criticised Eisenhower, Kennedy and Johnson for outright rejection of the idea of a **neutralised Vietnam**. Gelb and Betts (1979), like other 'stalemate theory' historians, say Johnson and his advisers knew the prospects were poor, but kept escalating lest they appeared weak. Logevall (1999) emphasised how Johnson rejected the idea of a negotiated settlement in 1964 and in 1965, and guessed that Kennedy would have chosen negotiation.

Key term

Neutralised Vietnam Some contemporaries advocated taking Vietnam out of the Cold War context and allowing it to decide its own future, without influence or input from Moscow, Beijing or Washington, DC.

Some key books in the debates

D. Anderson, *The Vietnam War* (Palgrave Macmillan, 2003).

D. Barrett, *Uncertain Warriors: Lyndon Johnson and his Vietnam Advisers* (Kansas, 1993).

L. Berman, *Lyndon Johnson's War* (New York, 1989).

J.P. Burke and F.I. Greenstein, *How Presidents Test Reality* (New York, 1989).

D. Di Leo, *George Ball, Vietnam and the Rethinking of Containment* (North Carolina, 1991).

L. Gelb and R.K. Betts, *The Irony of Vietnam* (Washington DC, 1979).

G. Herring, *America's Longest War* (New York, 1979).

G.M. Kahin, *Intervention: How America Became Involved in Vietnam* (New York, 1986).

D. Kearns, *Lyndon Johnson and the American Dream* (1976).

D. Kennard, *The Certain Trumpet: Maxwell Taylor and the American Experience in Vietnam* (Washington DC, 1991).

Yuen Foong Khong, *Analogies at War* (Princeton, 1992).

F. Logevall, *Choosing War* (1999).

H.R. McMaster, *Dereliction of Duty* (New York, 1997).

R. McNamara, *In Retrospect* (New York, 1995).

E. Moise, *Tonkin Gulf and the Escalation of the Vietnam War* (North Carolina, 1996).

D. Schmitz, *The Tet Offensive* (Lanham, 2005).

R.D. Schulzinger, *A Companion to American Foreign Relations* (Oxford, 2003).

B. VanDeMark, *Into the Quagmire: Lyndon Johnson and the Escalation of the Vietnam War* (New York, 1991).

E. Windchy, *Tonkin Gulf* (New York, 1971).

Study Guide: AS Questions

In the style of AQA

(a) Explain why the American Congress passed the Gulf of Tonkin resolution in August 1964. (12 marks)

(b) 'Johnson alone bears the responsibility for the escalation of war in Vietnam in the years 1965–8.' Explain why you agree or disagree with this statement. (24 marks)

Exam tips

The cross-references are intended to take you straight to the material that will help you to answer the questions.

(a) You should re-read pages 135–40 and 141–2 before answering this question. You are required to provide a range of reasons here and it would be helpful to think of long- and short-term factors in your answer. In the short term, the resolution was passed because of attacks on American shipping in the Gulf (pages 141–2). However, the longer term reasons are connected with the USA's commitment to support South Vietnam against the Communist North Vietnamese and President Johnson's personal decision to increase US involvement so as not to be the first president to lose a war (pages 135–40). It would also be helpful to refer to the public doubts that had to be appeased, and in your conclusion you might consider whether Johnson had merely been looking for an excuse. Try to offer some personal judgement on the relative importance of the factors you cite.

(b) The dates here direct you specifically to developments during Johnson's presidency, but to answer this question successfully you will need to consider other reasons for the escalation of war at this time and this would include some outline of the scale of US commitment before this date and consideration of whether the Americans could have ever avoided the increasing commitment of these years. You might like to begin with Johnson's own explanation of the escalation (page 147) and then move on to assessing Johnson's responsibility by evaluating:

- longer term and personal influences on Johnson (pages 135 and 137–8)
- the Kennedy inheritance (pages 137–9)
- Johnson and his advisers (pages 138–9) and the debates, doubts and opponents (pages 139–40 and 145)
- the importance of the Tonkin resolution and the presidential election (pages 141–3)
- the incompetence of the Saigon government and the Working Group recommendations (pages 144–5)
- concerns over the security of US bomber bases (pages 146–7).

Try to offer thoughtful and balanced comments and do remember that Johnson never had complete control and that others shared responsibility. The historiographical debate on this issue is provided on pages 151–3. Read this carefully before you begin so that you are able to offer a fair appraisal and appropriate conclusion.

In the style of Edexcel

How accurate is it to say that the USA increased its involvement in Vietnam in the period 1954–64 primarily for ideological reasons? (30 marks)

Exam tips

The cross-references are intended to take you straight to the material that will help you to answer the question.

Examiners frequently ask why the US got involved and escalated that involvement. Sometimes they simply ask 'why?' Sometimes they suggest one reason why, and ask you to debate whether that specified factor is crucial. Perhaps most difficult to answer is the question where two factors are specified and you are asked to pick the one that you consider more important.

For all three types of question you need to know why the United States got increasingly involved. When preparing an essay on this you should think of it either in terms of topical paragraphs or in chronological paragraphs.

The chronological approach would cover the motives of Eisenhower, Kennedy and Johnson:

- Eisenhower: anti-Communism, domino theory, rollback, Asia-firsters, French exit (pages 95–7 and 104).
- Kennedy: as Eisenhower, adding commitment trap, memories of Republican attacks on Truman for his 'loss of China', youth and inexperience, Cuba and Laos, advisers (pages 115–22).
- Johnson: as Eisenhower and Kennedy, adding Kennedy legacy, 'first president to lose a war', stalemate theory (pages 110, 135–9 and 141–3).

However, chronologically organised answers can degenerate into description. In order to show off your analytical skills, it is better to use thematic or topical paragraphs. Thematic paragraphs will certainly be needed for this question, where you are asked to weigh the significance of the stated factor 'ideological reasons' against other factors which drew the USA into the conflict. Your paragraph topics for both factors would probably be:

- anti-Communism (pages 96, 104, 115 and 135)
- domino theory (pages 97, 115, 130 and 135)
- French exit (page 104)
- domestic politics (pages 97, 115, 126, 130 and 143)
- president's personal position (pages 97, 117–19, 121–2 and 137–9)
- commitment trap and stalemate theory (pages 109–10 and 130).

Although you will encounter many different questions essentially asking you to explain US involvement in Vietnam, it is important not to approach this sort of question thinking that you will always be able simply to write out exactly the same six paragraphs on why the USA became involved in the war. Essentially you will always be selecting from the same bank of material, but a good essay writing technique involves the organising of that material to meet a particular question. For this question you should devote about a third of your answer to 'ideological reasons' since they are your given stated factor. Note that the first two bullet points above relate to ideological reasons – be careful to make that clear.

In order to gain high marks you need to weigh up the relative importance of these factors against each other, and to decide on which is or which are the most important, giving persuasive arguments for your choice. But your reading of Chapters 4, 5, 6 and 7 will have shown you that historians are themselves divided over the reasons for US involvement. There is not a 'right' answer here. It is a real opportunity for you to decide which factor seems more significant to you.

In the style of OCR

(a) Compare Sources A and B as evidence for the problems faced by South Vietnam.   (30 marks)
(b) Using your own knowledge, assess how far the sources support the interpretation that the *main* reason America began and continued its involvement in Vietnam was to defend democracy.   (70 marks)

Source A

From a letter from Dwight Eisenhower, 23 October 1954.
The American president writes to Ngo Dinh Diem, the president of the Republic of South Vietnam, expressing his support for the new South Vietnamese government.

Dear Mr President: I have been following with great interest the developments in Vietnam, particularly since the conclusion of the Geneva conference. The implications of the agreement concerning Vietnam have caused grave concern regarding the future of a country temporarily divided by an artificial military grouping, weakened by a long, exhausting war and faced with external enemies and internal collaborators. We have fulfilled your recent requests for aid in the formidable task of moving several hundred thousand loyal Vietnamese citizens away from areas ruled by a Communist ideology they hate. I am glad that the United States is able to assist in this humanitarian effort.

Source B

From a programme of the National Liberation Front of South Vietnam, January 1962. A statement of the goals of the NLF, the united front that brought together Communists and non-Communists to liberate Vietnam from foreign control.

The present South Vietnamese regime is a camouflaged colonial regime dominated by the Yankees, and the South Vietnamese government is a servile government, implementing faithfully all the policies of the American imperialists. Therefore, this regime must be overthrown and a government of national and democratic union put in its place composed of representatives of all social classes, of all nationalities, of various political parties, of all religions; patriotic, eminent citizens must take over for the people the control of economic, political, social, and cultural interests and thus bring about independence, democracy, well-being, peace, neutrality, and efforts toward the peaceful unification of the country.

Source C

From a statement by President de Gaulle, 23 July 1964. At his tenth press conference in Paris the French president expresses his views on American policy in Vietnam.

Vietnam was shocked by the withdrawal of French administration and forces. The south was exposed to new perils by the existence of a Communist state in Tonkin, from where our troops withdrew. It tried to find, in itself, a solid national government. It was then that the Americans arrived, bringing their aid, their policy and their authority. The United States considered itself the worldwide defender against Communism. The regime established in the north aimed to impose itself also in South Vietnam, and America wanted to help this state to protect itself. Also, without intending to criticise, the American conviction of fulfilling a sort of vocation, their disapproval of other countries' colonialism, and the natural desire among such a powerful people to expand, made the Americans determined to take our place in Indochina.

Source D

From a speech by Lyndon Johnson in 1965. The US president explains why the USA continued to be involved in Vietnam.

We have a promise to keep. Since 1954 every American president has offered support to the people of South Vietnam. We have helped to build and defend its independence. To dishonour that promise and abandon this small, brave nation to its enemies, and the terror that must follow, would be an unforgivable wrong. We are also there to strengthen world order. Around the globe are people whose well-being rests partly on believing they can count on us if attacked. To leave Vietnam to its fate would shake these people's confidence in the value of America's word. Let no one think for a moment that retreat from Vietnam would bring an end to conflict. The battle would be renewed in one country and then another. The appetite of aggression is never satisfied. In Southeast Asia, as we did in Europe, we must follow the words of the Bible: 'Hitherto shalt thou come, but no further.'

Exam tips

The cross-references are intended to take you straight to the material that will help you to answer the questions.

(a) This question asks you to compare two sources as evidence by using their content and provenance to explain your answer to the question. Focus clearly on '*problems* faced by South Vietnam' and make it the heart of your answer. A true comparison needs sustained cross-reference of the two sources point by point, not one source after the other. Your answer should be balanced, and references to context are only valuable in helping you compare the sources.

Provenance:

- Authors and dates: subjective, national and ideological. Source A: Eisenhower, American attitudes in 1954 (pages 104–6); Source B: Vietnamese attitudes in 1962 in the Kennedy era (page 124).
- Nature, purpose, style. Source A: official, impersonal, self-congratulatory in justifying American policy to solve problems (pages 104–6); Source B: secret war plans, summarising aims to solve a broader range of political, cultural and social problems (page 126).

Textual content on problems faced by South Vietnam:

- Points of agreement on problems: disunity, external enemies and internal collaborators (of which the authors of Source B are an example), military activity.
- Points of disagreement: hatred of militant Communism in Source A versus American imperialism in Source B; external enemies seen as North Vietnam (and implicitly foreign Communists) in Source A, versus the USA in Source B; subsidiary role of the USA in aiding Diem to solve problems in Source A versus servile Diem government and US intervention itself as key problems in Source B.

(b) This question asks you to use your own knowledge and *all four* sources to create a balanced argument evaluating the interpretation in the question. Focus clearly on '*reasons* why America began and continued its involvement in Vietnam' during the period covered by the sources.

The sources should drive your answer, and your factual knowledge should be used to support and exemplify the points in your argument.

There will be one reason given in the question, and your first task is to evaluate it. Group the sources by their side of the argument: Sources A and D support the interpretation, whereas Sources B and C refute it. Use factual knowledge to exemplify and discuss each point. Suggest a range of other reasons, picking up the clues in the sources. Cross-reference phrases across the sources and use them to argue a case for and against the view that democracy was the main reason, using factual knowledge to develop and explain your points (Chapters 4, 5, 6 and 7). Reach an evaluative judgement on the relative importance of each, at the end of each paragraph – remembering to link back to the question.

Other reasons might include:

- Imperialism (Sources B and C); humanitarian concerns (Sources A and D; pages 104–6; domestic politics (pages 117, 126, 130 and 143); presidents' personal stances (Sources A and D; pages 97, 117, 121–2 and 137–9).
- Anti-Communism (Sources A, C and D; pages 96, 115 and 135); domino theory; rollback (Source D; page 97); French exit (Source C; page 104).
- Economics and domestic politics, including defence and moral issues (Sources C and D; pages 96, 97, 115, 135 and 141); commitment trap; 'loss of China'; and stalemate theory (Source D; page 110).

In your conclusion, link together the reasons, weigh up their relative importance and reach a supported judgement to answer the question.

8 Why the USA Failed: I – The People in Vietnam

POINTS TO CONSIDER

The second great debate about Johnson and Vietnam concerns the reasons why Johnson's America (and its South Vietnamese ally) could not defeat the Communists. Despite Johnson's dramatic escalation of the American war effort, his advisers concluded that the war was unwinnable and Johnson halted the escalation in 1968. This chapter looks at why he halted the escalation, through sections on:

• The Vietnamese
• The Americans in Vietnam
• The key debates

This chapter must be read in conjunction with the next chapter, which looks at further reasons why Johnson halted the escalation.

Key dates

1965	November	Battle of la Drang
1967	January	Americans found Communist tunnel network near Saigon
		Operation Cedar Falls
1968		Operation Phoenix
	January	Battle of Khe Sanh
	March	My Lai massacre
1969		An American company refused to fight
		Fragging began
	May	Battle of Hamburger Hill
1971	February	ARVN retreated from Laos because of heavy losses

1 | The Vietnamese

a) Winning the hearts and minds of the South Vietnamese people

i) The decisive factor

One of the main reasons the Americans could not defeat the Communists was because they were unable to win the hearts and minds of the Vietnamese people. General Giap said that Hanoi won because it waged a people's war, a total war in which every

Key question
Why were the Americans and the Saigon regime unable to win the hearts and minds of the South Vietnamese people?

An American soldier helping a South Vietnamese child in 1966.

man, woman and even child was mobilised, whether militarily or emotionally. He maintained that human beings were the decisive factor.

There were thousands of American civilian 'experts' in Vietnam during the war: doctors, school-teachers and agricultural advisers. They felt that too little was done to win the hearts and minds of the people. Understandably, the military men thought in terms of force. 'Grab 'em by the balls and their hearts and minds will follow', said the American military.

ii) Understanding the Vietnamese

Most Vietnamese were rice-growing peasants, who lived in small villages, in small mud and bamboo houses with dirt or wooden floors. The dirt paths between the houses were piled with stinking human and animal ordure for fertilising the fields. There was neither running water nor electricity. American soldiers could not conceive of 'real' people living like this, which goes a little way towards explaining why Americans sometimes treated the Vietnamese peasants as sub-human (see page 163) and were consequently unable to win many of them over to their side.

Maxwell Taylor admitted years later that Americans never really knew or understood any of the Vietnamese. When Thieu told Johnson that the Communists would win any South Vietnamese elections. Johnson's response was significant: 'I don't believe that. Does anyone believe that?' Johnson never really understood what motivated Ho and his armies. In April 1965 he promised Ho economic aid if he would stop the war: 'Old Ho can't turn that down'. Johnson did not seem to understand that Ho was fighting for a united Communist Vietnam and would not compromise. The North Vietnamese knew why they fought and were willing to wait, suffer and persevere to achieve their aims in a way that many Americans and South Vietnamese were not. Naturally, the Vietnamese Communists understood their fellow countryman.

The peasants had always been used to struggling to provide sufficient food for their families, and this had led to an emphasis upon collective discipline and endeavour. Harvesting was best approached communally, so many villages adapted with relative ease to the principles of Communism. The Communists worked hard to win over the peasantry, offering them a fairer distribution of land and urging Communist soldiers to avoid the rape and pillage characteristic of the ARVN.

iii) Carrot and stick

Although the Communists were generally better at winning the hearts and minds of the peasantry, they were ruthless when necessary. During the 1968 Tet Offensive (see pages 182–3), the Vietcong dragged 'unfriendly' people out of their houses in Hue and shot them, clubbed them to death or buried them alive. Over 3000 bodies were found in the river or jungle. A judicious mixture of ruthlessness and frequent good behaviour gained the Vietcong the sullen acquiescence or support of the peasants that was vital in guerrilla warfare. Giap's strategy was to use the Vietcong for incessant guerrilla warfare to wear down Saigon and its American allies, while the PAVN would only fight conventional set-piece battles at times and places when it was sufficiently strong. Villagers often gave them the food, shelter and hiding places necessary for survival. Greater success in winning peasant hearts and minds or simply peasant acquiescence helps to explain why the Communists defeated Washington and Saigon.

> **Key dates**
>
> Operation Phoenix: 1968
>
> My Lai massacre: March 1968

iv) 'They are all VC'

The circumstances of the war tended to make American soldiers dislike the people they were supposed to be helping, which then made it very difficult to win the war. In 1965 some marines were supposed to search hamlets for VC and dispense food and medical care, but one marine recalled how the villages were often Vietcong, and so the marines would treat the villagers badly, 'and if they weren't pro-Vietcong before we got there, they sure as hell were by the time we left'. Another marine recalled, 'Our emotions were very low because we'd lost a lot of friends', so when his unit

Vietnamese villagers lie dead after the massacre at My Lai, 16 March 1968.

entered a village suspecting of supporting the VC, 'we gave it to them … whatever was moving was going to move no more'.

The most famous, but by no means the only, example of American hatred of the Vietnamese was the massacre at apparently pro-Communist My Lai on 16 March 1968. Three hundred and forty-seven unarmed civilians were beaten and killed by American soldiers and their officers: old men, women, teenagers and even babies. Women were beaten with rifle butts, raped and shot. Water buffalo, pigs and chickens were shot then dropped in wells to poison the water.

War inevitably bred brutality. In 1968 the CIA introduced a system codenamed 'Operation Phoenix', whereby tens of thousands of VC were sought out and interrogated. Few taken for interrogation came out alive. Torture was the norm.

v) The American high-tech war

American technology created formidable new fighting weapons, such as the cluster bombs, which the Vietnamese called 'mother bombs' because after exploding in mid-air they released 350–600 baby bombs. Each one exploded on impact into thousands of metal pellets. Later, fibreglass replaced the metal; X-rays could not detect fibreglass, so it was harder and more painful to remove. American bombing forced many peasants to move away from the homes, crops and ancestral graves which meant so much to them.

Ironically, American firepower was concentrated more on South than North Vietnam. The dependent Saigon regime was unlikely to complain. In their search for VC the Americans killed and wounded tens of thousands of civilians who might or might not have been Communist sympathisers. When asked about civilian casualties Westmoreland agreed it was a problem, 'but it does deprive the enemy of the population, doesn't it? They are Asians who don't think about death the way we do.'

Neither the American army nor the ARVN would take responsibility for wounded civilians, who were left to get what (if any) primitive medical care was available. Bombing obliterated five towns with populations over 10,000, and many villages. Some civilians lived like moles in caves and tunnels, emerging to work but ready to go back down when planes appeared. Children were kept down for days at a time.

From 1962 Agent Orange was used to defoliate South Vietnam's jungles so that the enemy could be more easily seen, and to kill the rice crops that were partly used for feeding the VC. Bombs and chemicals best suited American technological superiority, wealth and reluctance to lose American lives, but they were not the way to win this war: these methods alienated friendly and neutral Vietnamese and Americans themselves, contributing greatly to American failure in Vietnam. It was not surprising that the Communists controlled most of the countryside, as the JCS admitted in February 1968. In 1995 McNamara wrote that the administration was wrong to allow an arrogant American military to attempt a high-tech war of attrition against a primarily guerrilla force willing to absorb massive casualties, in a state like

One of the most famous photos of the war: 10-year-old Kim Phuc (centre) ran away from her village, badly burned by napalm dropped from American bombers in 1972.

South Vietnam which lacked the political stability and popularity necessary to conduct effective military and pacification operations.

vi) Life in Saigon

Incessant fighting and bombing drove roughly one-third of South Vietnam's peasant population out of the countryside into the towns and cities. Many were put up in camps where primitive sanitation bred disease. Many lived off Americans, particularly in Saigon. Mid-twentieth-century Saigon was a strange and lovely mixture of Southeast Asia and provincial France, with tree-shaded streets, lined with quiet shops and sleepy pavement cafés and beautiful villas with lush tropical gardens of scented jasmine and purple and red bougainvillaea.

   Saigon became an unsavoury city in the American war years. Drugs were sold in its bars. Many hotels were brothels. The streets were awash with black-market goods, American soldiers, orphans, cripples, beggars and 56,000 registered prostitutes. The beggars targeted 'rich' Americans, tugging at them and making crying sounds. Limbless Vietnamese victims of the war crawled along crab-like, seeking handouts from Americans.

American GIs with their Vietnamese girlfriends.

The war had destroyed the social fabric of South Vietnam, uprooting peasants to the cities and dividing families. Poor peasant girls who turned to prostitution dismayed their families, despite earning more in a week than the whole family did in a year. American dollars distorted the economy. The salary of the lowest ranking American was gigantic by Vietnamese standards. Taxi drivers would not stop for other Vietnamese if it was possible to be hailed by an American. Vietnamese professionals lost status and influence in this new dollar-dominated world. Doctors earned less than waiters who served big-tipping Americans. Garbage and sewage disposal suffered as municipal workers sought higher wages working for Americans. On one pavement pile of rat-covered garbage was a sign: 'this is the fruit of American aid'. One Vietnamese nun told an American relief worker that Vietnam was a beautiful country 'until *you* arrived'.

Saigon was full of Vietnamese and American officials. There was much talk but little real communication. The Americans would put forward plans and, so long as America financed them, the Vietnamese would agree, although not necessarily co-operate. One jaundiced American official said, 'We report progress to Washington because Washington demands progress.'

vii) The Saigon government – corruption and 'democracy'
The Vietnamese peasants were often politically apathetic. Their concern was their day-to-day struggle for existence. When a leader offered ideas (especially the fairer redistribution of wealth) that might ease that struggle, many were attracted. Although Ho was greatly aided by Moscow and Beijing, their help was not as visible as American help in the South. Ho thus combined the appeal of nationalism and equality in a way that the South Vietnamese regimes never managed.

Washington talked of bringing democracy to Vietnam but the concept was meaningless to the Vietnamese who had no tradition of American-style political democracy. The strongest Vietnamese political tradition was the hatred of foreigners. What Americans insisted on seeing as a South Vietnamese state went against that most powerful tradition, for the South Vietnamese regimes were all too clearly bound up with and dependent on the American foreigners.

Ky's government was corrupt and averse to reform. During 1966–7 there were many protests in Saigon. A Buddhist nun sat cross-legged, her hands clasped in prayer, in a temple in Hue. A friend doused her with petrol. The nun lit a match to set herself alight while the friend poured peppermint oil on her to disguise the smell of burning flesh. The dead nun's letters were widely circulated; they blamed Johnson for her death because he helped the repressive Saigon regime. 'What are we doing here?' asked one American official when American marines helped Ky to attack Buddhist strongholds. 'We are fighting to save these people and they are fighting each other.'

At Johnson's insistence, Ky held democratic elections. The elections were observed by American politicians, one of whom kept calling the country 'South Vietcong'! Although Ky ran the election, his candidate for president, Thieu, still managed only 37 per cent of the vote. Not surprisingly, many South Vietnamese wanted negotiations with Hanoi.

When he fled Vietnam in April 1975, President Thieu carried away millions of dollars in gold. Some of his money came from American aid, which rarely reached the peasants for whom it was primarily intended. Much of that aid found its way into the pockets of the military and urban élites. An investigation revealed that the amount of cement supposedly needed by and given to Vietnamese officials in one year could have paved over the whole country. The endemic corruption owed much to the Vietnamese emphasis on family duty. Poorly paid officials and even the highly paid president wanted to provide well for their relations. Thieu's cousin ran a wealthy province: for a fee he would let VC out of jail or keep ARVN men out of battle.

The unpopularity of the Saigon regime was perhaps the main reason for the American failure in Vietnam.

viii) The ARVN

The corruption and mismanagement that characterised South Vietnam's government naturally permeated its armed forces.

Saigon wanted to avoid losses. In February 1971, 30,000 ARVN invaded Laos with orders to retreat if over 3000 died. They retreated, halfway to their objective (see page 214). The Americans described their own tactics as '**Search and Destroy**' but those of the ARVN as 'Search and Avoid'. Poor results damaged morale and led to further failure.

Many military leaders were appointed for political rather than military reasons. The high command spent more time fighting among themselves than against the enemy. The urban middle-class officers did not get on well with the peasants in the lower ranks. Although Buddhists constituted 80 per cent of the South Vietnamese army, they made up only five per cent of the ARVN leadership.

ARVN wages were so low that some ARVN officers pocketed the pay of thousands of deserters, sick or dead men. Lower ranks bullied and robbed the population. Some deserted to the Communists.

The ARVN were compromised in the eyes of the Vietnamese people by their association with the Americans, while Americans such as Westmoreland were frequently unwilling to use ARVN assistance because they despised them and preferred to use Americans. In Westmoreland's headquarters in Saigon there were hidden nozzles to spray his 'élite' ARVN guards with tear gas if they defected.

While the ARVN were often remarkably tenacious when cornered (many ARVN fought often and bravely, and tens of thousands of them died), generally, the morale and performance of the ARVN constitutes a major factor in explaining the defeat of the Washington–Saigon alliance.

Key date

ARVN retreated from Laos because of heavy losses: February 1971

Key term

Search and destroy
General Westmoreland's tactics included finding and killing groups of Vietcong guerrillas.

b) Communist determination, heroism and ingenuity
i) Communist determination

Key question
Why were the Communists so difficult to defeat?

Inspired by Communism and nationalism, the VC won admiration from their American foes. One American general was impressed by some besieged Communists in a bunker, who 'didn't even give up after their eardrums had burst from the concussion [from American fire-power] … and blood was pouring out of their noses'. The Vietnamese had always struggled for their existence against both nature and other, hostile peoples such as the Chinese. Continuous struggle ensured unusual patience in the face of adversity, which helps to explain Hanoi's refusal to be beaten. As Giap said:

> We were not strong enough to drive out a half million American troops, but that was not our aim. Our intention was to break the will of the American government to continue the war.

America did not understand that determination. American strategy never took it into account, and this was an important factor in the American inability to win.

ii) The Ho Chi Minh Trail

Most of Giap's men and women spent time on the **Ho Chi Minh Trail** (see the map on page 136), which came southward via Cambodia and Laos.

Ho Chi Minh Trail North Vietnamese Communist supply route going south from North Vietnam through Cambodia and Laos to South Vietnam.

Key term

Both sides knew that keeping the trail open was vital to the Communist war effort. Men and materials came south and the wounded were sent north on the trail. Giap's porters carried most of the war materiel down the trail from 1959 to 1964, then the trail was widened and sometimes even covered with asphalt to accommodate the thousands of trucks supplied by China and the USSR.

The trail was never a single route. There were several branches, along which were dotted repair workshops, stores depots, hospitals and rest camps. Around 50,000 women were employed at any one time to repair the road. If one part was damaged by American bombing, the traffic would be switched to other branches while repairs were done. Vehicles and parts of the trail were camouflaged with foliage. Giap's trails, troops and trucks melted into the landscape.

While Hanoi lost many $6000 trucks, America lost many several million-dollar bombers, which were far harder and more expensive to replace. American bombers perpetually sought to obliterate the trail but failed. The battle of the trail was a vital one, in which people could be said to have triumphed over technology.

iii) The battle of Ia Drang, 1965

In 1965, a PAVN regiment clashed with the US army. In the 34-day battle of Ia Drang, 305 Americans and 3561 North Vietnamese died. Both sides thought they had won, that the

Battle of Ia Drang: November 1965

Key date

People power in action: Hanoi kept supplies moving south, on bikes if necessary.

other would not be able to sustain such losses. It was the North Vietnamese who were eventually proved right. Ia Drang is a good illustration of the Communist determination which helped to ensure their eventual victory.

iv) Communist ingenuity

Communist ingenuity and preparedness was vitally important. In many areas supposedly controlled by the Saigon government, the Communist Party had a web of informants and a multitude of social organisations which helped to comfort, control and motivate the people. The Communists had a network of tunnels in which VC could hide, shelter and regroup. In January 1967 the Americans found a maze of tunnels north of Saigon. These were like an underground city, full of stoves, furniture, clothing and paperwork. An exploring American officer was killed by a booby trap so the Americans just pumped in tear gas, set off explosives, then got out. They had just missed the VC headquarters, several miles of tunnels away.

In Hanoi itself the government made excellent preparations against air raids. The ground was riddled with concrete bolt-holes, each with a thick concrete cover which could be pulled over the top. When the sirens sounded, most of Hanoi's population could vanish. Two million northerners, mostly women, were in the 'Shock Brigades' that repaired the effects of air-raid damage to roads and railways. Communist ingenuity was vital in the American failure to win.

Key date

Americans found Communist tunnel network near Saigon: January 1967

Summary diagram: The Vietnamese

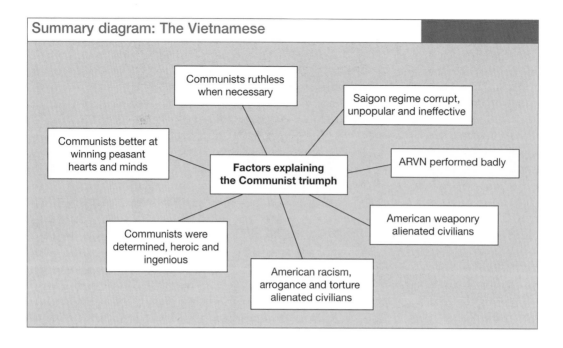

2 | The Americans in Vietnam

American disunity, the insistence on a 'comfortable' war and problems particular to fighting in Vietnam help to explain why the Americans were unable to defeat the Communists.

a) American disunity

Although many Americans fought with conviction and bravery, the American and allied forces were frequently disunited. The marines were traditionally linked with the navy and were not keen to obey orders from Westmoreland's army. The unconventional Green Berets aroused antagonism. Americans distrusted the ARVN. At Khe Sanh (see pages 183–4) in 1968, Westmoreland sent for ARVN representation as an afterthought, and then deployed them somewhere unimportant.

Ordinary soldiers served 365 days, marines 13 months. Many stencilled the return dates on their helmets. This short term of service meant that units never attained the feeling of unity vital to morale and performance. Thirteen per cent of Americans in Vietnam were black but they constituted a disproportionate 28 per cent of those in combat units (rather than desk jobs). This naturally led to resentment.

Key question
How did American disunity contribute to failure?

Battle of Khe Sanh: January 1968

An American company refused to fight: 1969

Key dates

UUUU

American soldiers frequently painted UUUU on their helmets. The initials stood for 'the unwilling, led by the unqualified, doing the unnecessary, for the ungrateful'. Black soldiers often wrote on their helmets, 'NO GOOK [Vietnamese] EVER CALLED ME NIGGER'.

Disagreement with the war or tactics led to indiscipline. An underground newspaper offered a $10,000 bounty for the death of the officer responsible for Hamburger Hill (see page 174). Things got much worse under Johnson's successor. In 1969 an entire company sat down on the battlefield, and, in full view of the TV cameras, another company refused to go down a dangerous trail.

Americans of different ranks had different experiences. An American army officer did five months in the front line. He would probably be less experienced than some of the soldiers he commanded. Five months was too little to get to know his men properly. He would then be moved on to a training, organisation or desk job. Unpopular officers were shot in the back in action or had fragmentation grenades thrown at them. Under Johnson's successor, between 1969 and 1971, there were 730 '**fraggings**', killing 83 officers. Often they were simply trying to get their men to fight. Obviously, it was hard to win a war with so many inexperienced and increasingly unpopular officers.

Many American soldiers did not like their country's manner of waging war and became confused about why they were fighting. Others felt that America had no right to intervene in Vietnam. Some disapproved of the mistreatment of civilians on humanitarian or military grounds.

In the late 1960s anti-war feeling grew in America. Many soldiers returned home to find themselves ostracised, jeered at ('baby killer' was a favourite insult) and spat on if they wore their uniform. Some found the families they had left at home had been victimised by opponents of the war. Homes belonging to soldiers might have broken glass spread across their lawns, or objects thrown at their windows.

The collapse of the home front (see pages 186–90) was a crucial factor in America's failure in Vietnam. It damaged troop morale and hamstrung the government in Washington.

b) Trying to fight a 'comfortable' war

Ironically, the American desire to keep their soldiers as comfortable as possible in Vietnam helps to explain their defeat there. President Nixon said:

> If we fail it will be because the American way simply isn't as effective as the Communist way … I have an uneasy feeling that this may be the case. We give them the most modern arms, we emphasise the material to the exclusion of the spiritual and the Spartan life, and it may be that we soften them up rather than harden them up for the battle.

Many soldiers never actually fought. They had to organise the American lifestyle for everyone else, for example, running clubs and cinemas. Every week, several thousand combat soldiers were sent for **R&R** to Saigon or Japan. When the last American soldier left Vietnam, there were 159 basketball courts, 90 service clubs, 85 volleyball fields, 71 swimming pools, 40 ice-cream plants, and two

Key date

Fragging began: 1969

Key terms

Fragging
When enlisted men tried to kill officers by throwing fragmentation grenades at them.

R&R
Rest and recuperation for American soldiers in Vietnam.

Key question
How did trying to fight a 'comfortable war' contribute to failure?

bowling alleys. All this led to an air of unreality and disorientation. A soldier could be airlifted from the horrors of the jungle to a luxurious base where the air-conditioning was so cold there were homely fireplaces. He could have steak, French fries, ice-cream and Coca-Cola. Sometimes cigarettes and iced beer were dropped by helicopters in mid-siege, and hot meals were landed at remote jungle camps. One colonel got a Silver Star bravery award for delivering turkeys by helicopter for Thanksgiving.

The American soldier was fighting a different war from his enemy. Every soldier suffers great personal hardship in the field, but while many North Vietnamese and VC spent years away from their families, existed on a basic diet and lacked decent medical treatment, the typical American soldier served a short term in Vietnam, and had good food and medical treatment. One PAVN soldier thought this was the difference between the two sides:

> You ask me what I thought of the Americans ... it was difficult for them to suffer all the hardships of the Vietnamese battlefront. When we had no water to drink, they had water for showers! We could suffer the hardships much better than they could. That probably was the main reason we won.

Westmoreland said this was the only way you could get Americans to fight.

Frustration with the war led many American soldiers to seek comfort elsewhere. Around a quarter of American soldiers caught sexually transmitted diseases. Drug abuse became common. In 1970 an estimated 58 per cent of Americans in Vietnam smoked 'pot' (marijuana), and 22 per cent shot up heroin. One colonel was **court-martialled** for leading his squadron in pot parties. In 1971, 5000 needed treatment for combat wounds, 20,529 for serious drug abuse. It was hard to take action over the drug market as so many prominent government officials in Saigon were involved, including Ky. It was hard to win a war when army discipline deteriorated: the process began under Johnson, then accelerated under his successor as troops were withdrawn and those remaining wondered why they were still there.

c) Problems for the 'grunts'

The young foot soldier or '**grunt**', like Ron Kovic (whose autobiography, *Born on the Fourth of July*, was made into a powerful anti-Vietnam War film, starring Tom Cruise), was often horrified by what he saw in 'Nam' and was keen to get out. Many hoped for a small wound and some shot themselves in the foot. What was particularly awful about this war?

The average age of the grunt in Vietnam was 19, compared to a less vulnerable 26 in the Second World War. In the Second World War the folk back home cheered their soldiers as they worked their way towards Berlin or Japan. Those soldiers could see

Key terms

Court-martialled
Tried by an army court for breaking army regulations.

Grunt
Ordinary ground trooper or footsoldier.

Key question
What problems faced the 'grunts'?

themselves making progress. In contrast, American soldiers in Vietnam fought for ground, won it, and left knowing the VC would move in again. Meanwhile, many folks back home jeered rather than cheered.

Key term

Booby traps
Disguised traps.

The grunt never felt safe. Twenty per cent of American wounded were victims of **booby traps** rather than direct enemy fire. There were booby traps all around, including the 'Bouncing Betty', which shot out of the earth, exploded after being stepped on, and blew away limbs. The VC wired up dead bodies with mines in the hope that Americans would trigger them off. They camouflaged holes on trails so Americans would fall in and be impaled on sharpened bamboo stakes. These were positioned so the victim could not get out without tearing off flesh. The patrolling infantryman was thus in almost continuous danger, with enemy mines, booby traps or snipers likely to get him at any time.

Sweat-drenched grunts hated the physical problems of patrolling the ground. They carried 20–30 kg of equipment, and were plagued by heat, rain and insects. The heat was often suffocating, making breathing difficult. Salt tablets were chewed to counter sweat loss. In the paddy fields metal gun parts burned in the sun. In the jungle thick foliage blotted out the sun and moving air, and thorn scratches bled. Uniforms rotted because of the dampness.

Not knowing which of the local people were the enemy was one of the biggest and most demoralising differences from the Second World War. One admiral said:

> We should have fought in the north, where everyone was the enemy, where you didn't have to worry whether or not you were shooting friendly civilians. In the south, we had to cope with women concealing grenades in their brassieres, or in their baby's diapers. I remember two of our marines being killed by a youngster who they were teaching to play volleyball.

It was hard to win the war when many of the grunts were terrified and demoralised.

d) American military strategy

Key question
Did the US adopt the wrong military strategy?

The American conventional forces, like the French before them, struggled to defeat Giap's army and guerrillas.

i) Search and destroy

Under Johnson, US troops engaged in 'search and destroy' missions, in which they would try to clear an area of VC. However, it was very hard to find the guerrillas. A 1967 CIA report said under one per cent of nearly two million small unit operations conducted between 1965 and 1967 resulted in contact with the enemy. Furthermore, the ratio of destruction was usually six South Vietnamese civilians for every VC soldier.

The large-scale use of helicopters and the blasting of the zones where they were to land was not conducive to searching out guerrillas, who simply went elsewhere on hearing all the noise. In Operation Cedar Falls in 1967, 20 American battalions entered an area north of Saigon. Defoliants, bombing and bulldozers cleared the land. Six thousand people were evacuated and their homes and lands destroyed. Thus 'friendly' civilians were made hostile to Saigon and its American ally and only a few VC were found.

Key dates

Operation Cedar Falls: 1967

Battle of Hamburger Hill: May 1969

It is notoriously difficult to try to wipe out a guerrilla movement, particularly when the guerrillas are sent in from another 'state' (North Vietnam) and when the guerrillas have a sympathetic, supportive or simply apathetic reaction from the local community. Frequently, US troops would 'clear' an area of VC. However, as soon as the Americans moved out, the Communists would move back in. A famous example of this is the bloody battle for 'Hamburger Hill' (so-called because of the bloody carnage) in 1969. The Americans 'won', but the ground was quickly retaken by the VC when the Americans left.

ii) Reliance on superior technology

Bombing was a favourite tactic during Johnson's presidency. North Vietnam, the Ho Chi Minh Trail and South Vietnamese villages suspected of harbouring Communist sympathisers were all heavily bombed. However, the bombing failed both to damage North Vietnamese morale and to stop the flow of men and materials coming down the trail from North Vietnam to South Vietnam. The Johnson administration ignored warnings (for example, from the CIA in 1966) about that lack of impact. Furthermore, the bombing alienated many people in South Vietnam and in America.

iii) The wrong strategy

Years later, McNamara admitted that US tactics were wrong, that it was unwise to use a high-tech war of attrition against a primarily guerrilla force that never considered giving up their war for independence. McNamara's successor Clark Clifford said that it 'was startling to me that we had no military plan to win the war'.

iv) What if … ?

Americans, particularly ex-soldiers, frequently debate what might have happened if the United States had done things differently in the Vietnam War.

What if President Johnson had gone beyond limited war and declared war on North Vietnam? Could the United States have won?
The war might have become even more unpopular. The USSR and China might have entered the war, something Johnson was

determined to avoid. He clearly did not think South Vietnam was worth a Third World War, and the American public certainly would not have thought so. Congress would probably not have declared war for South Vietnam.

What if, as General Bruce Palmer contended in 1986, the United States had cut South Vietnam off from Communist infiltration, thereby giving South Vietnam time to build itself up into a viable state?

That 'cutting off' might have been possible in flatter terrain, as in Korea. However, to 'cut off' the jungles and mountains on the Cambodian and Laotian borders would have been impossible. Furthermore, the PLAF (see page 107) would have been 'trapped' inside South Vietnam, and would have continued guerrilla warfare. The strategic hamlets had been infiltrated by Communists, which proved that it was impossible to isolate the South Vietnamese population from South Vietnamese (or North Vietnamese) Communists. In 1967 the CIA established that most of the supplies used by the Communists originated in the South, so 'cutting off' supplies would have been difficult.

What if the United States Army had worked harder to win the hearts and minds of the people, as the historian Andrew Krepinevich suggested in 1986?

The historian Richard Hunt pointed out in 1995 that this would have taken too many American soldiers too long, and that the American public would have run out of patience. One commander pointed out that if he and his men became 'mayors and sociologists worrying about hearts and minds', they would not be much use if they had to fight the Soviets!

v) Questions Americans ask today

Americans still argue today about the Communist victory in Vietnam. Was it inevitable? Are guerrillas impossible to beat when much of the population is sympathetic to them? Or was it just that the Americans were not the people to win this war? Were American tactics wrong? Was Westmoreland's war of attrition the way to defeat determined nationalists and guerrillas? Should America have concentrated upon winning the hearts and minds of the people? Were bombing and 'search [for Communists] and destroy' tactics wise? Did the American public lose the war for America? Or the American media? Or American politicians? This chapter will probably have made up your mind about the answer to those questions which centre upon events in Vietnam. The next chapter will give you more ideas about the 'home front' and the loss of the war.

Summary diagram: The Americans in Vietnam

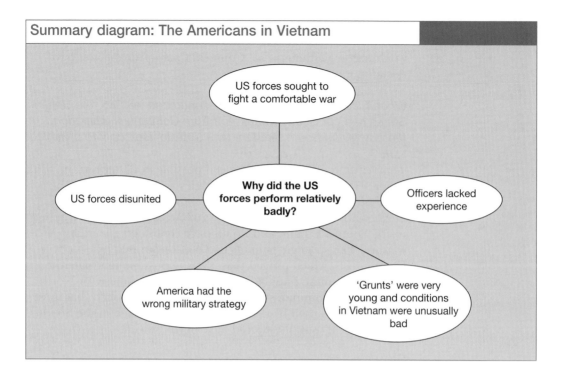

US forces sought to fight a comfortable war

US forces disunited

Why did the US forces perform relatively badly?

Officers lacked experience

America had the wrong military strategy

'Grunts' were very young and conditions in Vietnam were unusually bad

3 | Key Debates

a) Was the war unwinnable?

Some historians believe the war was unwinnable. They contend that America was fighting in the wrong place, against the wrong enemy, and that Americans never understood Vietnam or the Vietnamese.

On the other hand, those who fought in Vietnam and subsequently wrote about it often disagree. Orthodox historians generally accept that US intervention was morally justifiable in the struggle against Communism and that greater use of force would have been acceptable. In his memoirs, Westmoreland (1976) claimed that he was too restricted by orders from Washington, DC, and that more ground troops and air power would have defeated Hanoi. Colonel Harry Summers (1982) blamed civilian officials for dispersing US military power in the search for guerrillas. Summers advocated greater use of greater force.

b) Could military solutions solve Saigon's problems?

Historians such as Herring (1996) point out that military historians err in imagining that military solutions could have solved the political problems of the unpopular Saigon regime. Some historians actually blame overuse of American military power for the US failure, for example, Thomson (1980). They point out that the bombing in particular served to alienate the South Vietnamese people. Others criticise US confidence in high-tech warfare and managerial techniques, for example, Gibson (1986).

Key terms

Pacification
Paying greater
attention to the
security and
government of the
South Vietnamese
people.

Reunification
Vietnam was
reunited in 1975
when the North
took over the
South.

c) Did Westmoreland use the correct strategy?

Some (such as Cable in 1991) contend that Westmoreland should have concentrated more on **pacification** and counter-insurgency, rather than on the war of attrition. However, Bergerud (1990) studied Hau Nghia province, where American troops worked closely with villagers on pacification but still failed to win greater support for the Saigon regime.

d) Did America lose the war, or did the Communists win it?

Bergerud contends that the outcome of the Vietnam War is not so much an American failure, but rather a Vietnamese success. Several American historians, such as Duiker (2000), emphasise the Communist advantages: their undoubted patriotism, superb organisation, ruthlessness when necessary and effective military strategy.

e) Which was the villain: Saigon or Hanoi?

Some historians point out the frequently unpleasant nature of the Communist government in Vietnam after **reunification**, while others suggest that the Saigon regime was not as bad as is often thought (Hatcher, 1990).

Some key books in the debates
E. Bergerud, *The Dynamics of Defeat* (Boulder, 1990).
L. Cable, *Unholy Grail* (New York, 1991).
W. Duiker, *Ho Chi Minh* (New York, 2000).
J.W. Gibson, *The Perfect War* (New York, 1986).
P. Hatcher, *The Suicide of an Elite* (Stanford, 1990).
G. Herring, *America's Longest War* (New York, 1996).
H. Summers, *On Strategy* (California, 1982).
J.C. Thomson, *Rolling Thunder* (North Carolina, 1980).
W. Westmoreland, *A Soldier Reports* (New York, 1976).

9 Why the USA Failed: II – US Politicians and People

POINTS TO CONSIDER

In 1963, the Johnson administration believed America could 'win', that is, defeat the Communists in South Vietnam and sustain a strong and independent state there. However, by the end of Johnson's presidency, the administration had concluded that the war was unwinnable. Like Chapter 8, this chapter analyses why America could not win the war in Vietnam, with sections on:

- The problems with Johnson's aims and methods
- Why and how Johnson was forced to retreat
- Johnson's last months
- Conclusions about Johnson and the war

Key dates

1965	March	First American combat troops landed in South Vietnam
	August	'Poisonous reporting' from Vietnam
1966		Increased domestic opposition to US involvement in Vietnam
	February	Senate hearings on war dominated by doves
	November	Democrats did badly in the congressional mid-term elections
	December	Nearly 400,000 US soldiers in South Vietnam
1967	January	Martin Luther King Jr publicly criticised US involvement in the war
	August	Unpopular tax rises to help to finance the war
	August	Senate hearings on the war dominated by hawks
	November	McNamara resigned
1968	January	Clark Clifford selected as Secretary of Defence (took office in March)
	Jan–Feb	Tet Offensive shook US confidence
	January	Battle of Khe Sanh
	March	'Wise Men' advised Johnson against further escalation
		Johnson sought peace talks not re-election
	August	Riots during Democratic Convention in Chicago

Key question
Were Johnson's aims and methods conducive to victory?

1 | Problems with Johnson's Aims and Methods

a) Johnson's aims

It is not always easy to discover Johnson's aims. Nearly half of Americans polled in 1967 did not know for sure what the war was all about. McNamara's assistant privately quantified American aims as:

> seventy per cent to avoid a humiliating US defeat (to our reputation as a guarantor). Twenty per cent to keep South Vietnamese (and the adjacent) territory from Chinese hands. Ten per cent to permit the people of South Vietnam to enjoy a better, freer way of life.

Johnson publicly said that he aimed to defeat Communist aggression, build a nation in South Vietnam and search for peace there. His other aims were best kept private. He wanted to save American face, which he believed necessitated continuing and winning the war. He also wanted to ensure that his conduct of the war did not adversely affect the electoral prospects of any Democrat (especially himself). The problem was that the publicly stated American aims did not particularly inspire the American public and were probably impossible to achieve – especially with the methods Johnson used and the criticism they aroused.

b) Johnson's methods

Johnson's methods were to advise, support, and try to strengthen the Saigon governments, both politically and militarily. As has been seen in Chapter 8, Johnson's military men used the wrong methods in Vietnam: 'Bomb, bomb, bomb – that's all they know', Johnson sighed. These military methods did not bring in American victory, especially as they were so unappealing to the people of South Vietnam and of the United States. Similarly, his political methods alienated many South Vietnamese and some Americans: the US-sponsored Saigon regime had few supporters.

Between 1965 and 1968 Johnson's administration slowly became convinced that their aims and methods were inappropriate. It became clear that the escalation of US military involvement in support of the Saigon regime was not going to stop Hanoi and that the involvement was becoming increasingly unpopular amongst Americans and South Vietnamese. Johnson would be forced to retreat because his aims and methods in Vietnam were inappropriate and increasingly unpopular.

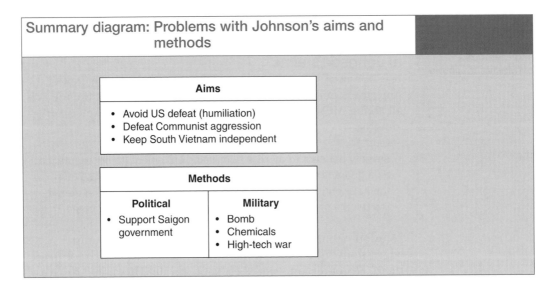

Summary diagram: Problems with Johnson's aims and methods

Aims

- Avoid US defeat (humiliation)
- Defeat Communist aggression
- Keep South Vietnam independent

Methods

Political	Military
• Support Saigon government	• Bomb • Chemicals • High-tech war

2 | Why and How Johnson was Forced to Retreat

Even as Johnson was building up American forces in Vietnam in 1965–7, the problems which would eventually defeat him were becoming obvious. The Saigon government remained ineffective and unpopular, and increasing numbers of Americans doubted the wisdom of continuing to support it.

a) Problems in South Vietnam in 1966–7

In 1967, the Johnson administration was publicly optimistic, claiming that the '**cross-over point**' had been reached in South Vietnam: American and ARVN troops were killing the enemy faster than they could be replaced. General Westmoreland said that there were only 285,000 Communists left fighting in the south (the CIA said over 500,000, but the administration kept that quiet to preserve morale).

Privately the administration was pessimistic. Its members disagreed over how the war should be prosecuted. 'Rolling Thunder' (see page 146) was causing tremendous divisions. Johnson railed against 'gutless' officials who leaked 'defeatist' stories to the press: 'It's gotten so you can't have intercourse with your wife without it being spread by traitors'. Things were clearly going badly in Vietnam and it was destroying confidence within the administration. Most worrying was Secretary of Defence McNamara's change of position.

Key question
How did problems in South Vietnam help to force Johnson to retreat?

Cross-over point
The point at which Americans anticipated that Communists would give up because they were being killed faster than Hanoi could replace them.

Key term

b) The loss of McNamara

Robert McNamara had been vital in the formulation of Kennedy and Johnson's Vietnam policies. However, Bobby Kennedy had become passionately anti-war and publicly opposed the war from January 1966, which greatly influenced his friend McNamara.

McNamara's health and family life had suffered because of the war. His daughter and son participated in the anti-war protests.

Key question
How did McNamara help to force Johnson to retreat?

Key dates

Senate hearings on the war dominated by hawks: August 1967

McNamara resigned: November 1967

Clark Clifford selected as Secretary of Defence (took office in March): January 1968

McNamara blamed himself for his wife's stomach ulcer. He seemed physically and mentally tortured, bursting into tears during discussions. He was losing his old certainty. McNamara told Johnson in early 1967:

> The picture of the world's greatest superpower killing or seriously injuring 1000 non-combatants a week, while trying to pound a tiny, backward nation into submission on an issue whose merits are hotly disputed, is not a pretty one.

In August 1967 hawks organised Senate hearings designed to force Johnson into lifting restrictions on the bombing of North Vietnam. Public opinion polls in spring 1967 revealed that 45 per cent of Americans favoured increased military pressure in Vietnam (41 per cent favoured withdrawal). During the hearings the military blamed McNamara and Johnson for tying their hands behind their backs, by limiting the bombing. McNamara testified that the bombing was not worth risking a clash with the Soviets. He said bombing would only stop Hanoi if the bombing totally annihilated North Vietnam and all its people. He pointed out that bombing of the Ho Chi Minh Trail did not stop Communist troops and supplies moving south.

Johnson and the JCS were furious with McNamara's performance. The president thought that McNamara had degenerated into 'an emotional basket case'. The JCS said his doubts were undermining all the rationale for America's previous and present efforts. Johnson decided McNamara had to go.

In November 1967, in a last tearful White House conference, McNamara condemned:

> the goddamned Air Force and its goddamned bombing campaign that had dropped more bombs on Vietnam than on Europe in the whole of World War II and we hadn't gotten a goddamned thing for it.

He had not advocated getting out of Vietnam, only halting the escalation. His administration colleagues considered the exit option unacceptable.

In January 1968 Johnson selected Clark Clifford as McNamara's replacement as Secretary of Defence. Like his predecessor, Clifford began to doubt the domino theory and the wisdom of US involvement. The Tet Offensive (see below) finally made Clifford conclude that he had to extricate America from this endless war.

US Allies in Vietnam

In July 1967, Clark Clifford had toured the countries helping the US in Vietnam. In exchange for enormous American aid, South Korea had contributed 45,000 troops, Australia 5000, Thailand 2000, the Philippines 2000 (non-combatants) and New Zealand under 500. Clifford told Johnson that 'more people turned out in New Zealand to demonstrate against our trip than the country had sent to Vietnam'.

c) The Tet Offensive, January 1968

i) Aims of the Tet Offensive

In January 1968 Hanoi launched an unprecedented offensive against South Vietnam. Tens of thousands of PAVN and VC attacked cities and military installations in the South. Hanoi dreamed that their great offensive would cause the Saigon government to collapse or, at the very least, demonstrate such strength that America would give up.

ii) Course of events

The attack broke the traditional **Tet** holiday truce. The Americans and South Vietnamese were preoccupied with the Tet festival. Saigon, Washington and the US public were shocked that the Communists could move so freely and effectively throughout the South. The American ambassador had to flee the embassy in Saigon in his pyjamas. It took 11,000 American and ARVN troops three weeks to clear Saigon of Communist forces. The attackers had even hit the US embassy and dramatic scenes there were headline news in America. The Tet Offensive cost a great many lives and caused incredible damage; 3895 Americans, 4954 South Vietnamese military, 14,300 South Vietnamese civilians, and 58,373 VC and PAVN died. Out of 17,134 houses in historic Hue, 9776 were totally destroyed and 3169 were seriously damaged.

iii) Results and significance of Tet

- The Tet Offensive was the largest set of battles fought in the Vietnam War up to that point.
- It was the first set of battles to be fought in the cities of South Vietnam.
- The Communists suffered grievous losses. It took Hanoi several years to get over this great effort.
- The South Vietnamese people had not risen *en masse* to help the Communists, which damaged the VC claim to be a liberation force.
- The Communist position in the South Vietnamese countryside was strengthened because of the Communist performance in Tet.
- The ordinary South Vietnamese had not rallied to the Saigon regime. Tet seemed to show that although the US could stop the overthrow of the Saigon government, it had failed to make it viable in the face of Communist determination.
- US intelligence officials had failed to notice clear warnings and their confidence was shaken. Had Americans and President Thieu known their Vietnamese history better, they would have remembered that during Tet in 1789 the Vietnamese defeated a Chinese occupation army distracted by the festival.
- One famous photo of a Saigon general shooting a bound captive in the head damaged Americans' faith in their side as the 'good guys' (see page 184): only later was it discovered that the captive was a VC death-squad member who had just shot a relation of the general.

Key question
How important was Tet in Johnson's decision to retreat?

Tet Offensive shook US confidence: January–February 1968

Key date

Tet
The most important Vietnamese festival. Americans use the word 'Tet' as shorthand for the 'Tet Offensive'.

Key term

- An anti-war newsman repeated a soldier's unforgettable and telling phrase about one South Vietnamese village: 'We had to destroy the town to save it'. That phrase made many Americans question what was being done in Vietnam.
- Tet so shook Westmoreland that one American official considered him almost broken.
- The administration had been claiming that America was winning the war but the TV pictures suggested US failure: even the US embassy was unsafe.
- Tet increased the credibility gap between the Johnson administration's explanations of events in Vietnam and the American public's understanding of those events.
- Some historians claim that US reporters presented a uniformly hostile and negative picture of the Tet offensive, so that Americans felt it was a great defeat. These historians say that it was a psychological rather than a military defeat.
- Johnson performed badly at the press conferences following Tet, admitting, 'It may be that General Westmoreland makes some serious mistakes or that I make some.' Johnson is often criticised for dishonesty but it has to be said that on this occasion, when he was honest, he was so uninspiring as to seem guilty of lack of leadership. After Tet his approval ratings plummeted. Clifford feared that the president and indeed the whole government of the United States was on the verge of coming apart.
- Tet encouraged anti-war presidential candidates to oppose Johnson in the forthcoming presidential election, and forced Johnson to withdraw from the 1968 presidential race. He said that he would concentrate upon the pursuit of peace.
- Tet forced the Johnson administration into a re-evaluation of US policy. By March Clifford was totally against the war and even Rusk (see page 119) was wavering. Back in September 1967 the CIA director had said America could get out of Vietnam without suffering any great loss of international standing. The Treasury said the nation could not afford to send more troops and even hawkish senators said 'no more men'. Tet had shaken the confidence of the American government and people. Pictures of destruction and death had turned many Americans against the war.
- After Tet, Johnson rejected repeated JCS demands that 200,000 more US troops be sent to Vietnam. Clifford questioned them about their plan for victory and concluded that they did not have one.

iv) The battle of Khe Sanh

Battle of Khe Sanh: January 1968

Key date

At the same time as Tet, the battle of Khe Sanh was being fought. Successfully designed to distract the Americans from the Tet Offensive, Khe Sanh was the biggest and bloodiest battle of the war: 10,000 Communists and 500 Americans died. Westmoreland wrongly thought that Khe Sanh was the great prize. This was the kind of fight he wanted, against uniformed and easily identifiable PAVN troops. Westmoreland wanted to use tactical nuclear

One of the most famous and most misinterpreted photos of the war. South Vietnam's police chief executed a VC in Saigon during the Tet Offensive in 1968.

weapons but Washington said no, 'kicked him upstairs' to a desk job and replaced him.

v) Key debates

Was Tet an American military defeat?

Although most historians agree that the Tet Offensive marked the start of an American de-escalation process that eventually got the United States out of Vietnam, they disagree over whether or not it was a US defeat.

Some historians (for example, Davidson, 1988) argue that Tet was a military victory for the US, on which feeble politicians failed to capitalise. On the other hand, Buzzanco (1996) pointed out that the US army chief of staff felt that the offensive showed the limits of US military power. Others (for example, Duiker, 1996) disagree, pointing out that Tet was a costly Communist miscalculation, as no popular rising occurred in South Vietnam, but lots of Communist men and material were lost.

Did the Tet Offensive change American opinion on the war?

Kolko (1985) stressed that Tet was exactly what Hanoi wanted – a psychological victory against the Americans.

Several journalists, for example, Braestrup (1997), claimed that for the first time ever, the media rather than battlefield events determined the outcome of a war. On the other hand, scholars such as Pach (1998) have found no evidence that TV reporting had a negative impact on public opinion and therefore consider that it did not affect the outcome of the war. However, Pach admitted that coverage of Tet exposed the credibility gap and exacerbated doubts about American policy that had begun to develop within the Johnson administration since the autumn and the resignation of McNamara.

Schmitz (2005) rejected claims of media bias in American reporting, and argued that it was not the impact of Tet on the public that was significant, but rather the impact of Tet on senior officials in the Johnson administration. Those officials brought about a dramatic change in Johnson's policies. Schmitz recorded that polls showed steadily declining popular support for the war throughout 1967 until the Johnson administration's public relations campaign of autumn 1967 stabilised the percentages. Then, at the time of Tet, after an initial patriotic rise in support for Johnson and his war policies, the decline in support continued once more.

Some key books in the debates
P. Braestrup, *Big Story* (Boulder, 1967).
R. Buzzanco, *Masters of War* (Cambridge, 1996).
P.B. Davidson, *Vietnam at War* (California, 1988).
W.J. Duiker, *Sacred War* (Stanford, 1994).
G. Kolko, *Anatomy of a War* (New York, 1986).
C. Pach, in C. Fink (editor), *1968: The World Transformed* (Cambridge, 1998).

Key question
Was a majority of the American public anti-war?

d) Public opinion

Johnson and Congress naturally paid great attention to public opinion. Many believe that opposition to the war from the public and in the press was the main reason why Johnson finally decided on retreat. However, the objectors were probably a minority, and supporters of the war also put pressure on Johnson to continue the fighting.

i) The conservative right-wing

Cold Warriors criticised Johnson for insufficient escalation, complaining that American boys were being forced to fight the Communists with one hand tied behind their backs. They were angry that America never used more than half of its combat-ready divisions and tactical air power in Vietnam. 'Win or get out' was a popular bumper sticker. Many believed that American boys, who fought out there on the orders of an elected president and funded by an elected Congress, deserved more support from the folk back home. Those who wonder why Johnson continued to escalate for so long often forget this right-wing pressure on him. On the other hand, not all conservatives approved of the war. Many considered developed areas such as Europe and Japan more important to America. One retired general argued that Asians did not want American ideas 'crammed down their throats'.

ii) Pacifist feeling

Many Americans hated the thought of themselves or their loved ones having to fight in Vietnam. Some were repelled by the sufferings of Vietnamese non-combatants, or believed America's international image was suffering.

iii) College students

College students were in the forefront of protest, especially after February 1968 when the draft boards stopped automatic exemption for students. Many draft dodgers (some claim 50,000) slipped into Canada. College students used ingenious methods to avoid the draft: young men psyched themselves up to have apparent blood pressure problems when tested, or feigned mental instability. Claiming to have considered suicide usually did the trick.

iv) Debates about the protests

The extent to which (i) anti-war protesters and reporters were just a vociferous minority, and (ii) they affected American and North Vietnamese policy, are questions that require us to look at the American home front.

e) The collapse of the home front

i) 1964

The protests began in 1964 when 1000 students from prestigious Yale University staged a protest march in New York and 5000 professors wrote in support. However, the Gulf of Tonkin resolution and the presidential election (see pages 141–3) suggest that at this stage Johnson had near unanimous support for his Vietnam policy from the public and most congressmen.

ii) 1965

During 1965 many universities held anti-war lectures and debates; 20,000 participated in **Berkeley**. However, thousands of students signed pro-Johnson petitions, including one-quarter of Yale undergraduates. Thousands of other citizens participated in protests. In April 1965, 25,000 protesters marched on Washington. Johnson insisted that the protests were financed by Communist governments, and that protesters encouraged the enemy.

During 1965, congressional unanimity developed cracks. One congressman reported 'widened unrest' among colleagues in January 1965. With the introduction of American ground troops to Vietnam, the increasing number of casualties meant that in 1965 the press and TV networks went to Vietnam in full force. The war became America's first fully televised war. People talked of 'the living-room war' as Americans watched it on every evening news. In August 1965 Johnson was informed that increasing

Key question
To what extent did anti-war protests affect Johnson's Vietnam policy?

Key dates

First American combat troops landed in South Vietnam: March 1965

'Poisonous reporting' from Vietnam: August 1965

Key term

Berkeley
A leading Californian university.

numbers of American reporters in Saigon were 'thoroughly sour and poisonous in their reporting'. However, as yet the opposition had little practical impact on American involvement, and fewer than 25 per cent of Americans believed that the US had erred in sending troops to Vietnam.

iii) 1966

During 1966 public and congressional support for the war dropped dramatically. In February 1966, during **Senate Foreign Relations Committee** hearings on the war, senators spoke against the bombing, and many said that Vietnam was not vital to America and withdrawal would do no great harm.

The Democratic Party suffered a sharp defeat in the Congressional mid-term elections of November 1966 and congressmen blamed Vietnam. They urged Johnson to end the war before it damaged the Great Society and the party. Congress nevertheless continued to fund the war, unwilling to face accusations of betraying the 400,000 American boys in the field.

Westmoreland complained that 'The enemy leaders were made to appear to be the good guys' by the media. Government propaganda was pedestrian and ineffective and (unlike the Second World War) Hollywood gave minimal assistance, with the exception of two ageing national institutions: comedian Bob Hope entertained troops in Vietnam, and John Wayne made a pro-war film, *The Green Berets*.

During 1966, Johnson felt bound to limit his public appearances to avoid chants of 'Hey, hey, LBJ, how many boys have you killed today?' On the other hand, there were relatively few marches and only one state governor refused to declare his support for government policy.

iv) 1967

As yet, the criticism had not caused Johnson to alter his policies, but during 1967 opposition to the war grew. Tens of thousands protested in the great cities of America. Congressmen put ever more pressure on Johnson. The churches and black civil rights leader Martin Luther King Jr led the opposition. Black people resented the disproportionate number of black casualties in Vietnam and, as victims of white racism, felt kinship with the poor, non-white Vietnamese. When King saw a picture of Vietnamese children showing burn wounds from American napalm bombs in January 1967 he became publicly critical. He lamented that federal funds that would help the black ghettos were being diverted to the war.

In August 1967, tax rises turned more Americans against the war. In October 1967 draft cards were publicly burned throughout the country. Between 4000 and 10,000 Berkeley students tried to close down the draft headquarters in Oakland and clashed with the police. The students vandalised cars, parking meters, newsstands and trees. Many were high on drugs. In Washington, Johnson had 2000 policemen, 17,000 **National Guard** troops and 6000 regular army men to meet 70,000 protesters. Most of the protesters just listened to speeches but some extremists were involved in violence outside the **Pentagon**. McNamara watched from his office window and found it 'terrifying. Christ, yes, I was scared'. The government's bill for the operations was just over $1 million. There were 625 arrests. Many middle-class Americans were antagonistic towards all protesters, but particularly the extremists. Conservative California Governor Ronald Reagan said that protesters' activities, 'can be summed up in three words: Sex, Drugs and Treason'.

Johnson's friend Abe Fortas possibly got it right when he said McNamara was one who had been overinfluenced by the protesters. During August 1967 hawkish senators had conducted hearings aimed at pressurising Johnson into lifting all restrictions on bombing in Vietnam. The respected and experienced group of elder statesmen nicknamed the '**Wise Men**' and including Acheson (see page 14) and Rusk, all assured Johnson that they supported his Vietnam policy. Such support for the war and escalation is too often forgotten because it is overshadowed by the drama of the protests. On the other hand, a growing number of Johnson's friends and supporters were changing their views on the war because of the loss of someone close to them, or because their children opposed the war. Dean Rusk's son disagreed so intensely with his father over Vietnam that his psychiatrist told him, 'You had your father's nervous breakdown [for him].'

Key terms

Pentagon
Headquarters of the US Department of Defence.

Wise Men
A group of experienced politicians, generals and others who had previously held high office, frequently consulted by Johnson over the Vietnam War.

v) Was 1967 a turning point?

Pinpointing turning points in support for the war is difficult, but 1967 was probably crucial. Some influential newspapers and TV stations shifted from support to opposition. Draft calls, deaths in Vietnam and taxes all increased, arousing more discontent, but it is difficult to know exactly how many opposed Johnson's policies. Polls can be misleading. In October 1967, 46 per cent of Americans felt that the Vietnam commitment was a mistake, yet a massive majority wanted to stay there and get tougher – so, one could say that this poll indicated both widespread support and widespread opposition to the war. 'I want to get out but I don't want to give up', said one housewife. After a successful November public relations offensive by the Johnson administration, in which Westmoreland said, 'We are winning a war of attrition now', the White House was pleasantly surprised by a poll which showed considerable support for the war in early 1968:

- 49 per cent to 29 per cent favoured invading North Vietnam
- 42 per cent to 33 per cent favoured mining Haiphong (the main port in North Vietnam) even if Soviet ships were sunk as a result
- 25 per cent did not oppose bombing China or using atomic weapons.

There were nearly half a million Americans in Vietnam and nearly 17,000 had died there, but Johnson's policies still had considerable support.

vi) 1968 – was Tet a turning point?

Perhaps the media coverage of the Tet Offensive in early 1968 was the crucial turning point. Walter Cronkite, the most respected TV journalist, had been strongly supportive of the war until a February 1968 visit to Vietnam made him conclude the war could not be won. 'What the hell is going on?' Cronkite asked. 'I thought we were winning the war.' Johnson knew the significance of Cronkite's change of mind: 'If I've lost Cronkite, I've lost America.' Some saw his defection as a great turning point.

In the weeks after Tet, Johnson's approval rating fell from 48 to 36 per cent. The Communists might have been defeated militarily, but Tet suggested that Johnson was losing the battle for the hearts and minds of an important percentage of his people. Some were against the war altogether, others wanted him to wage it differently. A minority were protesting vociferously.

It is difficult to trace the interrelationship between the protests and rising dissatisfaction in Congress and in the White House itself, but there is no doubt that politicians were sensitive to the wishes of the voters, and the protesters probably played a part disproportionate to their numbers in bringing the war towards an end. By the spring of 1968, Johnson had lost confidence if not in the rectitude of his policies then at least in his capacity to maintain continued support for them. The protesters and the media had suggested that his war and his way of conducting it were wrong and this played an important part in loss of confidence amongst White House officials and the troops in Vietnam.

The massive anti-war protest outside the Pentagon, October 1967. The 'war criminal' is President Johnson.

vii) Key debate
Historians disagree over the extent of press responsibility for the US inability to win in Vietnam.

Johnson criticised the American press for failing to support the war effort. Journalist Peter Braestrup (1997) argued that media coverage of Tet helped to convince Americans that what was actually a victory was instead a US defeat. In contrast, Hammond's 1998 study of the press found most reporters supportive of the war until the public and government members started questioning it. Hammond said that the press reflected rather than shaped public opinion.

Studies of the anti-war movement (for example, Wells, 1994) often suggest that the protests did not end the war but did restrain Johnson and his successor. Small (1988) found presidents more influenced by protests than they cared to admit. On the other hand, Garfinkle (1995) contended that the radicalism of some protesters alienated the majority of Americans, discredited the anti-war movement, and may even have helped to prolong the war.

Some key books in the debate
P. Braestrup, *Big Story* (Boulder, 1997).
A. Garfinkle, *Tell-tale Hearts* (New York, 1995).
W. Hammond, *Reporting Vietnam* (Kansas, 1998).
M. Small, *Johnson, Nixon and the Doves* (Rutgers, 1988).

f) Financial and economic problems
The war cost a great deal of money and distorted the economy. Johnson did not want to admit how much he was spending lest conservatives in Congress cut off payments for his Great Society programmes, so he was slow to ask for the necessary wartime tax rises. In 1965 the government deficit had been $1.6 billion. By 1968 it was $25.3 billion. Such deficits caused inflation and endangered America's economic well-being. The Treasury warned him that this should not go on and taxpayers grew resentful, increasing the pressure on him to change direction in Vietnam.

g) Johnson's loss of confidence
Back in November 1967, after optimistic briefings from the JCS and CIA, the 'Wise Men' had declared their support for the continuation of US efforts in Vietnam. Now, however, at a meeting on 25 March 1968, the majority of them were in the process of changing their minds, and most advocated some kind of retreat in Vietnam. One said that the US could not 'succeed in the time we have left' in Vietnam, because that time was 'limited by reactions in this country'.

Johnson could not believe that 'these establishment bastards have bailed out'. Congress was pressing hard for retreat, and the polls were discouraging: 78 per cent of Americans believed that America was not making any progress in the war, 74 per cent that

Key question
Was the American press responsible for the US failure to win in Vietnam?

Key question
How did the cost of the war impact on Johnson?

Key question
Why did Johnson finally decide to halt escalation?

Key dates

'Wise Men' advised Johnson against further escalation: March 1968

Johnson sought peace talks not re-election: March 1968

Key term

Balance of payments deficit
When the value of a country's imports exceeds that of its exports.

Johnson was not handling it well. The war-induced **balance of payments deficit** had dramatically weakened the dollar on the international money market, causing a gold crisis which was the final straw for many Americans. From now on Johnson knew there would have to be some sort of a reversal in Vietnam.

Johnson agonised over how to announce any change in US policy, unwilling to admit that his country had been in error and unwilling to betray those Americans who were fighting and dying in Vietnam. On 31 March 1968 he said, 'I am taking the first step to de-escalate the conflict'. He offered to stop bombing North Vietnam if Hanoi would agree to talks. He said that he would not be running for re-election. Some think Johnson's decision not to run was a reaction to the unpopularity of his Vietnam policies, but his poor health was also a factor.

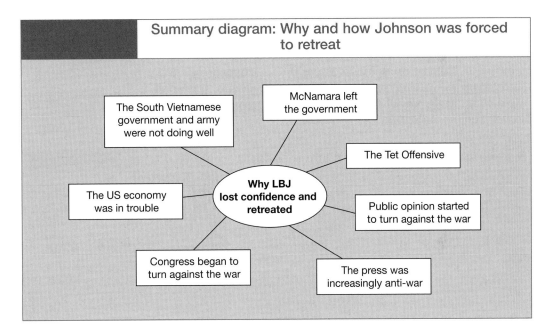

Summary diagram: Why and how Johnson was forced to retreat

Key question
Why could Johnson not end the war?

3 | Johnson's Last Months

a) Peace talks

With Johnson's loss of confidence by spring 1968, the prospects for successful peace talks improved. Hanoi was exhausted after Tet, anxious to divide Americans, and keen to negotiate. Talks began in Paris in May 1968. Johnson demanded a North Vietnamese withdrawal from South Vietnam and rejected Communist participation in the Saigon government. North Vietnam demanded American withdrawal from South Vietnam and insisted on Communist participation in the Saigon government. These mutually exclusive demands explain why the talks continued intermittently for five years.

b) The disintegration of Johnson's presidency

Events in the final few months of Johnson's presidency confirmed the need for a dramatic change in America's Vietnam policy. The fighting had reached maximum intensity in the first half of 1968. In two weeks in May alone, 1800 Americans were killed and 18,000 seriously wounded. US forces, now numbering over half a million, had began to suffer the severe morale problems that left the forces near to collapse.

There were protests and riots in Chicago in August 1968, during the Democratic Party convention. Continuation of the war seemed to be leading to the disintegration of American society. The Democrats' presidential nomination, Johnson's vice-president Hubert Humphrey, lost the election, partly because of his inability to dissociate himself sufficiently from Johnson's Vietnam policy. However, like polls, elections are notorious for not telling the whole story. The Republican candidate Richard Nixon pledged to bring an honourable end to the war in Vietnam, but a vote for him was not necessarily a vote against the war. Some voted according to habit or on domestic issues. All we can conclude is that in 1968 the voters remained divided over Vietnam. Johnson's presidency and the war effort had disintegrated primarily because of these American divisions.

> **Key date**
>
> Riots during Democratic Convention in Chicago: August 1968

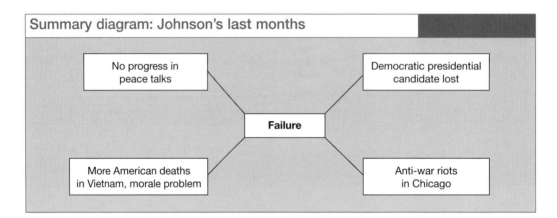

Summary diagram: Johnson's last months

- No progress in peace talks
- Democratic presidential candidate lost
- **Failure**
- More American deaths in Vietnam, morale problem
- Anti-war riots in Chicago

4 | Conclusions about Johnson and the War

a) Why had Johnson failed to win the war?

Perhaps the main reason why Johnson failed to win the war was that the establishment of a viable South Vietnamese state was beyond America's capabilities. Johnson considered real escalation an impossibility: it might bring the Soviets and Chinese in, and attacking 'little' North Vietnam would damage America's international image. So America just continued to fight a limited and ineffective war to support a series of unpopular Saigon regimes. The nature of the warfare and criticism back home led to the apparent collapse of the home front and the American forces in Vietnam.

b) Had Johnson's Vietnam policy been a total failure?

It could be argued that Johnson's Vietnam policy was not a total failure. He had restrained American hawks, whose policies might have led to full-scale war with China or the USSR. Perhaps Communist insurgents in other parts of Southeast Asia did badly in the 1960s because American actions in Vietnam encouraged anti-Communists and kept China busy.

c) Why did Johnson not get out?

Johnson did not get out because Hanoi was not going to give up, so neutralisation or peace would mean a coalition government containing Communists, which was unacceptable to Johnson and many other Americans. Johnson thought getting out of Vietnam on those terms would damage the credibility of himself, his party and his country, and be a betrayal of the Americans who had fought and died there.

d) What had the war done to America?

The war damaged America's armed forces, image, morale, national unity and economy. It also damaged the presidency and American society.

e) How did Johnson and the Vietnam War damage the presidency?

During 1965 the media became increasingly hostile, partly because of the Vietnam policies, partly because of Johnson and McNamara's lack of straightforwardness in describing them. When the marines landed in Danang in March 1965, the State Department readily admitted it, to Johnson's fury. He said there had been 'no change', which was untrue. The 'credibility gap' was the difference between what Johnson said and what actually was. One wit said that Johnson lost the most important battle of the Vietnam War, the 'Battle of Credibility Gap'! It had an adverse impact on the presidency; respect for the office decreased because of the increasingly unpopular and apparently dishonest person who held it.

f) How did the war damage American society?

'Vietnam took it all away', said Kennedy's brother-in-law, Sargent Shriver, 'every God-damned dollar. That's what killed the war on poverty'. Between 1965 and 1973, $15.5 billion was spent on the Great Society, compared to $120 billion on the war in Vietnam. During Johnson's presidency 222,351 US military were killed or wounded in Vietnam. Returning American veterans had physical and/or mental disabilities that for the most part would remain with them for the rest of their lives. Many veterans returned with drug problems and with sharpened class and racial antagonisms (see page 170). Ethnic minorities and poor whites knew that middle-class white males were under-represented in Vietnam, except in the officer class, which they dominated. The middle class had frequently used their money and intelligence to avoid combat whether by continuing education or convincing the draft board of their uselessness. The unpopularity of the war divided friends and families. Many of these social wounds and divisions remain. A Johnson aide said that the war was like a fungus or a contagion: it infected everything it touched and seemed to touch everything. He was right.

As Johnson left the presidency he admitted he had made mistakes. He said history would judge him after current passions had subsided. The passions have still not subsided, for the impact of the war remains with Americans. Johnson is still greatly blamed and frequently reviled.

Study Guide: AS Questions

In the style of AQA

Source A

From a speech by President Johnson in 1965 explaining why Americans must fight in Vietnam.

Why must this nation hazard its ease, its interest, and its power for the sake of a people so far away? We fight because we must fight if we are to live in a world where every country can shape its own destiny, and only in such a world will our own freedom be secure. This kind of world will never be built by bombs or bullets. Yet the infirmities of man are such that force must often precede reason and the waste of war, the works of peace.

Source B

Adapted from G.B. Tindall, America, *published in 1988.*

In May 1967 even Secretary of Defence McNamara was not convinced about Johnson's policies in Vietnam. 'The picture of the world's greatest superpower killing or injuring 1000 non-combatants a week, while trying to pound a tiny backward nation into submission on an issue whose merits are hotly disputed, is not a pretty one.' Then, a few months later Walter Cronkite, the most important of American television journalists, confided to his viewers that he no longer believed the Vietnam War was winnable. 'If I've lost Walter', Johnson was reported to say, 'then it's over. I've lost Mr Average Citizen.' Polls showed that Johnson's popularity declined to 35 per cent. Johnson was increasingly isolated over his failing policies. Clark Clifford, the new Secretary of Defence, reported to Johnson that a task force of prominent soldiers and citizens saw no prospects for military victory.

Source C

From Vivienne Sanders, The USA and Vietnam, *published in 2007.*

Perhaps the main reason why Johnson failed to win the war was that the establishment of a viable South Vietnamese state was beyond the powers of Johnson's America. Johnson considered real escalation an impossibility: it might bring the Soviets and Chinese in, and attacking 'little' North Vietnam would damage America's international image. So America just continued to fight a limited and ineffective war to support a series of unpopular Saigon regimes.

(a) **Use Sources A and B.**
   Explain how far the views in Source B differ from those in Source A in relation to the US involvement in Vietnam.
   (12 marks)

(b) **Use Sources A, B and C and your own knowledge.**
   'President Johnson failed in Vietnam because he lacked support from "Mr Average Citizen".' Explain why you agree or disagree with this view.
   (24 marks)

Exam tips

(a) You should identify clearly what the views of each source are, providing direct comparisons where possible. Try to make a broad general statement, such as, according to Source B the fighting is unjustifiable – whereas in Source A it is justified on the grounds of helping to transform the world to preserve freedom. Then define aspects of disagreement more closely, with reference to the text:

   • Source B is hostile to US involvement: the image of killing non-combatants and pounding a tiny nation into submission 'is not a pretty one'.
   • Source A is in favour of US involvement and believes that 'force must often precede reason' and war must precede peace.

   Finally you should consider the extent of disagreement by looking at any similarities:

   • both sources are hostile to war as such
   • both appreciate that the Vietnam War involves 'hazarding' American interests.

   You will need to decide on the extent of disagreement the sources show and provide an overall conclusion.

(b) In answering this question you need to construct a balanced argument that uses both evidence from the given sources and your own knowledge. Source A shows Johnson working hard to gain popular support, which suggests that his policies were not always popular. Source B indicates that by 1967, Johnson was losing support amongst his advisers, the press and 'Mr Average Citizen', but it could be argued that this loss of support was a slow process, and that the war was once a relatively popular war, for example, in the months following the death of Kennedy. Source C provides additional information that suggests other reasons for the failure of the war: the impossibility of establishing a viable South Vietnamese state and the fear of antagonising China and the USSR by attacking the North. According to this source the war was bound to be limited and unpopular because of the Saigon regimes. Another argument that disagrees with the quotation is the fact that support for Johnson actually increased in the early days of the Tet Offensive.

While you should make a clearly supported case for agreement or disagreement, you do need to balance such points for and against to provide a full and convincing answer.

In the style of Edexcel

1. How accurate is it to say that the US failure in Vietnam resulted primarily from losing the hearts and minds of the American people? (30 marks)
2. How important was the Tet Offensive of 1968 in changing US policy in Vietnam? (30 marks)

Source: Edexcel specimen paper 2007. (Edexcel Ltd, accepts no responsibility whatsoever for the accuracy or method of working in the answers given.)

Exam tips

The cross-references are intended to take you straight to the material that will help you to answer the questions.

These two questions will need very different plans, although they are dealing with much the same period.

Question 1 is asking you why the US failed. Question 2 is asking you to look at the way the US government decided to approach the conflict – its aims and plans – and to assess the significance of the Tet Offensive in bringing about a change.

1. Plan to devote about one-third of your answer to the role of public opinion in the USA, showing that the 'hearts and minds' of the American people had turned against the conflict (pages 185–90). You could cover: growing anti-war protests; resentment of war costs; the intensification of hostile press coverage after the Tet Offensive and the sharp decline in public support for the war. Resist the temptation simply to describe the growth of anti-war feelings. In order to show its significance, it will be important to link it directly to its impact on government policy: Johnson's loss of confidence (pages 190–1).

Next, plan to deal with other factors that played a part; factors which had a bearing on how the conflict was going in Vietnam itself:

- The Washington/Saigon failure to win the hearts and minds of the South Vietnamese people (pages 160–7).
- Communist determination, heroism, ingenuity and popularity (pages 168–9).
- The performance of the ARVN and the disunited Americans, who tried to fight a comfortable war in awful conditions and with the wrong methods (pages 167 and 170–5).
- The loss of confidence by the Johnson administration, especially after Tet (pages 182–5 and 190–1).
- American financial and economic problems (page 190).

You could then bring both groups of factors together, showing how they interacted by dealing with the impact of the failure of the Tet Offensive (pages 182–5 and 189–90). You might choose to argue that ultimately the lack of military success in Vietnam was significant in increasing the opposition in the USA and hence was directly and indirectly responsible for the US failure in Vietnam.

2. The key words to note when planning your answer to this question are: 'Tet Offensive' and 'changing US policy'. You need to be clear about the ways in which policy changed after Tet, and you also need to be able to make an assessment of how influential the Tet Offensive was in bringing about those changes.

You could plan to deal briefly with the change in policy from increasing involvement in 1966–7 prior to Tet, to de-escalation afterwards and Johnson's decision in 1968 to hold negotiations and halt bombing. It will be important not to overemphasise the change here, since attempted negotiations and temporary halts were not altogether new (page 150), but you could use Johnson's attitude to these in 1968, combined with the election of a president in 1968 committed to American troop withdrawal (pages 191–2) to show a policy change which was permanent.

In order to show that the Tet Offensive was significant in bringing about this change, you will need to show that Tet had an influence on public opinion, military thinking and government opinion (pages 182–5 and 189–90). Remember to focus your coverage on the impact of Tet on US policy. For example, you should resist the temptation to describe the impact of Tet on the media and public opinion. You need to make this directly relevant by showing that the pressure of media and public opinion influenced government policy (pages 189–90).

In order to assess the significance of the Tet Offensive you will also need to show that these trends were in place prior to Tet:

- The impact of protests and hostile media coverage prior to Tet (pages 187–8).
- Questioning of US policy by senior military and political figures prior to Tet (pages 180–1 and 187–8).

In coming to your overall assessment you can choose to see Tet as an accelerator of pre-existing trends or an event responsible for a decisive change in policy. If you feel that public attitudes were crucial in influencing government policy (page 188), the link between Tet and this might be a point to highlight in a conclusion which deals with the interaction of a number of factors.

In the style of OCR

(a) Compare Sources A and C as evidence for military morale during the Vietnam War. (30 marks)
(b) Using your own knowledge, assess how far the sources support the interpretation that the *main* reason America failed to win the Vietnam War was the strength of their opponents. (70 marks)

Source A

From a letter by Le Duan, Thu Vao Nam, November 1965. The Hanoi Politburo writes to the Communist Party in the South, outlining the party's commitment to a protracted war strategy.

Dear brothers,
Militarily, destroying the puppet government's troops is easier than American troops who have not fought us much, so are optimistic, proud of their weapons and keep their nationalist pride. The puppet troops, after many defeats, have low morale and little enthusiasm to fight. Therefore, we must strengthen our resolve to wipe out the puppet troops as fast as possible. However, our propaganda must emphasise the slogan 'Find Americans to kill'. We must thoroughly research suitable methods to destroy American troops in particular battlegrounds. Our guerrilla forces encircle the American troops' bases. Brothers and sisters must be encouraged and praised, so as to heighten their resolve to kill American troops.

Source B

From a lecture by Robert F. Kennedy, 18 March 1968. Senator Kennedy expresses his opinion on the reasons why America was losing the Vietnam War in a lecture at Kansas State University.

Our control over the rural population has evaporated. The Saigon government is now less of an ally. Our victories come at the cost of destroying Vietnam. Its people are disintegrating under the blows of war. The war is weakening our position in Asia and the world, and eroding international co-operation that has directly supported our security for the past three decades. The war is costing us a quarter of our federal budget and tens of thousands of our young men's lives. Higher yet is the price we pay in our own innermost lives, and in the spirit of America.

Source C

From a speech by Clark Clifford, 1969. The US Secretary of Defence addresses the Council on Foreign Affairs concerning the impact of the 1968 Tet Offensive.

The enemy's Tet Offensive was beaten back at great cost. The confidence of the American people was badly shaken. We questioned whether the South Vietnamese government could restore order, morale and army discipline. President Johnson forbade the invasion of North Vietnam because this could trigger their mutual assistance pact with China. He forbade the mining of the principal port through which the North received military supplies, because a Soviet ship might be sunk. He forbade our forces pursuing the enemy into Laos and Cambodia, for this would spread the war. Given these circumstances, how could we win?

Source D

Adapted from Time *magazine, 5 December 1969. An American magazine article reports the impact of the My Lai Massacre a year after it occurred.*

The massacre at My Lai was an atrocity, barbaric in execution. Yet as chilling to the American mind was that the culprits were not obviously demented men, but were almost depressingly ordinary and decent in their daily lives. At home in Ohio or Vermont they would never maliciously strike a child, much less kill one. Yet men in American uniforms slaughtered the civilians of My Lai, and in so doing humiliated the US and called in question the US mission in Vietnam in a way that all the anti-war protesters could never have done.

Source E

From a statement by John Kerry of Vietnam Veterans Against the War, 23 April 1971. Kerry addresses the Senate Committee of Foreign Relations, recalling the observations of some American soldiers during the Vietnam War.

We found most people didn't even know the difference between Communism and democracy. They only wanted to work in rice paddies without helicopters strafing them and bombs with napalm burning their villages and tearing their country apart. They wanted America to leave them alone in peace. They survived by siding with whichever military force was present at a particular time, be it Viet Cong, North Vietnamese or American. We saw first hand how American taxes supported a corrupt dictatorial regime. We saw America lose its sense of morality as it accepted My Lai very coolly.

Exam tips

The cross-references are intended to take you straight to the material that will help you to answer the questions.

(a) This question asks you to compare two sources as evidence by using their content and provenance to explain your answer to the question. Focus clearly on '*military morale* during the Vietnam War' and make it the heart of your answer. A true comparison needs sustained cross-reference of the two sources point by point, not one source after the other. Your answer should be balanced, and references to context are only valuable in helping you compare the sources.

Provenance:

- Authors and dates: subjective, national and ideological. Source A: the North Vietnamese Communists – military tactics and propaganda in the lead-up to the Tet Offensive (pages 160–1, 168 and 182); Source C: US Secretary of Defence – looking back on the impact of the Tet Offensive after Johnson had left office (pages 182–5 and 189–90).
- Nature, purpose, style: Source A – secret, official, ideological propaganda to raise morale (pages 146–7); Source C – public, with hindsight, excusing failures, recording loss of confidence (page 192).

Textual content on problems faced by South Vietnam:

- Points of agreement on morale: weakness of the South Vietnamese government; the high cost in lives and damage to morale from military defeats.
- Points of disagreement: Source A refers to a time when US troops had not yet seen much combat, whereas Source C refers to the impact of destructive battles fought in South Vietnamese territory; in Source A the positive tone contrasts with US defeatism in Source C. In Source A the target is becoming the US troops now that the South Vietnamese troops have lost morale, but the war effort seems internal, whereas in Source C the American government sees the enemy in international terms, banning any provocative military strategy which might extend the war to China or the USSR, so undermining morale and hindering US military tactics. The sense of Source C is that confidence in the US ability to win has been lost, with lack of ARVN order, morale and army discipline, in contrast to Source A, where American troops are seen as nationalist, optimistic and proud of their weapons.

(b) This question asks you to use your own knowledge and *all five* sources to create a balanced argument evaluating the interpretation in the question. Focus clearly on '*reasons* America failed to win the Vietnam War' during the period covered by the sources. The sources should drive your answer, and your factual knowledge should be used to support and exemplify the points in your argument.

There will be one reason given in the question, and your first task is to evaluate it. Group the sources by their side of the argument: Sources A, C and to some extent E support the interpretation, whereas Sources B, D and E refute it. Use factual knowledge to exemplify and discuss each point. Suggest a range of other reasons picking up the clues in the sources. Cross-reference phrases across the sources and use them to argue a case for and against the view that 'the strength of their opponents' was the main reason, using factual knowledge to develop and explain your points (Chapters 8 and 9). Reach an evaluative judgement on the relative importance of each, at the end of each paragraph – remembering to link back to the question.

The other side of the argument concerns the weaknesses of America and its allies:

- Loss of confidence and moral opposition from both American troops and public opinion (Sources B and C; pages 171, 182 and 187); loss of South Vietnamese support (Sources B, C, D and E; pages 160–7); domestic politics (page 189); the president's personal loss of confidence and status (Sources B and C; pages 190–1).
- International attitudes (Sources B, C and D; page 181).
- Reliance on superior technology, brutalisation and indiscipline among American troops (Sources A, D and E; pages 163–4, 171–2 and 174).
- Economics (Sources C and D; pages 190–1).

In your conclusion, link together the reasons, weigh up their relative importance and reach a supported judgement to answer the question.

10

1969–73: Nixon – Diplomatic Genius or Mad Bomber?

POINTS TO CONSIDER

American involvement in Vietnam finally ended under President Richard Nixon. The issues that historians debate about Nixon and Vietnam are covered in this chapter. Why was it Nixon, the great Cold Warrior and supporter of escalation, who ended the war? Having decided from the outset of his presidency that the war had to be ended, why did Nixon take so long to do so? Did he delay peace until the eve of the 1972 presidential election in order to get re-elected? Why did he apparently escalate the war by bombing Cambodia? Was his Vietnam policy a total failure? Also covered is another bigger question. Was he, as some Americans believe, an evil man whose policies were characterised by 'secrecy, duplicity, and a ruthless attention to immediate political advantage regardless of larger moral issues', as the historian Marilyn Young, writing in 1991, considered? These questions are covered through sections on:

- Nixon's changing views on Vietnam
- President Nixon, Kissinger and the Vietnam problem
- Vietnam, 1969–71
- 1972 – getting re-elected
- Assessment of Nixon's Vietnam policy

Key dates

1969	February	Communists launched offensive on South Vietnam
	March	Nixon secretly bombed Cambodia
	April	Nixon suggested secret Washington–Hanoi negotiations
	May	Nixon offered Hanoi concessions for peace
	June	Troop withdrawals began
	September	Nixon announced the withdrawal of 60,000 American troops from Vietnam
	October	Nixon started 'linkage'
	Oct–Nov	Widespread anti-war protests; My Lai massacre publicised

	November	Nixon's 'great silent majority' speech
1970	January	Heavy US bombing of the Ho Chi Minh Trail in Laos and Cambodia, and of North Vietnamese anti-aircraft bases
	February	Massive North Vietnamese offensive in Laos; US/ARVN invasion of Cambodia
	April	Nixon's 'pitiful helpless giant' speech
	May	Large-scale protests throughout US; students shot at Kent State University
1971	February	Lam Son Offensive by ARVN in Laos
	May	Nixon offered Hanoi more concessions
	December	Number of American troops down to 180,000
1972	March	PAVN offensive against South Vietnam
	April	Nixon bombed Hanoi and Haiphong
	August	Kissinger and Hanoi made concessions
	October	Kissinger said, 'Peace is at hand'
	October	Thieu rejected Kissinger and Hanoi's agreement
	November	Nixon re-elected president, but running out of money
	December	Nixon's 'Christmas bombing' of North Vietnam
1973	January	Paris Peace Accords ended US involvement in Vietnam War
1975		Vietnam reunified under Communism; Cambodia and Laos also Communist

Key question
What was Nixon's position on Vietnam before he became president?

1 | Nixon's Changing Views on Vietnam

a) Vice-president and Cold Warrior (1953–61)

As Eisenhower's vice-president, Nixon had an exceptional apprenticeship in foreign affairs, including the problem of Vietnam. He wanted to help the French at Dienbienphu (see page 108) with an American air strike and was even willing to use (small) atomic bombs. He said that if sending American boys to fight in Vietnam was the only way to stop Communist expansion in Indochina, then the government should take the 'politically unpopular position' and do it.

b) Republican foreign policy expert (1961–8)

After his defeat in the 1960 presidential race, Nixon held no political office for eight years but kept himself in the political news by foreign policy pronouncements. On Vietnam, he said:

> Victory is essential to the survival of freedom. We have an
> unparalleled opportunity to roll back the Communist tide, not only
> in South Vietnam but in Southeast Asia generally and indeed the
> world as a whole.

As the recognised leader of the Republican opposition on foreign
policy, Nixon spurred the Democrat Johnson to greater
involvement in Vietnam. Whatever President Johnson did, Nixon
urged him to do more. 'The United States cannot afford another
defeat in Asia', Nixon said. 'When [President] Nixon said, in
1969, that he had inherited a war not of his making, he was being
too modest', said his biographer Stephen Ambrose.

c) Republican presidential candidate (1967–8)
i) Vietnamisation
In 1967, presidential hopeful Nixon seemed the last man likely to
advocate withdrawal from Vietnam. He criticised the anti-war
protesters as a traitorous minority: 'The last desperate hope of
North Vietnam is that they can win politically in the United States
what our fighting men are denying them militarily in Vietnam.'
However, in early 1968, Nixon was as shocked as everyone else by
the Tet Offensive (see pages 182–3). This was a great turning
point for him. He realised that there would have to be changes in
American policy. He started to call (as had Kennedy and Johnson
before him) for the increased use of South Vietnamese soldiers.
This policy became known as **Vietnamisation**:

> The nation's objective should be to help the South Vietnamese fight
> the war and not fight it for them. If they do not assume the majority
> of the burden in their own defence, they cannot be saved.

Nixon said that American forces should be withdrawn while the
ARVN was built up. He stopped talking about escalation. There
was no more talk of a 'victorious peace', only '**peace with
honour**'. 'I pledge to you, new leadership will end the war and
win the peace.'

Did Nixon really believe that Thieu could maintain a strong
South Vietnam without the ever-increasing American aid that
Nixon had so strongly advocated until Tet? Or was he guilty of
duplicity? He probably genuinely believed that Thieu could
survive with the help of a change of emphasis in American aid
(more American bombing and fewer American soldiers) and a
radical change of diplomatic direction. Nixon hoped that
America could replace the era of confrontation with the era of
negotiation, and get Soviet and Chinese help in forcing Hanoi to
accept American peace terms.

ii) Johnson and peace talks in 1968
The final months of Johnson's presidency were dominated by the
Paris peace talks, and some have accused Nixon of sabotaging the
negotiations in order to stop the Democrats getting the credit for

Key terms

Vietnamisation
A phrase/policy
introduced by the
Nixon
administration; the
idea was that the
South Vietnamese
government and
forces should take
the main
responsibility for
the war against
Communism.

'Peace with honour'
Nixon always
claimed he would
get 'peace with
honour' in Vietnam,
by which he meant
that Thieu's
government must
stay in power in a
viable South
Vietnamese state.

peace. Hanoi was offering Thieu an opportunity to remain in power with a coalition government. Privately, Nixon encouraged Thieu not to participate in the talks. 'We don't want to play politics with peace', said Nixon, but, he subsequently admitted, 'that was inevitably what was happening'. So, had Nixon sabotaged the talks? Although Nixon might have tried to do so, Thieu needed no persuasion to reject the idea of a coalition government.

d) Why Nixon decided to get out of Vietnam

Nixon made his name as a politician as an extreme anti-Communist, yet he got America out of Vietnam and drew closer to the Soviets and Chinese than any previous Cold War president. Was there a genuine conversion or 'ruthless attention to immediate political advantage'? A combination of events made Nixon change his Cold Warrior stance.

i) Tet

Tet (see pages 182–3) proved conclusively to Nixon that the Vietnam War was not going well, and made him decide that America needed to withdraw as soon as possible.

ii) The Sino-Soviet split

The Cold War world had changed. The **Sino-Soviet split** shattered the threat of a **monolithic Communist bloc**. Nixon decided that America could play off the two rival Communist giants against each other, by improving American relations with both China and the USSR, who could then press Hanoi to a 'peace with honour' settlement in Vietnam.

iii) Peacemaker

The political and dramatic impact of being a world peacemaker appealed to Nixon. In his inaugural address, Nixon said, 'The greatest honour history can bestow is the title of peacemaker'. Improved relations with China and the USSR and peace in Vietnam would reinvigorate America, and ensure Nixon's place in the history books and his re-election in 1972. He knew that the Vietnam War had ruined Johnson's presidency. On learning of Johnson's bugging and wiretapping in the White House, Nixon said privately, 'I don't blame him. He's been under such pressure because of that damn war, he'd do anything. I'm not going to end up like LBJ … I'm going to stop that war. Fast!'

An intelligent pragmatism, an element of idealism and political ambition all combined to make the old Cold Warrior ready to end the Vietnam War.

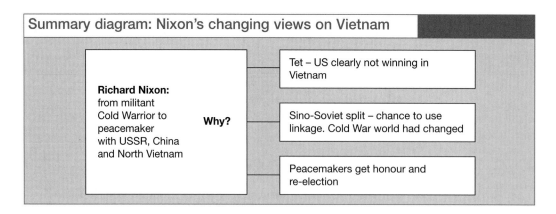

Summary diagram: Nixon's changing views on Vietnam

Richard Nixon: from militant Cold Warrior to peacemaker with USSR, China and North Vietnam

Why?

Tet – US clearly not winning in Vietnam

Sino-Soviet split – chance to use linkage. Cold War world had changed

Peacemakers get honour and re-election

2 | President Nixon, Kissinger and the Vietnam Problem

Key question
What was the role and significance of Henry Kissinger?

a) Nixon and Kissinger

Nixon thought that foreign policy was the most important and interesting task of any president, and he chose a national security adviser, Henry Kissinger, who agreed with him. In order to ensure White House control of foreign policy, Nixon chose his old friend and supporter William Rogers to be Secretary of State. Rogers knew little about foreign policy: when he got his first pile of foreign policy papers to read, he was amazed: 'You don't expect me to read all this stuff, do you?'

i) Kissinger and diplomacy

Kissinger was a great believer in personal and secret diplomacy. He distrusted bureaucrats and it was commonly said in Washington that he treated his staff as mushrooms: kept in the dark, stepped on, and frequently covered with manure. Like Nixon, Kissinger felt that foreign policy was usually 'too complex' for 'the ordinary guy' to understand. This conviction was a weakness. They did not always explain their diplomacy, and therefore did not always ensure popular support for their policies. Both thought in terms of American national interest with little apparent regard for moral considerations. Many have considered their *realpolitik* shocking. Unlike Johnson, neither seemed to worry about the deaths of Vietnamese civilians or even of American soldiers.

ii) The Nixon–Kissinger relationship

Nixon and Kissinger spent a great deal of time together and as Nixon's presidency wore on, Kissinger became ever more influential. Unlike Nixon, Kissinger was always treated with the utmost respect by the media. Such was Kissinger's power that on the occasions when he subverted Nixon's intentions, he got away with it. Led by two such hard-headed realists, American foreign policy became what many people would consider careless of 'larger moral issues' in its emphasis upon the ultimate survival and strength of American power. Nixon himself recognised that it would be called **Machiavellian**.

Key terms

Realpolitik
A realistic, rather than moralistic or legalistic approach to foreign policy; a belief that foreign policy should be dictated by the national interest.

Machiavellian
Machiavelli was a sixteenth-century Italian writer who once wrote, 'the end justifies the means' – in foreign policy, that would be considered as *realpolitik*.

Profile: Richard Nixon 1913–94

1913		– Born in California, son of a grocer
1937		– Practised law in California
1942		– Joined US Navy in the Second World War
1947–9		– Twice elected to House of Representatives; took a leading role in hounding Communists
1950		– Elected to Senate, defeating Helen Douglas, partly by accusing her of Communist ('pink') sympathies – he said she was 'pink right down to her underwear'
1953–61		– Eisenhower's vice-president
1954		– Advocated use of tactical (small) nuclear weapons to help France at Dienbienphu (see page 108)
1960		– Narrowly lost to Democrat John Kennedy in presidential election
1962		– Defeated in Californian **gubernatorial** election; told the press he was retiring from politics, so they would not 'have Richard Nixon to kick around any more'; gained reputation as Republican Party foreign policy specialist
1967		– Published article that advised improved relations with Communist China, which would soon be a leading world power
1968	Jan–Feb	– Shaken by Tet Offensive, decided America must get out of Vietnam
	November	– Presidential election victory; promised to bring 'peace with honour' in Vietnam
1969		– Began withdrawing American troops from Vietnam; emphasised Vietnamisation
1970		– Extended Vietnam War to Communist sanctuaries in neighbouring Cambodia; led to massive anti-war protests in US
1972	February	– Visited People's Republic of China, ending two decades of dangerous estrangement
	November	– Re-elected in landslide victory
1973	January	– Ended Vietnam War
	May	– Made arms limitation treaty with the USSR, as part of his **detente** policy
1974	August	– Nixon announced resignation because of **Watergate affair**
1994		– Died

Nixon is very important in the Vietnam War context as the president who finally got the United States out. Faced with the problem of getting out yet retaining US international credibility, his tactics included the promotion of detente and the massive bombing of Vietnam, Cambodia and Laos.

Key terms

Gubernatorial
Pertaining to being a state governor.

Detente
Relaxation of tension between the USA and the USSR in the Cold War in the 1970s.

Watergate affair
During Nixon's re-election campaign, Republicans authorised burglary and wiretapping of Democratic national headquarters at Watergate building in Washington, DC; the Nixon administration tried a 'cover-up'.

Profile: Henry Kissinger 1923–

1923	– Born in Germany
1938	– Family escaped Nazi persecution of Jews; fled to USA
1943	– Served in US Army in the Second World War
1954	– Harvard PhD; lectured in international relations
1959–69	– Served as defence consultant to several administrations
1962	– Professor of government at Harvard
1969–75	– Head of National Security Council; contributed greatly to detente with USSR and People's Republic of China
1970	– Major role in Vietnamisation
1973–7	– Secretary of State; arranged Paris Peace Accords, which ended Vietnam War; awarded Nobel Peace Prize
1974	– Secretary of State under President Gerald Ford
1977	– Became an international consultant, writer and lecturer

Kissinger's importance in the Vietnam War context is that he worked closely with Nixon in getting the United States out of Vietnam, supposedly 'with honour'.

b) Vietnam: the problems and solutions

Vietnam was Nixon's greatest single problem. He sought a peace settlement that would allow Thieu to remain in power in an independent South Vietnam. He hoped to achieve this through 'Vietnamisation' and through pressure on the USSR and China. Nixon would tempt the Soviets with promises of arms agreements and trade and the Chinese with a **normalisation of diplomatic relations**. He also had another ploy, one of his advisers recalled:

> I call it the '**Madman Theory**' ... I want the North Vietnamese to believe ... I might do anything ... We'll just slip the word to them that, 'for God's sake, you know Nixon is obsessed about Communism. We can't restrain him when he's angry – and he has his hand on the nuclear button' – and Ho Chi Minh himself will be in Paris in two days begging for peace.

America also needed peace at home. This was demonstrated in Nixon's presidential inaugural parade. Thousands of anti-war demonstrators chanted 'Ho, Ho, Ho Chi Minh, the NLF [see page 107] is going to win'. Demonstrators burned small American flags and spat at police. Nixon thus had two great tasks as president in 1969. He had to bring peace to America and to Vietnam.

Key question
What did President Nixon see as his great challenge and how did he plan to meet it?

Normalisation of diplomatic relations
It was not until the late 1970s that the USA established diplomatic relations with China. Once diplomatic relations were established, ambassadors were exchanged.

Madman Theory
Nixon wanted Hanoi to think he was capable of anything, in order to frighten them into making peace.

Key terms

Summary diagram: President Nixon, Kissinger and the Vietnam problem		
Nixon + Kissinger = Expertise and *realpolitik*		
Vietnam War + Division amongst Americans = The need for peace at home and abroad		

3 | Vietnam 1969–71

Although Nixon was determined to end the war, he wanted 'peace with honour'. It took time and tremendous effort to persuade Hanoi to agree to allow Thieu to remain in power without having to accept Communists in a coalition government. Nixon had to use great military and diplomatic pressure to gain a settlement in which Thieu was given a reasonable chance for survival, and whereby it could not be said that America had wasted its time and effort in Vietnam. While applying the military and diplomatic pressure, Nixon had also to take into account American left-wing opposition to the war, and right-wing opposition to losing it.

a) 1969
i) Military solutions in 1969
Nixon attempted three solutions to the military problem in 1969: bombing the trail in Cambodia, the 'madman' ploy and Vietnamisation.

In February 1969, the Communists launched another offensive on South Vietnam. 'Rolling Thunder' (see page 146) and the American ground offensive of 1966–8 (see pages 150–1) had clearly not worked, so in March Nixon decided to try a secret bombing offensive against the Ho Chi Minh Trail (see the map on page 136) in Cambodia. Nixon hoped to sever enemy supply lines, to encourage Hanoi to agree to an acceptable peace, and to destroy the supposed Vietnamese Communist headquarters in Cambodia – **COSVN** (the Central Office for South Vietnam). When the bombing failed to destroy COSVN or slow traffic on the trail, Nixon escalated it in late April.

'I can't believe', said the exasperated Kissinger, 'that a fourth-rate power like North Vietnam does not have a breaking point'. He advocated blockading Haiphong and invading North Vietnam. Nixon feared domestic opposition to this but deliberately leaked to the press that he was considering it – his 'madman' tactic.

ii) Diplomacy in 1969
On the diplomatic front, Nixon's first initiative was the April 1969 suggestion that, as the Paris peace talks had stalled amidst the public posturing by the representatives from Saigon and Hanoi,

---

Key question
How and with what results did Nixon try to end the war in 1969?

Key dates

Communists launched offensive on South Vietnam: February 1969

Nixon secretly bombed Cambodia: March 1969

Key term

COSVN
Central Office for South Vietnam – supposed Vietnamese Communist headquarters in Cambodia.

there should be secret Washington–Hanoi negotiations. Hanoi had always favoured that option as it excluded Saigon.

In secret talks in May, Nixon offered Hanoi new peace terms. Although still insistent that Thieu remain in power, he dropped Johnson's insistence that American troops would only withdraw six months after the PAVN. He offered simultaneous withdrawal. The North Vietnamese delegation was unimpressed. Nixon told Kissinger to warn them that as America was withdrawing troops and was willing to accept the results of South Vietnamese elections, they must do likewise or Nixon would have to do something dramatic. Kissinger set them a 1 November deadline. Hanoi responded that they had no troops in South Vietnam and that Thieu must give way to a coalition government.

As he was making little progress with Hanoi, Nixon turned to Moscow. In October Nixon put pressure on the Soviets, promising detente for their help in ending the Vietnam War (he called this exchange '**linkage**'). He warned them, 'The humiliation of a defeat is absolutely unacceptable to my country.'

Key terms

Linkage
Linking US concessions to the USSR and China to their assistance in ending the Vietnam War.

Moratorium
In this context, suspension of normal activities, in order to protest.

iii) The home front in 1969
Nixon used several tactics to keep the home front quiet.

Firstly, he made a series of American troop withdrawals from Vietnam. He timed the announcements to defuse public opposition: for example, in September 1969, anti-war activists and congressmen were preparing to protest, so Nixon announced the withdrawal of 60,000 troops. Kissinger opposed the troop withdrawals, saying it would decrease American bargaining power with Hanoi and would be like giving salted peanuts to the American public – they would just want more and more. Nixon said public opinion gave him little choice.

Secondly, Nixon judged that the heart of the anti-war movement was male college students threatened with the draft. He therefore adjusted it so that older students (whom he presumably considered to be more confident and articulate) were less hard-hit. This temporarily decreased protests and Nixon got a 71 per cent approval rating.

Thirdly, in order to forestall the anti-war protesters, Nixon tried to keep his actions secret, as with the 1969 bombing of Cambodia. When a British correspondent in Cambodia publicised it, Nixon, convinced it was an internal leak, ordered large-scale wiretapping.

However, troop withdrawals, adjustments to the draft and (attempted) secrecy failed to halt the protests. Nixon rightly claimed that the protesters were a minority, but their numbers were growing. In October 1969 the campuses were in uproar and the largest anti-war protest in American history took place. In this '**moratorium**' protesters took to the streets in every major city. Millions participated, many middle class and middle aged. The more radical waved VC flags, chanted defeatist slogans and burned American flags. Although such behaviour proved unpopular, it made Nixon drop the 1 November ultimatum to Hanoi. He backed down to keep the public happy, despite saying that:

Key dates

Nixon suggested secret Washington–Hanoi negotiations: April 1969

Nixon offered Hanoi concessions for peace: May 1969

Nixon started 'linkage': October 1969

Troop withdrawals began: June 1969

Nixon announced the withdrawal of 60,000 US troops from Vietnam: September 1969

Widespread anti-war protests; My Lai massacre publicised: October–November 1969

Nixon's 'great silent majority' speech: November 1969

to allow government policy to be made in the streets … would give the decision, not to the majority, and not to those with the strongest arguments, but to those with the loudest voices … It would invite anarchy.

Nixon used speeches to try to keep the home front quiet and on 3 November 1969 delivered one of his best. He asked for time to end the war:

And so tonight, to you, the great silent majority of my fellow Americans – I ask for your support. Let us be united for peace. Let us be united against defeat. Because let us understand: North Vietnam cannot defeat or humiliate the United States. Only Americans can do that.

Nixon's approval rating shot up to 68 per cent, but although he exulted, 'We've got those liberal bastards on the run now, and we're going to keep them on the run', protests soon began again.

Between 14 and 16 November, a quarter of a million peaceful protesters took over Washington. Forty thousand marchers carrying candles filed past the White House, each saying the name of an American soldier. Nixon wondered whether he could have thousands of helicopters fly low over them to blow out their candles and drown their voices. Simultaneously, news of the My Lai massacre (see page 163) surfaced. Although Nixon reminded everyone that the VC often behaved similarly, many thought that if the price of war was making murderers out of American youths, it was too high.

In 1969, diplomatically as well as militarily, Nixon made no real progress. He had tried changes, concessions and threats, but seemed no nearer to peace; 1970 was no better.

b) 1970 – the Cambodian offensive
i) Nixon's aims and methods

<table>
<tr><td>

Key question
How and with what results did Nixon try to end the war in 1970?

</td><td>

Nixon's goals were clear. He wanted to be out of Vietnam before the presidential election of November 1972, leaving pro-American governments in South Vietnam, Cambodia and Laos. He also wanted Hanoi to release American prisoners of war (POWs). His only means of persuasion were 'Mad Bomber' performances and linkage, and neither worked in 1970.

</td></tr>
<tr><td>

Key date

Heavy US bombing of the Ho Chi Minh Trail in Laos and Cambodia, and of the North Vietnamese anti-aircraft bases: January 1970

</td><td>

ii) Escalation in Laos and Cambodia

Having announced the withdrawal of 150,000 American troops from Southeast Asia, Nixon nevertheless appeared to be extending the war to Laos and Cambodia when in January 1970 he escalated the air offensive in January 1970, heavily bombing the trail in Laos and Cambodia, and North Vietnamese anti-aircraft bases. Why? He believed that demonstrations of American power would counter Saigon's pessimism about American troop withdrawals, help to protect the remaining Americans in Vietnam, intimidate Hanoi and gain better peace terms. Nevertheless, on

</td></tr>
</table>

12 February the North Vietnamese launched another great offensive in Laos. Desperate for some success, especially as Congress was considering cutting off his money, Nixon sent 30,000 American and ARVN forces into southwestern Cambodia (less than 50 miles from Saigon), but they encountered neither enemy resistance nor COSVN.

iii) The 'pitiful, helpless giant' speech

This invasion of Cambodia caused unrest within the United States, which Nixon tried to defuse with a speech in April 1970. He said America had respected Cambodian neutrality for five years ('a whopper', says Ambrose), but the Vietnamese Communists had vital bases there, so the US had to do a clean-up operation. He denied that this constituted an invasion of Cambodia and said America's first defeat in its 190-year existence would be a national disgrace:

> If, when the chips are down, the world's most powerful nation, the United States of America, acts like a pitiful, helpless giant, the forces of totalitarianism and anarchy will threaten free nations and free institutions throughout the world.

This emotive language was effective. The speech proved quite popular, but again the success was short-lived.

iv) Achievements of the Cambodian offensive

What had Nixon's Cambodian offensive achieved? The capture and destruction of vast quantities of Communist war materiel meant that it was nearly two years before Hanoi launched another major offensive in South Vietnam, which theoretically gave the ARVN time to grow stronger. Nixon claimed that intervention in Cambodia had occupied PAVN troops who would otherwise have been killing Americans. However, COSVN had not been found. Perhaps it had never existed. The Americans had expected to find a miniature Pentagon, but there were just a few huts. Furthermore, 344 Americans and 818 ARVN died, and 1592 Americans and 3553 ARVN were wounded. Nixon's critics said that it had widened the war. The *New York Times* queried whether the offensive had won time for America or just boosted Hanoi by revealing American divisions and the restraints on the president.

One totally unexpected result of the Cambodian invasion was that it forced the Communists further inland, where they destabilised the Cambodian government. Furthermore, American bombing increased the popularity of the Cambodian Communists.

v) Kent State and campus riots

When Secretary of State Bill Rogers finally heard about the planned invasion of Cambodia, he said, 'This will make the students puke.' The Cambodian offensive did indeed cause trouble on campuses across America. On 5 May 1970 four

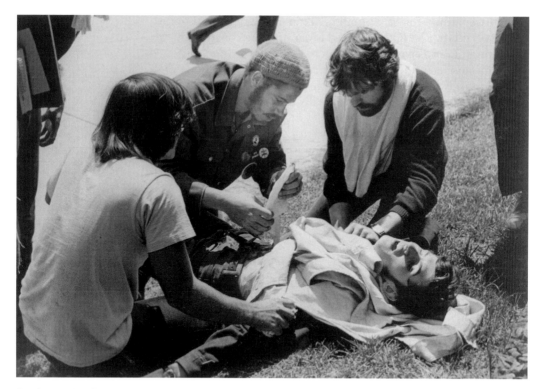

Students give first aid to a young demonstrator shot and wounded by Ohio National Guardsmen on the Kent State University campus.

students at Kent State University, Ohio, were shot dead by the National Guard. Some had been participating in an anti-war rally, some just changing classes. Student protests escalated. All Californian colleges were closed down by Governor Reagan. As students rioted, Nixon backed down and declared that he would get American troops out of Cambodia by June. Again, government policy was made in the streets. The military were furious. In New York City, 100,000 pro-Nixon people demonstrated and construction workers (traditionally Democrats) beat up students from the East's leading colleges in support of the Republican president's policies.

vi) President, public opinion and Congress

Polls showed how the Cambodian intervention had divided Americans: 50 per cent approved Nixon's Cambodian offensive, 39 per cent disapproved. As the Cambodian offensive appeared to be a dramatic escalation of the war authorised solely by the president, it aggravated relations between the president and Congress. Under pressure of the Cold War, the president had been acquiring near absolute control over foreign policy and America had been developing what many historians call the **'imperial presidency'**. It was inevitable that Congress would attempt to reassert its power, especially when presidential foreign policy was unpopular. Congress rightly said that the constitution gave them alone the power to declare war and to raise and to

Key term

'Imperial presidency'
Some Americans felt that under the pressure of the lengthy Cold War, the president gained greater power and became like some old European king or emperor.

finance the armed forces, although Nixon also had a good point when he said that he had inherited a war and the constitution gave him powers as commander-in-chief. Whatever the constitutional rectitude, throughout 1970 and 1971 the Senate enthusiastically supported bills to stop Nixon waging war in Cambodia, Laos and Vietnam. 'Virtually everybody wants out', said one hawk.

Nixon's dilemma was that he could not get re-elected unless he extricated America from Vietnam: he told Republican senators, 'I will not be the first President of the United States to lose a war'. However, he would not be able to save Thieu, honour or peace if he just withdrew.

c) Vietnam 1971
i) US Army morale, 1971

Key question
How and with what results did Nixon try to end the war in 1971?

By 1971 the morale of the army in Vietnam had plummeted. This is not surprising. Eighteen-year-olds were still being asked to fight a war that everyone in America agreed was just about finished, in order to allow time for the army of a corrupt dictatorship in Saigon to improve. Nixon warned the West Point graduating class that it was no secret that they would be leading troops guilty of drug abuse and insubordination.

ii) The Lam Son Offensive, 1971

Determined not to be the first president to lose a war and desperate to gain peace with honour, Nixon decided to go on the military offensive again.

The JCS had long been tempted to attack the Ho Chi Minh trail in southern Laos. Although Westmoreland had said that it would require four American divisions, the JCS argued that the ARVN could do it if protected by American air power. Cutting the trail would help ARVN morale, show that Vietnamisation was working, and damage Hanoi's ability to stage an offensive in 1971. Rogers warned that Hanoi expected it (there had been leaks in Saigon), and that Nixon was sending only one ARVN division to do a job which Westmoreland refused to do without four American divisions, but Nixon and Kissinger ignored him, and the Lam Son Offensive began on 8 February 1971.

Key date
Lam Son Offensive by ARVN in Laos: February 1971

Initially the 5000 élite ARVN troops did well, but then the PAVN got the upper hand, thanks especially to new armoured units using Soviet equipment. Within two weeks, the ARVN was routed. Half the force died. American TV viewers saw ARVN troops fighting each other for places on American helicopters lifting them out of Laos. American crews coated the skids with grease so the South Vietnamese would stop hanging on in numbers sufficient to bring down the choppers. Kissinger was particularly furious with Thieu, who had refused to send the number of troops the US recommended. 'Those sons of bitches. It's their country and we can't save it for them if they don't want to.'

iii) Diplomacy in 1971

After three years of offensives and Vietnamisation, Nixon did not seem to have made any progress on the military front. However, in spring 1971 it seemed as if linkage might be working. Nixon's planned *rapprochement* with both the USSR and China was becoming a reality and the USSR and China were urging Hanoi not to insist on Thieu's removal as a prerequisite for peace.

In May, Nixon offered Hanoi another concession: the United States would get out by a set date without demanding mutual withdrawal. In return Hanoi should stop sending additional troops or materials to South Vietnam, observe a ceasefire, and guarantee the territorial integrity of Laos and Cambodia (just when the Communists were about to win in both). Thieu would have to stay in power and the American POWs would be returned. Hanoi was unimpressed, especially as there was no mention of stopping the bombing.

iv) The home front in 1971

The American home front was equally dispiriting for Nixon in 1971: his approval rating dropped to 31 per cent. Influenced by the spring protests (300,000 marched in Washington, DC), some senators tried to halt all aid to South Vietnam unless there was a presidential election. Thieu held one in October 1971, but only allowed one candidate – himself! Nixon could only say that democracy took time to develop.

After three years, then, a frustrated Nixon seemed no closer to bringing peace to America or Vietnam. Public opposition was hampering the military offensives that he hoped would get Hanoi to make concessions at the peace talks. As yet, his diplomatic offensives were not paying off. The USSR and China could not or would not persuade Hanoi to give in. Aware of American national honour and credibility, and fearful of alienating the right wing, Nixon insisted that Thieu remain in power, but Hanoi said 'No'.

Key dates

Nixon offered Hanoi more concessions: May 1971

Number of American troops down to 180,000: December 1971

Summary diagram: Vietnam 1969–71

	Military	Diplomatic	Home front
1969	• Communist offensive • Nixon bombed Cambodia	• Madman ploy • Secret talks • Nixon concessions • Linkage	• Troop withdrawals • Moratorium • 'Silent majority speech' • News of My Lai
1970	• Nixon bombed Laos, Cambodia and North Vietnam's anti-aircraft bases • US/ARVN invaded Cambodia • Cambodian offensive	• Linkage	• 'Pitiful giant' speech • Protests, e.g. Kent State • Congress critical of Nixon and the war
1971	• Lam Son Offensive	• Nixon concessions	• Congress critical

4 | 1972 – Getting Re-elected

1972 was the presidential election year. Nixon needed some great breakthrough to ensure that he won, but that looked unlikely.

a) Problems in early 1972

In January 1972, Nixon's combination of military and diplomatic pressure still seemed unsuccessful. His bombing offensive on the North antagonised many Americans. Many American pilots were shot down during the air offensive, increasing the number of POWs held by Hanoi. Many congressmen were willing to abandon South Vietnam in exchange for the POWs, but Nixon used their existence and safety to help convince others of the need to continue the war.

Key question
Why did an end to the war look unlikely in early 1972?

i) Hanoi's spring offensive

The USSR and China were pressing Hanoi to settle, to let Nixon out with honour and to let Thieu remain for a while. However, Hanoi did not want to face a superbly equipped ARVN perpetually supplied by America, so the PAVN began a great March offensive against South Vietnam, using tanks and artillery as never before. The ARVN crumbled. Nixon's policy of Vietnamisation was discredited in the presidential election year. Nixon therefore decided that these 'bastards have never been bombed like they are going to be bombed this time'.

Key dates

PAVN offensive against South Vietnam: March 1972

Nixon bombed Hanoi and Haiphong: April 1972

ii) Bombing and mining in the North

B-52s were used on North Vietnam for the first time since 1968 and inflicted heavy casualties, but nevertheless the PAVN still advanced. Nixon escalated the bombing. He bombed oil depots around Hanoi and Haiphong. On 16 April, American bombers hit four Soviet merchant ships at anchor in Haiphong, but as Nixon anticipated, the Soviets were so keen to have the planned **summit** that their protests were low key. Linkage was working.

Nixon then mined North Vietnam's ports. One Democrat spoke of flirting with a Third World War to keep General Thieu in power and save Nixon's face for a little longer. However, it was Nixon who understood the Soviets best. Moscow was tired of financing Hanoi's war, desperate for detente, and impressed by a great Nixon concession (he hinted that he was willing to accept a coalition containing Communists). Meanwhile, Nixon tried to rally the American public, saying:

Key terms

B-52s
Large American bomber planes.

Summit
During the Cold War, meetings or conferences between the US and Soviet leaders were known as summit meetings.

> If the United States betrays the millions of people who have relied on us in Vietnam … it would amount to renunciation of our morality, an abdication of our leadership among nations, and an invitation for the mighty to prey upon the meek all around the world.

He said that if America was strong, the world would remain half instead of wholly Communist. His approval rating shot up to 60 per cent.

iii) Concessions plus force

One of the ways in which Nixon intended to get America out of Vietnam 'with honour' was by disguising concessions with simultaneous shows of force. So, while continuing the bombing throughout the Moscow summit (May 1972), he secretly offered Hanoi yet another vital concession: the PAVN would be allowed to stay in South Vietnam.

iv) Hanoi faltering

Hanoi was finally being driven towards a settlement by a combination of American concessions, Soviet and Chinese pressure, their offensive's failure to take big cities, Operation Phoenix (see page 163), the destructiveness of the B-52s and the probable re-election of the unpredictable 'Mad Bomber'. After three years, Nixon's combination of military and diplomatic pressure and concessions appeared to be working. It was just as well. He was running out of time and money.

> **The end of Operation Phoenix**
> Nixon had been delighted by the success of Operation Phoenix, saying, 'We've got to have more of this. Assassinations. Killings. That's what they [the Communists] are doing.' However, when the press exposed the programme, there was considerable American outrage, so Nixon had to cancel Phoenix operations in 1972.

Key question
Why was peace 'at hand' in autumn 1972?

b) Autumn 1972: running out of time and money

By the second half of 1972 Nixon was running out of time and money. Troop withdrawals meant that Congress could no longer be shamed into granting funds to help 'our boys in the field'. Nixon begged them not to damage his negotiating capabilities, and pointed out that it would be immoral to walk away from Vietnam as there would be a bloodbath for former Thieu supporters. Polls showed that most Americans agreed with Nixon: 55 per cent supported continued heavy bombing of North Vietnam and 64 per cent the mining of Haiphong. Seventy-four per cent thought it important that South Vietnam should not fall to the Communists.

i) Both sides agree to compromise

Key dates
Kissinger and Hanoi made concessions: August 1972

Kissinger said, 'Peace is at hand': October 1972

Both sides now compromised. Hanoi would let Thieu remain in power while America would let the PAVN stay in South Vietnam and not insist upon a ceasefire in Cambodia and Laos. However, Hanoi insisted on a voice in the Saigon government and there seemed no chance of Thieu accepting that, despite Nixon's promise that America would never desert him. Kissinger rejected the idea of a coalition government but offered a Committee of National Reconciliation (to be one-third South Vietnamese, one-third Communist and one-third neutral) to oversee the constitution and elections. Kissinger thereby agreed that the

Communists were a legitimate political force in South Vietnam, which Thieu had always denied. Nixon reminded the tearful Thieu of what had happened to Diem. Nixon shared Thieu's doubts but felt that his ally had to make some concessions and threatened him with the withdrawal of American support. 'We're going to have to put him through the wringer … We simply have to cut the umbilical cord and have this baby walk by itself.'

ii) 'Peace is at hand'

In October, Kissinger thought he had an agreement:

Thieu rejected Kissinger and Hanoi's agreement: October 1972

Nixon re-elected president, but running out of money: November 1972

Key dates

- America would withdraw all its armed forces but continue to supply the ARVN.
- There would be a National Council of Reconciliation with Communist representation.
- The American POWs would be released.
- Thieu would remain in power.
- The PAVN would remain in South Vietnam.
- America would help with the economic reconstruction of North Vietnam as a humanitarian gesture.

Nixon said that it was 'a complete capitulation by the enemy', but then got cold feet and rejected the terms. Why? He was worried about accusations that he had given in to protesters, or that peace at this time was an electoral ploy. Some advisers feared that if peace came before the election, people might vote Democrat as the Democrats were supposedly better at peace-time governing. American Cold Warriors opposed the National Council, as did Thieu, who wanted the PAVN out of South Vietnam and loathed the National Council. Nixon himself was unsure that this constituted peace with honour.

Kissinger was as keen as Nixon for the latter to be re-elected. It meant four more years for both of them. However, when on the eve of the American presidential election, Kissinger assured the press that 'Peace is at hand', Nixon was furious, believing that it would make Hanoi and Thieu more intransigent. He also resented Kissinger gaining the glory from the announcement. Some Democrats were cynical. Why was peace suddenly at hand on the eve of the election? Nixon had had four years to do this. Kissinger pointed out that Hanoi's recent concessions allowing Thieu to remain in power were the difference. He omitted to mention that America had also made concessions.

iii) Persuading Thieu

In November 1972, Nixon was re-elected, but the new Democratic Congress was not going to carry on funding the war. The only way forward was to force Thieu to accept the unacceptable. Nixon gave Thieu his 'absolute assurance' that if Hanoi broke the peace, he would take 'swift and severe retaliatory action'. Thieu knew that any agreement was inevitably going to be a temporary ceasefire so long as the PAVN remained in South

Vietnam, and that the American political system could invalidate Nixon's promise of future aid against North Vietnamese aggression. Some of Kissinger's staff were so exasperated by Thieu's stubbornness that they suggested assassinating him!

Hanoi was still willing to accept the October agreement that Nixon and Kissinger had initially considered satisfactory. However, having once rejected that agreement, America could hardly accept it now without looking rather foolish.

iv) Christmas bombing

On 18 December, Nixon bombed and mined Haiphong again. Although American planes tried to avoid civilian casualties in Hanoi, 1000 died. The North Vietnamese shot down 15 B-52s with 93 American airmen, a rate of losses the US air force could not sustain for long. There was no public explanation for this Christmas 1972 bombing, which caused worldwide uproar. Kissinger was cracking: he leaked to the press that he opposed the Christmas bombing, which was untrue. One adviser thought that 'we look incompetent – bombing for no good reason and because we do not know what else to do'. Why did Nixon do it? He was probably trying to reassure Thieu of American strength and support, to weaken Hanoi so that it could not speedily threaten South Vietnam after peace was concluded, and/or to disguise American retreats and compromises in the negotiations. Several congressmen and influential newspapers rejected such suggestions and questioned Nixon's sanity and accused him of waging 'war by tantrum'.

v) Peace at last

The accord that was finally reached in Paris in January 1973 was basically the same as that of October 1972 with a few cosmetic changes for both sides (one Kissinger aide said, 'We bombed the North Vietnamese into accepting our concessions'). Knowing his funding would soon be cut off, Nixon had to tell Thieu that he was going to sign with or without him. On 22 January Thieu agreed, although he regarded it as virtual surrender.

The 27 January 1973 Paris Peace Accords declared a ceasefire throughout Vietnam (but not Cambodia or Laos). POWs would be exchanged, after which America would remove the last of its troops. The PAVN was not required to leave the South, but had to promise not to 'take advantage' of the ceasefire or increase its numbers. Thieu remained in power, but the Committee of National Reconciliation contained Communist representation, and would sponsor free elections. Nixon secretly promised billions of dollars worth of reconstruction aid to Hanoi.

Key dates

Nixon's 'Christmas bombing' of North Vietnam: December 1972

Paris Peace Accords ended US involvement in Vietnam War: 27 January 1973

Summary diagram: 1972 – getting re-elected

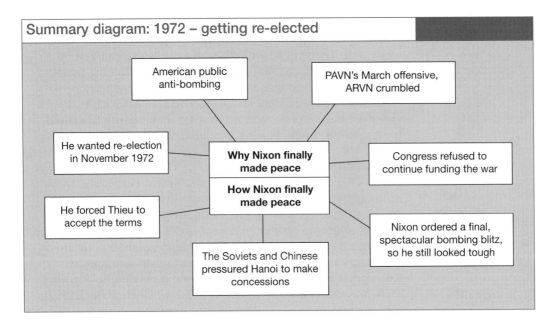

5 | Assessment of Nixon's Vietnam Policy

Key question
Was Nixon's policy a success or failure? Can it be defended?

a) Nixon and Kissinger – heroes or villains?

Kissinger was awarded the highly prestigious Nobel peace prize for ending the Vietnam War, which caused some to deny that he deserved it more than Nixon, and others to deny that he deserved it at all.

At the very least Nixon's critics have to admit that he got the American troops out of Vietnam. He did not always get much thanks for it (**doves** criticised his slowness) and he perhaps did not have much choice, but it was very significant indeed. It was difficult for any president to preside over the retreat of American power. Perhaps retreat from America's uncompromising and impossibly expensive Cold War militancy was one of Nixon's greatest achievements.

Doves
Americans more inclined to peace during the Cold War.

Key term

Some felt that Nixon and Kissinger were barely rational in their Vietnam policies, but it is not difficult to find reasons for their actions. They were motivated by the desire to do what they thought was best for America, which for the most part was what they thought was best for themselves also. Although one might not agree with their interpretation, and although one might be particularly upset by what it meant for the victims of their slow withdrawal and saturation bombing, one cannot help but conclude that all was accomplished with rational calculation of what was politically acceptable and best for America and the Western world.

b) Why did Nixon take so long to get out of Vietnam?

During 1968, Nixon had decided that America had to get out, but it took him four years to do it, during which time 300,000 Vietnamese and 20,000 Americans died. Most of the names on the left-hand side of the Vietnam War memorial wall in Washington died during Nixon's presidency, in a war he had decided from the first he could not win. Having decided on retreat, would it not have been less painful if Nixon had done it speedily? The slow retreat ensured a dramatic drop in the morale of American forces in Vietnam. It antagonised American anti-war activists. Some argue that it created the division, discontent and the presidential paranoia that helped to bring about Watergate (see page 207).

However, Nixon felt that American honour required that Thieu be left in power and that South Vietnam be left with a good chance of survival. Why else had America fought at such great cost in men and money? Nixon wrote to Rogers: 'We simply cannot tell the mothers of our casualties and the soldiers who have spent part of their lives in Vietnam that it was all to no purpose.' He was convinced that a first American defeat would lead to a collapse of confidence in American leadership and to Communist expansion throughout the world. He wanted peace, but not at any price.

Although the slow withdrawal was painful, there were clearly many who understood what Nixon was trying to do and sympathised with him. Like so many Americans, Nixon genuinely believed that the USSR and China presented a threat to America and its allies. Given the lack of political freedom within those two countries and Eastern Europe, those American fears were comprehensible and vital to understanding why America got into Vietnam and insisted on getting out 'with honour'. Although Kissinger and Nixon believed in detente, they thought that it was dangerous if the Soviets and Chinese thought that America was weak; and they were probably right.

c) Had Nixon gained peace with honour?

Nixon had got the American ground forces out without abandoning Saigon. He had forced Hanoi to agree that Thieu could remain in power with the world's fourth largest air force and an improved ARVN. On the other hand, Nixon had aimed to get the PAVN to withdraw and to nullify the VC in South Vietnam, but he had failed to do so. By late 1972 his freedom was limited: he knew that Congress would cut off his money early in 1973, so he had to make peace on whatever terms he could get, and thanks to his 'mad bomber' and linkage tactics the terms were quite probably better than he could have got in 1969.

d) What did the peace cost Nixon?

It could be argued that the peace cost Nixon the presidency itself. The difficulties of gaining 'peace with honour' in the face of domestic opposition and Vietnamese intransigence accentuated his tendency towards a siege mentality. During 1972 a Nixon organisation, the Campaign to Re-elect the President (CREEP) indulged in dirty tricks and got caught breaking into the Democrats' offices in the Watergate building. The scandal simmered relatively quietly in late 1972, but during Nixon's second term it exploded and brought the president down. Many Americans believed that had Nixon not felt besieged and battered by the Vietnam War, had he not believed that Vietnam might cost him re-election, Watergate would not have happened.

e) Had Nixon really won peace for Indochina in January 1973?

Nixon had not really won peace for Indochina in January 1973. The fighting continued in South Vietnam, and Nixon bombed Communist sanctuaries in Cambodia until 15 August 1973 when his money was cut off. Within months, Cambodia had become Communist, and so had South Vietnam, which was overrun by the Communists in 1975. There was no help from America. Nixon had resigned because of Watergate in 1974. Had he still been president, would Nixon have saved Saigon? Or had he (like Kissinger) just wanted a decent interval to elapse before the inevitable Saigon collapse? In 1977 Nixon said that he did not think he could have saved South Vietnam because Congress was opposed to any more American actions there. Nixon's expensively gained 'peace with honour' was thus untenable. Preoccupied with his foreign policy and international relations, Nixon had failed to engineer the domestic consensus necessary to save the incompetent Thieu.

> **Key date**
> Vietnam reunified under Communism; Cambodia and Laos also Communist: 1975

6 | Key Debate

Nixon felt that, 'History will treat me fairly. Historians probably won't, because many historians are on the left.' He was right in guessing that historians would usually be hostile towards him.

Does President Nixon's Vietnam policy deserve praise?

Kimball (1998) felt that, despite his electioneering promises, Nixon had no new Vietnam policy and never really developed one: he and Kissinger constructed *ad hoc* and often contradictory strategies in reaction to events. The 'madman theory' was the closest thing resembling a consistent approach. Morgan (2002) criticised the 'madman theory'. 'The use of insanity as an instrument of diplomacy is at best a contradiction in terms and at worst dangerous brinkmanship that could rebound disastrously in a crisis.'

The 'peace with honour' is disputed by most historians, for example, Berman (2001). Many historians, for example, Small (1999), felt that Nixon could have made peace on equally 'favourable' terms in 1969, and saved many lives. 'Because of his faith in mad strategies and triangular diplomacy', says Kimball (1998), 'he had unnecessarily prolonged the war, with all the baleful consequences of death, destruction and division for Vietnam and America that this brought about'. Similarly, Nixon's biographer Ambrose said that Nixon's slow retreat from Vietnam was, 'One of the worst decisions ever made by a Cold War president and the worst mistake of his presidency' (1989, 1991).

Small (1999) contends that the most remarkable of Nixon's feats was not ending the war, but managing to maintain support for his policies for over four years and to win the landslide victory in 1972. Small points out that Nixon used public anger at the 'hippies' in the anti-war movement to get support for his bombing. Since the end of the war, prominent Vietnamese have revealed that Hanoi counted on the American public to tire of the war, and Hanoi believed that the anti-war movement was more of a brake on Nixon than on Johnson.

Morgan (2002) said Nixon was 'guilty not of losing Vietnam but of trying ... to save a regime that was beyond salvation', and that, 'if Nixon inherited the Vietnam War, he did much to create the Cambodian War'. Morgan emphasises the horrific impact of US bombing on Cambodia, blaming Nixon, and disagreeing with those such as Hitchens (2001) who blame Kissinger for being the architect of the policy.

Some key books in the debate

S. Ambrose, *Rise to Globalism* (New York, 1989).

L. Berman, *No Peace, No Honour* (New York, 2001).

C. Hitchens, *The Trial of Henry Kissinger* (London, 2001).

J. Kimball, *Nixon's Vietnam War* (Kansas, 1998).

I. Morgan, *Nixon* (London, 2002).

M. Small, *The Presidency of Richard Nixon* (Kansas, 1999).

Study Guide: AS Questions

In the style of AQA

(a) Explain why Henry Kissinger became a highly influential national security adviser. (12 marks)

(b) How important was the anti-war movement in the decision to end the Vietnam War during the Nixon administration? (24 marks)

Exam tips

The cross-references are intended to take you straight to the material that will help you to answer the questions.

(a) Re-read pages 206–8. There are a number of reasons that can be cited:

- Nixon believed foreign policy to be of prime importance and had a personal need for an adviser in extricating the USA from Vietnam.
- Kissinger was a respected academic and specialist in international relations.
- Kissinger sought power on his own account and provided Nixon with what he needed.
- Kissinger's *realpolitik*/Machiavellian attitude, using personal/secret diplomacy, bypassing traditional diplomatic machinery, made him particularly suitable to a complex situation which involved trying to influence public opinion.

Try to provide a conclusion in which you show how these factors are interlinked and assess the most important.

(b) In order to provide an effective answer, you will need not only to address the anti-war movement, but also to balance its part against other factors encouraging an end to the Vietnam War. In this way you can show how far you agree or disagree with the given premise. In support of the quotation you might cite:

- Nixon's concern not to 'end up like LBJ' (Johnson) (page 205)
- the protests of 1969 and 1970 (pages 210–13)
- the link between the trouble in the streets in spring 1970 and Nixon's decision to pull out of Cambodia (pages 212–13).

Factors disagreeing with the quotation include:

- Nixon's personal concerns and his need for a 'place in history' (page 205)
- the changing Cold War world (page 205) – there was no longer a monolithic Communist bloc
- the 'unwinnable' war problem (see page 179)
- the military situation and Nixon's decisions prior to the 1969 protests (pages 209–11)
- US economic problems with the dollar in trouble because of the war by 1972 (page 190)
- US diplomacy (page 205).

Once you have decided which way you will argue, work through your points in a logical and linked manner so that your conclusion flows naturally from what you have written.

In the style of Edexcel

How accurate is it to describe President Nixon's handling of the Vietnam conflict as having achieved 'peace with honour'?

(30 marks)

Exam tips

The cross-references are intended to take you straight to the material that will help you to answer the question.

Nixon achieved peace if that is defined as getting American troops out of Vietnam, but you will need to decide what counts as 'with honour'. See pages 221–3 for the issues involved here.

You could plan to deal with the following factors:

- Nixon's view that confidence in American world leadership must be maintained to prevent Communist expansion (page 216).
- The combination of diplomacy plus force enabled him to secure some gains (page 221).
- He maintained support for Thieu and refused to abandon Saigon (page 221).
- In dealing with these last two points you could refer to the terms achieved at the Paris Peace Accords (page 219).

However:

- North Vietnam overran South Vietnam in 1975 (page 222).
- Many lives were lost in 1969–73 (pages 220–1) and what was the rationale for the Christmas bombing (page 219)?

What is your conclusion? Could President Nixon have made peace in 1969? He was responsible for prolonging the conflict. You could base your final assessment on how far what was achieved in 1973 represented a better peace with more honour than the position in 1969. Re-read pages 221–3 to clarify your thinking here. Again, this is an area of debate amongst historians and not one where there is a right answer to be found. It will depend on the criteria you apply for assessing 'with honour'.

In the style of OCR

(a) **Study Sources C and D.**
Compare these sources as evidence for reactions to the sending of US troops into Cambodia in 1970.

(b) **Study all of the sources.**
Use your own knowledge to assess how far the sources support the interpretation that the Nixon administration achieved an honourable peace in Vietnam.

Source A

In a speech accepting the nomination as Republican candidate for president of the USA, 8 August 1968, Richard Nixon outlines what his policy on Vietnam would be as president.

For four years this administration has had the support of the loyal opposition for the objective of seeking an honourable end to the struggle. Never has so much military and economic and diplomatic power been used so ineffectively. And if after all of this time, and all of this sacrifice, and all of this support, there is still no end in sight, then I say the time has come for the American people to turn to new leadership not tied to the mistakes and policies of the past. That is what we offer to America. And I pledge to you tonight that the first priority foreign policy objective of our next administration will be to bring an honourable end to the war in Vietnam.

Source B

From President Nixon's televised talk to the American people, 3 November 1969. Nixon public outlines his policy for 'Vietnamisation'.

We have adopted a plan which we have worked out in co-operation with the South Vietnamese for the complete withdrawal of all US combat ground forces and their replacement by South Vietnamese forces on an orderly scheduled timetable. This withdrawal will be made from strength and not from weakness. As South Vietnamese forces become stronger, the rate of American withdrawal can become greater.

Source C

From a speech by Wallace Bennett, Senator (Republican) for Utah, 2 May 1970. A US politician comments on sending troops into Cambodia.

In expanding the war, our commanders are co-operating with the armed forces of South Vietnam. The attack being launched will clear out major enemy strongholds on the Cambodian–Vietnam border. We are not invading Cambodia. The areas being attacked are completely occupied and controlled by the forces of North Vietnam. Our troops will not occupy these areas. They will defeat the enemy there and destroy his military supplies. Then our troops will withdraw. Intervention in Cambodia is necessary to bring the war in Vietnam to an end. It will shorten the war and save the lives of our soldiers.

Source D

From the St. Louis Post Dispatch, *3 May 1970. A US newspaper comments on sending troops into Cambodia.*

President Nixon now has his own Indochina war and his own credibility gap. Neither one is inherited any longer. In asking the American people to support the expansion of the Vietnam war to Cambodia, as he has already expanded it to Laos, he asks them to believe the same false promises which have repeatedly betrayed them against their will into ever deeper involvement on the mainland of Asia. They are asked to seek peace by making war; to seek withdrawal of our troops by enlarging the arena of combat; to diminish American casualties by sending more young men to their death; to save the lives of 450,000 American troops by one more round of escalation. And all this Mr Nixon asks in the name of preserving the credibility of America as a great power!

Source E

From the Toronto Star, *24 January 1973. A Canadian newspaper comments on the Paris Peace Accords.*

It's evidently impossible for a president of the United States to come clean about Vietnam; there is too much shame and failure in the American record there to be even hinted at. Thus President Nixon kept proclaiming the achievement of 'peace with honour' last night, when all he can really promise is that the Americans are going to pull out of that wretched area in fairly good order, with their prisoners returned, instead of fleeing in abject humiliation.

'Exit with face saved' would have been a more accurate phrase than peace with honour; for, whatever the terms of the Paris agreement may say, it's obvious that there is no guarantee of peace between North and South Vietnam. Hanoi maintains its goal of unifying all Vietnam under Communist rule, while the government of South Vietnam and a considerable number of its people mean to resist that dubious blessing.

Exam tips

The cross-references are intended to take you straight to the material that will help you to answer the questions.

(a) Your task is the comparison of two sources. No set answer is expected, but you should compare the contents, evaluating such matters as authorship, dating, utility and reliability, so using both sources 'as evidence for ...'. Use the headings and attributions to help your evaluation.

First of all, compare the sources as evidence for what they agree and disagree on. A better answer will do this thematically, comparing them both on each point. For example, both Sources C and D agree that sending troops into Cambodia will expand the war. After that, however, they differ on every point about the President's policy:

- The Senator (Source C) supports the president's policy while the newspaper (Source D) opposes it, and their disagreements are all about the consequences of this expansion into Cambodia.
- Bennett in Source C argues this act will shorten the Vietnam War and save US lives, while the *St. Louis Post Dispatch* in Source D argues the exact opposite.
- Bennett (Source C) sees action in Cambodia not as an invasion but as a limited operation on the border. By contrast, the newspaper (Source D) argues that this move opens a whole new war that will drag the US into even deeper involvements in Asia.
- Source D directly criticises the president, arguing Nixon cannot be trusted, talking of his 'false promises'. At first sight, Source C is silent on this, but implicit in Source D's argument is the belief that Nixon knows what he is doing. These two sources offer completely different perspectives on the wisdom of Nixon's move into Cambodia.

You must also consider the quality of the evidence each source offers. Looking at the date of each, they were spoken/written only a few days apart, when intervention in Cambodia was being argued over fiercely, and each represents a very different response.

Consideration of provenance might stress that a Republican senator (Source D) would be expected to support a Republican president, especially given the context of disturbed times: problems of morale among US troops (page 214); rising domestic opposition – Source D was written at a time of large-scale protests throughout the US (page 212).

Bennett (Source C) may be more typical of views still held by most Americans (as argued in Nixon's 'silent majority' speech), but the nation was increasingly divided – polls showed 50 per cent of Americans approved of Cambodian intervention while 39 per cent did not. If Source D's hostile claims did not yet represent majority opinion, they soon would.

(b) Your task is to give a judgement set in context. No set conclusion is expected, but if your essay is to score a high mark, it must use all five sources, judging them against your own knowledge as well as evaluating their strengths and weaknesses, and any limitations as a set they offer as evidence for or against the question.

Like the question, your focus must always be on Nixon's ending of the war. The sources offer a variety of useful points, explicitly or implicitly, and if your answer is to be strong you need to sort them out and group them according to their view.

- Source A sets the base for the argument, giving Nixon's own ambition for Vietnam and how the war was to be ended. That line is carried on through Source B in which Nixon justifies what he saw as a key step towards achieving his honourable peace. Source C backs up that line of argument, defending another of the major initiatives Nixon took to end the war quickly and in America's favour.
- Against Sources A–C, Sources D and E point in the other direction. Both are highly critical of Nixon's Vietnam policies and what they might be said to have achieved:
  - Source D opens up two different flanks. It pinpoints Nixon's failure to get the US out of Vietnam quickly enough – quite the opposite to the claims in Sources B and C that Nixon's policies brought a swifter end. Second, Source D also sets out a view that historians would later come to call the 'quagmire' interpretation: successive US presidents taking steps intended to solve the Vietnam problem but which only made things worse. Against that, you might want to consider another wider point that Source D raises: the extent to which domestic opposition delayed an end to the war and prevented military victory.
  - In Source E, the *Toronto Star* offers a direct and very bleak judgement on what had happened to Nixon's promised aim in Source A. As a Canadian source, it stands outside the internal US debate, offering the international perspective of the many Western democracies highly critical of US policy in Vietnam. It stands with its fellow (if American) newspaper (Source D) in condemning Nixon. According to Source E, there was no honour in the peace, and no peace either when, as you might add from your own knowledge, Nixon in his inauguration address had stated 'the greatest honour history can bestow is the title of peacemaker'.

So there are alternative explanations on offer here. You have sorted them out. It is up to you to test them against the question and make a clear judgement, justified by clear reference to the evidence and your own knowledge, for example, the claims that the US abandoned its South Vietnamese ally and that Nixon had to end the war at any price because public opinion had become so hostile that Congress pulled the plug on funding (page 217).

11 Conclusions: The USA in Asia, 1950–73

POINTS TO CONSIDER

Activity in Asia was central to American foreign policy between 1950 and 1973. While content with and/or forced to accede to continued Soviet domination of Eastern Europe, the US believed it could contain further Communist expansionism in Asia, with varying degrees of involvement in countries such as Korea, the Philippines and Vietnam. There are many important topics relating to this involvement, including those covered in this concluding chapter:

- Why the United States was involved in Asia, 1950–73
- The role of Congress, public opinion and the press
- The achievements of the United States in Asia, 1950–73

Key question
Why was the United States involved in Asia, 1950–73?

1 | Why the United States was Involved in Asia, 1950–73

In 1947, President Truman advocated the containment of Communism. He and his successors viewed the world through a Cold War perspective that made events in what would normally be considered insignificant countries in Asia seem very important. The 'fall' of China to Communism was the trigger event for the US preoccupation with Asia between 1950 and 1973. Communist activity in and by other countries (especially North Korea, Vietnam, the Philippines and Malaya) seemed to confirm that Asia had replaced Europe as the centre of the struggle between Communism and anti-Communism. This was why Truman took the United States into war in Korea and began the intervention in Vietnam. Truman felt the containment of Communism in Asia was essential to US security.

It could be said that Truman misread the situation in Asia, that the Korean War was triggered by a Korean civil war, rather than by Communist expansionism. It could also be argued that the Vietnamese Communists were nationalists first and Communists second. Nevertheless, successive administrations in Washington believed that letting the Communists win in Vietnam would affect the world balance of power in favour of Communism and lead to the fall of other Asian 'dominoes'.

Some argue that American motivation in intervening in Asia was primarily ideological, although views differ as to whether the ideological motivation was aggressive and expansionist or defensive and based on security fears. Those who play down the ideological motivation say that naked power and greed (the capitalist obsession with access to raw materials and markets) were equally if not more important. Also, as the war in Vietnam went on, US motivation changed in emphasis. The longer the US involvement lasted, the more it was felt that American credibility was at stake: getting out without victory would endanger the nation, as allies would lose confidence in the United States and the USSR would then take advantage of perceived American weakness. Soviet expansionism (in areas such as Angola and Afghanistan) after the United States withdrew from Vietnam seemed to confirm this. Domestic politics also played a part in presidential policies in Asia. Presidential credibility was deemed to be at stake in Korea and in Vietnam. No one wanted to be 'the first president to lose a war'.

2 | The Role of Congress, Public Opinion and the Press

Key question
What role did Congress, the public and the press play in US policy in Asia?

Successive presidents did not intervene in Korea and Vietnam alone and unaided. Congress, public opinion and the press all played a large part in getting the US involved in two wars, in the escalation of those wars, and in the American exit from them.

Congress, the public and the press were all initially supportive of entry into the Korean and Vietnam Wars, and also of escalation, whether by crossing the 38th parallel in September 1950 or by sending in several hundred thousand troops to Vietnam from 1965. Indeed, it could be argued that several Cold War presidents increased US involvement in Asia because of fears that the electorate would be hostile if they did not: the memory of the accusations that Truman had 'lost' China resonated with Eisenhower, Kennedy and Johnson.

Many people believe that public pressure played a big part in the exit from both the Korean War and Vietnam. It could be argued that this was the case in 'Truman's War' in Korea, although Truman certainly did not rush to get out. Similarly, while some claim that the anti-Vietnam War protesters forced Johnson to cease escalation and Nixon to get out altogether, it could be argued that Nixon's 'great silent majority' believed that some kind of victory in Vietnam was vital to the United States. Polls showed that a majority of Americans still felt saving Vietnam was important in the Nixon presidency.

The press did not play a great role in the Korean War, but Vietnam was the 'first televised war'. Many claim that 'poisonous reporting' and TV coverage played a part in disillusioning the public, Congress and the president about the prospects for victory, although it could be said that the coverage simply recorded events that had already made it obvious to people such as McNamara that the United States could not win.

Key question
Was the United
States successful in
combating
Communism in Asia,
1950–73?

3 | The Achievements of the United States in Asia, 1950–73

In some ways, it can be argued that the United States was successful in containing Communism in Asia. South Korea and perhaps Japan and some other potential dominoes were 'saved' from Communism. On the other hand, North Korea, Vietnam, Laos and Cambodia were 'lost'. Furthermore, the cost in men, money and divided and damaged society was great in the United States.

If one believes that Communism was evil and a great threat to the United States and to the Western world, then US policy could be adjudged to be a success, at the very least in South Korea. Communist rule in Eastern Europe, the USSR and China was certainly oppressive, although US allies in Asia in the struggle (such as Syngman Rhee, Diem and Chiang Kai-shek) were arguably little better. As has been said, the Soviet Union entered an expansionist phase after the US exit from Vietnam and had Communism spread to more countries then perhaps US security might have been compromised, although it is significant that Communist countries frequently failed to get along with each other, as evidenced by the Sino-Soviet split and the Sino-Vietnamese war that occurred within four years of Vietnam becoming a Communist country. Such divisions perhaps suggest that the United States probably did not need to fear Communist expansionism, as Asian Communists were usually nationalist first and Communists second.

Perhaps we can only conclude that it is exceptionally difficult to reach conclusions about the Cold War and that American administrations faced with a worldwide hostile ideology had a complex task.

Glossary

Administration   Rather than refer to a president's 'government', Americans refer to a president's 'administration'.

Agrovilles   New and well-defended villages set up by Diem's regime to keep Communists out.

Amphibious assaults   Attacks using land and sea forces.

Ap Bac   An important battle, the first major clash between the Vietcong and ARVN, in which American advisers and materials played a big part.

Approval rating   American pollsters continually check the public's opinion (approval) of the president's performance.

Armistice   The laying down of arms in a war, usually as a prelude to a peace treaty.

ARVN   Diem's Army of the Republic of Vietnam.

Asia-firster   An American who, during the Cold War, thought that Asia was the most important arena of conflict.

B-52s   Large American bomber planes.

Balance of payments deficit   When the value of a country's imports exceeds that of its exports.

Berkeley   A leading Californian university.

Bill   In order to make a measure law, the suggested measure has to be presented to Congress. Once this bill is passed by both houses of Congress, and assented to by the President, the bill becomes an act or law.

Bipartisan   When both Republicans and Democrats co-operate.

Booby traps   Disguised traps.

Bugout fever   The tendency of inexperienced and frightened American troops to flee the battlefield out of formation in the early days of the Korean War.

Bunco man   A con-man.

Capitalist   One who believes in a free market economy with no state intervention – the opposite of the Communist economic philosophy.

CIA   The Central Intelligence Agency, established in 1947, was responsible for collecting and evaluating intelligence data for the federal government.

Cold Warrior   One who wanted the US to wage the Cold War with even more vigour.

Collective security   An international system whereby all countries agree to collectively protect any one of their number that is a victim of aggression.

Colonialist   Also known as Imperialist. Believer in the acceptability of one country making a colony out of another country.

Commander-in-chief   Under the US constitution, the president commands the US armed forces.

Commitment trap   The theory that each president after Truman was bound to continue the US involvement in Vietnam.

Communiqué   In diplomatic and military terms, a statement issued by a commander or leader.

Communist   A believer in economic equality brought about by the revolutionary redistribution of wealth.

Congress   The US equivalent of the British Parliament; Congress makes laws and grants money to fund the President's policies.

Congressional mid-term elections   The US president and some members of

Congress are elected every fourth year, but the US Constitution (aiming to prevent a single party dominating US politics) requires that the other members of Congress are to be elected in the middle of that four-year cycle.

Congressman Member of the House of Representatives, where he or she votes on laws.

Containment Truman's policy of seeking to prevent the spread of Communism, for example, in Korea.

COSVN Central Office for South Vietnam – supposed Vietnamese Communist headquarters in Cambodia.

Counter-insurgency Style of warfare geared to dealing with guerrillas.

Coup A *coup d'état* is the illegal overthrow of a government, usually by violent and/or revolutionary means.

Court-martialled Tried by an army court for breaking army regulations.

Cross-over point The point at which Americans anticipated that Communists would give up because they were being killed faster than Hanoi could replace them.

Democrat Member of a US political party characterised by greater sympathy for the poor.

Detente Relaxation of tension between the USA and the USSR in the Cold War in the 1970s.

Dienbienphu Site of decisive Vietminh military victory over France in 1954.

Diplomatic In international relations, 'diplomacy' means relations between nations; a diplomat represents his or her nation abroad; nations that fully recognise each other have diplomatic relations.

Doves Americans more inclined to peace during the Cold War.

DPRK The Democratic People's Republic of Korea, also known as the DPRK or North Korea.

Draft The US term for what the British call conscription (the enforced call-up of civilians to be soldiers).

Egalitarian In this context, a Vietnam in which people had greater social, economic and political equality.

Europe-firster An American who, during the Cold War, thought that Europe was the most important arena of conflict.

Executive order In certain areas, such as military matters, the US constitution gives the president the power to act alone, through issuing executive orders.

Expansionist In the Cold War, each side considered the other to be aggressive and anxious to expand its power and influence.

Fragging When enlisted men tried to kill officers by throwing fragmentation grenades at them.

Friendly fire When a force's own side or an ally fires on the force by mistake.

Geneva Accords Agreements reached at Geneva in 1954 by France, China, Ho Chi Minh and the USSR, that Vietnam should be temporarily divided, with national elections held in 1956.

Geopolitical Political positions governed by the United States' geographical location in the world.

GIs US soldiers were issued with certain equipment by their superiors. 'GI' stood for 'government issue' and was used to describe American soldiers.

Great Society Johnson hoped to decrease American economic and racial inequality.

Ground commander While MacArthur was in charge of US forces in the Pacific, Walker then Ridgway commanded the American troops in Korea.

Ground troops In March 1965, President Johnson sent the first few thousand regular soldiers (rather than just 'advisers') to Vietnam.

'Group-think' When the herd instinct halts independent thought or disagreement.

Grunt Ordinary ground trooper or footsoldier.

Gubernatorial Pertaining to being a state governor.

Guerrillas Soldiers who try to avoid conventional warfare (that is, one army directly confronting another), preferring methods such as sabotage to counter the enemy's superior forces.

Hawks Militant Cold Warriors in the USA; those at the other end of the spectrum were known as doves.

Ho Chi Minh Trail North Vietnamese Communist supply route going south from North Vietnam through Cambodia and Laos to South Vietnam.

Ideologies Sets of political beliefs, for example, Communism.

Impeachment Process whereby Congress has the constitutional power to remove an errant president.

'Imperial presidency' Some Americans felt that under the pressure of the lengthy Cold War, the president gained greater power and became like some old European king or emperor.

Indochina The countries now known as Vietnam, Cambodia and Laos.

Internationalised Korean War The war between North Korea and South Korea led to intervention by the US/UN and China.

Iron Curtain After the Second World War, the USSR established Communism in, and took control of, Eastern Europe. Churchill said that it was as if an 'iron curtain' had come down across the European continent.

JCS The Joint Chiefs of Staff were the heads of the US armed forces.

Land reform Even anti-Communist Americans saw the need for a more equal distribution of land in Vietnam: an

estimated 1 per cent of the population owned all the cultivable land in the south.

Linkage Linking US concessions to the USSR and China to their assistance in ending the Vietnam War.

Machiavellian Machiavelli was a sixteenth-century Italian writer who once wrote, 'the end justifies the means' – in foreign policy, that would be considered as *realpolitik*.

Madman Theory Nixon wanted Hanoi to think he was capable of anything, in order to frighten them into making peace.

Mandarin A high-ranking civil servant.

Military Assistance Command, Vietnam MACV was created by Kennedy to co-ordinate US efforts in South Vietnam in February 1962.

Monolithic Communist bloc During the 1950s, many Americans believed that Moscow and Beijing were united in their foreign policies; by the 1960s, it was increasingly clear that with the Sino-Soviet split (in which other Communist nations took sides) there was no longer a united/monolithic Communist bloc.

Moratorium In this context, suspension of normal activities, in order to protest.

Multi-party state Nation in which voters have a free choice between several political parties.

Napalm Flammable liquid used in warfare.

National Guard US Armed Forces reservists, called up by the president in times of crisis.

National Liberation Front From 1960, Ho's southern supporters gave themselves this name.

National Security Council Established in 1947 to co-ordinate US government work on internal and external security; members included the president, vice-president, secretary of state, secretary of defence, and the chiefs of the CIA and JCS.

NATO   The North Atlantic Treaty Organisation was an anti-Communist Western military alliance established by the United States in 1949.

Neocolonialism   Whereas old-style colonialism was usually openly exploitative, neocolonialism had a kinder face.

Neutralised Vietnam   Some contemporaries advocated taking Vietnam out of the Cold War context and allowing it to decide its own future, without influence or input from Moscow, Beijing or Washington, DC.

'New look'   Republican policy emphasising nuclear weaponry rather than conventional forces for defence.

Non-aligned nations   Countries that remained neutral in the Cold War.

Normalisation of diplomatic relations It was not until the late 1970s that the USA established diplomatic relations with China. Once diplomatic relations were established, ambassadors were exchanged.

Operation Killer   Ridgway's February 1951 plan to inflict morale-damaging losses on the Chinese.

Orthodox historians   American historians who see the United States as resisting Communist aggression in the Cold War.

Orthodox viewpoint on the Korean War US historians who see the Korean War as a war of Communist aggression have the orthodox viewpoint.

Pacification   Paying greater attention to the security and government of the South Vietnamese people.

'Peace with honour'   Nixon always claimed he would get 'peace with honour' in Vietnam, by which he meant that Thieu's government must stay in power in a viable South Vietnamese state.

Pentagon   Headquarters of the US Department of Defence.

People's Army of Vietnam   Formal name of Ho's North Vietnamese Army by 1956.

People's Liberation Armed Forces   The name which Ho's southern supporters called their forces after 1960.

Politburo   The Chinese Communist government's equivalent of the British or US cabinet.

Popular mandate   Clear evidence that a political leader has the majority of the people behind him and his policies.

Post-revisionists   Historians who do not 'blame' one side of the Cold War.

POWs   Prisoners of war.

Protocol   In this context, an agreement between signatory nations.

Pusan Perimeter   The area on the southeastern corner of the Korean peninsula, into which the US/UN/ROK forces were forced in the early weeks of the Korean War.

Quagmire theory   Belief that the US got slowly and increasingly trapped in Vietnam, due to ignorance, overconfidence and credibility concerns.

R&R   Rest and recuperation for American soldiers in Vietnam.

Realpolitik   A realistic, rather than moralistic or legalistic approach to foreign policy; a belief that foreign policy should be dictated by the national interest.

Republicans   US political party characterised by conservatism on domestic issues.

Reunification   Vietnam was reunited in 1975 when the North took over the South.

Revisionist historians   American historians who criticise US motives in the Cold War as aggressive and acquisitive.

Revisionist viewpoint on the Korean War
Historians who see the origins of the
Korean War in a Korean civil war, rather
than blaming the North Korean attack on
Communist aggression, have a revisionist
viewpoint.

Rhetoric Stylised speech, designed to
impress and persuade.

ROK The Republic of Korea, also known
as the ROK or South Korea.

Rollback The Eisenhower administration
verbally rejected President Truman's
containment of Communism and
advocated pushing back Communism in
places where it was already established.

'Rolling Thunder' Heavy, often non-stop
US bombing of Vietnam.

SCAP General MacArthur was Supreme
Commander for the Allied Forces (SCAP)
in Japan. The acronym was used to
describe the whole US occupation regime.

Search and destroy General
Westmoreland's tactics included finding
and killing groups of Vietcong guerrillas.

SEATO Defensive alliance between USA,
Britain, France, Australia, New Zealand
and Pakistan, 1954.

Secretary of State The US equivalent of
Britain's Foreign Secretary, he had
responsibility for foreign policy and was in
charge of the State Department.

Security Council The UN chamber that
contained the great powers; the other
members were only represented in the
General Assembly.

Self-determination When the people
have the right to decide how they will be
governed.

Senate Foreign Relations Committee
Highly influential body of recognised
specialists in foreign policy in the US
Senate.

Sino-American Chinese–American.

Sino-Soviet Chinese–Soviet.

Sino-Soviet split In the early 1960s,
Chinese–Soviet mutual hostility became
increasingly obvious to the rest of the
world.

Stalemate theory Belief that the US
continued to fight an unwinnable war in
Vietnam, simply to avoid being seen to be
defeated.

Strategic hamlets Fortified villages in
South Vietnam, similar to agrovilles.

Summit During the Cold War, meetings
or conferences between the US and Soviet
leaders were known as summit meetings.

Taiwan Straits The stretch of water
between mainland (Communist) China
and Chang Kai-shek's island of Taiwan.

Tet The most important Vietnamese
festival. Americans use the word 'Tet' as
shorthand for the 'Tet Offensive'.

Third World Cold War-era name for
developing nations.

Ticker-tape parade When national
heroes returned to the United States, the
citizens of New York City would shower
them with bits of paper (ticker-tape) as
they drove through the streets of the city
in an open-top car.

Trustees In an international context,
countries who take responsibility for
another country.

UNC The United Nations Command,
under MacArthur, co-ordinated the
US/UN/ROK forces in the Korean War.

United Nations (UN) The UN was set
up in 1945. The 50 nations that signed its
founding charter pledged to assist any
other member that was a victim of
aggression.

US/UN Although theoretically a 'UN'
force in Korea, it was the US that provided
most of the forces and ordered their
deployment.

USSR Union of Soviet Socialist
Republics.

Vietcong   After 1960, Diem called the National Liberation Front 'Vietcong' (Vietnamese Communists or VC).

Vietminh   Ho's Vietnamese nationalist followers were known as the Vietminh after 1941.

Vietnamisation   A phrase/policy introduced by the Nixon administration; the idea was that the South Vietnamese government and forces should take the main responsibility for the war against Communism.

War of attrition   Westmoreland believed that US numerical and technological superiority would wear down the Vietcong who must, after losing a certain number of men, finally decide to give up.

Watergate affair   During Nixon's re-election campaign, Republicans authorised burglary and wiretapping of Democratic national headquarters at Watergate building in Washington, DC; the Nixon administration tried a 'cover-up'.

Wise Men   A group of experienced politicians, generals and others who had previously held high office, frequently consulted by Johnson over the Vietnam War.

Working Group   A group of experts brought together by President Johnson to study Vietnam and make suggestions for future policies in autumn 1964.

Index